The Renovation of Paintings in Tuscany, 1250–1500 focuses on several early Italian paintings of religious and civic importance that were physically transformed or reframed after their completion in order to accommodate cult practices and changes in taste. These images have traditionally been evaluated negatively because of their aesthetic impurity, an attitude that has often encouraged the removal of later additions by restorers and conservators. Cathleen Hoeniger argues that by investigating the religious and social motivations underlying these renovations, the historical significance of such practices can be revealed. The compound images that have resulted from transformations, therefore, can be viewed more positively as "carriers of history." Hoeniger's study also demonstrates how the methods of art history and conservation can be bridged to produce new and exciting conclusions about the form and meaning of artworks.

The Renovation of Paintings in Tuscany, 1250–1500

The Renovation of Paintings in Tuscany, 1250–1500

Cathleen Hoeniger
Queen's University, Kingston, Ontario, Canada

CAMBRIDGE
UNIVERSITY PRESS

Published by the Press Syndicate of the University of Cambridge
The Pitt Building, Trumpington Street, Cambridge CB2 1RP
40 West 20th Street, New York, NY 10011-4211, USA
10 Stamford Road, Oakleigh, Melbourne 3166, Australia

First published 1995

Printed in the United States of America

Library of Congress Cataloging-in-Publication Data

Hoeniger, Cathleen Sara.
The renovation of paintings in Tuscany, 1250–1500 / Cathleen Hoeniger.
p. cm.
Includes bibliographical references and index.
ISBN 0–521–46154–5 (hardback)
1. Altered paintings—Italy—Tuscany. 2. Painting, Gothic—Italy—Tuscany. 3. Painting, Renaissance—Italy—Tuscany. 4. Painting, Italian—Expertising. I. Title.
ND619.T9H64 1995
759.5′5—dc20 95–5258
CIP

A catalog record for this book is available from the British Library

ISBN 0-521-46154-5 Hardback

L'opera d'arte infatti si presenta alla nostra conscienza con due istanze, quella storica e quella estetica, nè l'una può essere sacrificata a scapito dell'altra.

– *Cesare Brandi*

Acknowledgments

This book began as a postdoctoral project generously supported by the Webster Fellowship in the Humanities at Queen's University and the Social Sciences and Humanities Research Council of Canada. It is with immense gratitude that I recall the congeniality of friends and colleagues at Queen's who helped to foster this study from the outset.

My research and writing were facilitated by many individuals and institutions. I offer my thanks to Andrea Bayer, Erin Blake, Jean Campbell, Keith Christiansen, Pierluigi Leone de Castris, Konrad Eisenbichler, Ed English, Bill Heckscher, Megan Holmes, Vojtech Jirat-Wasiutynski, the staff of the Kunsthistorisches Institut in Florence, Gordon Moran and Lucia Monaci, Kate Olivier, John Osborne, Joe Polzer, Maurizio Seracini and EDITECH, the staff of the Siena Soprintendenza, and Gail Solberg. The Publications Committee of the Department of Art and Archaeology, Princeton University, generously contributed for the publication of color plates.

Leonetto Tintori and Giuseppe Gavazzi shared a few of their restoration secrets with me. John Shearman and Patricia Brown offered invaluable advice. At an early stage, Norman Muller read through the manuscript, and his suggestions contributed in important ways to the final shape of the book. In conversations with Lynda Jessup, the notion of "living images" emerged. My father, David Hoeniger, combed through the manuscript on numerous occasions, patiently improving my prose. Last but not least, my husband, Byron Lew, supplied encouragement and good humor in the requisite amounts.

Contents

List of Illustrations

COLORPLATES

FIGURES

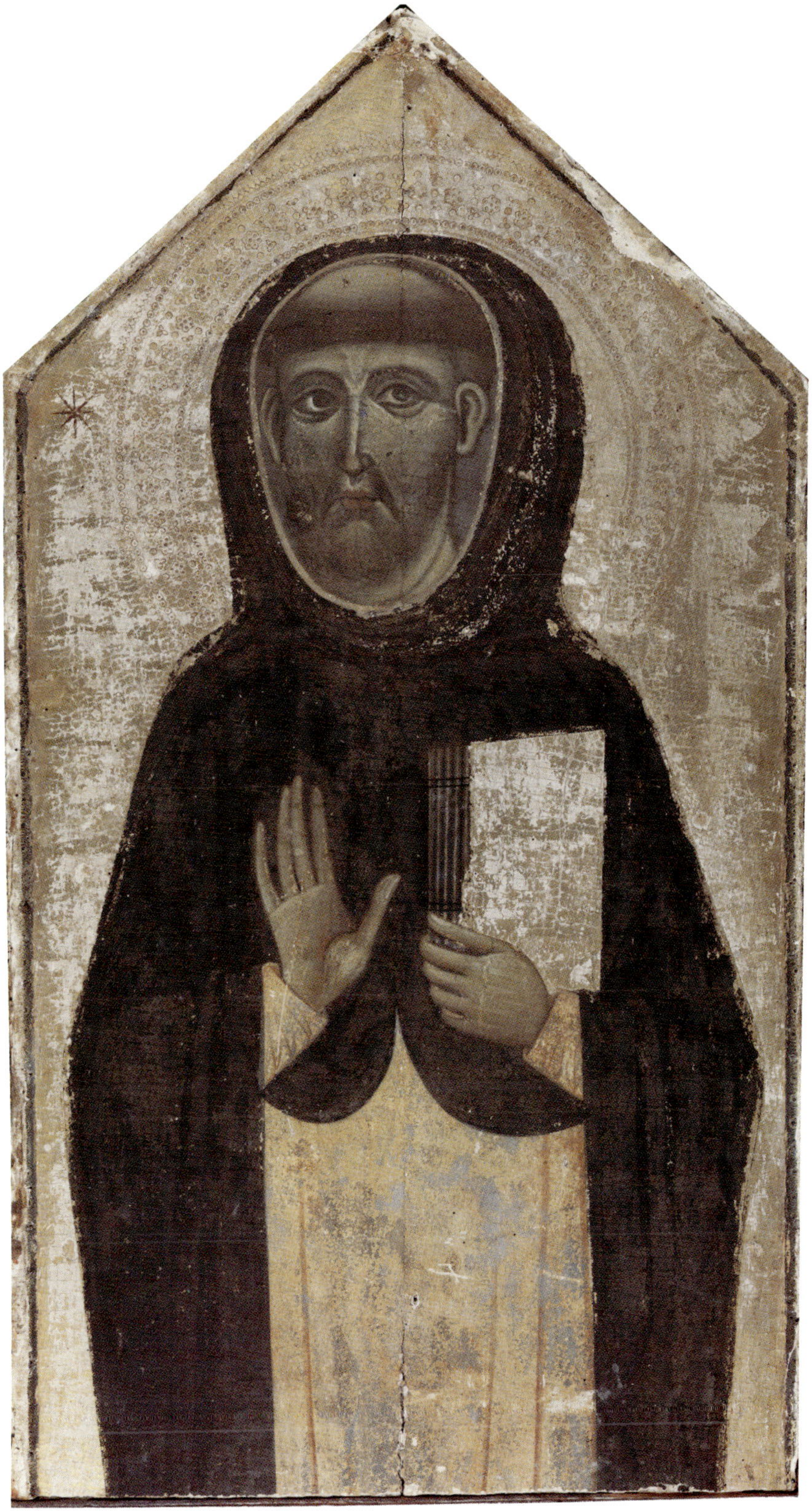

Plate 1. Sienese, *St. Dominic*, c. 1240–80, Cambridge, Mass., Fogg Art Museum (Courtesy of The Fogg Art Museum, Harvard University Art Museums, The Hervey E. Wetzel Bequest Fund)

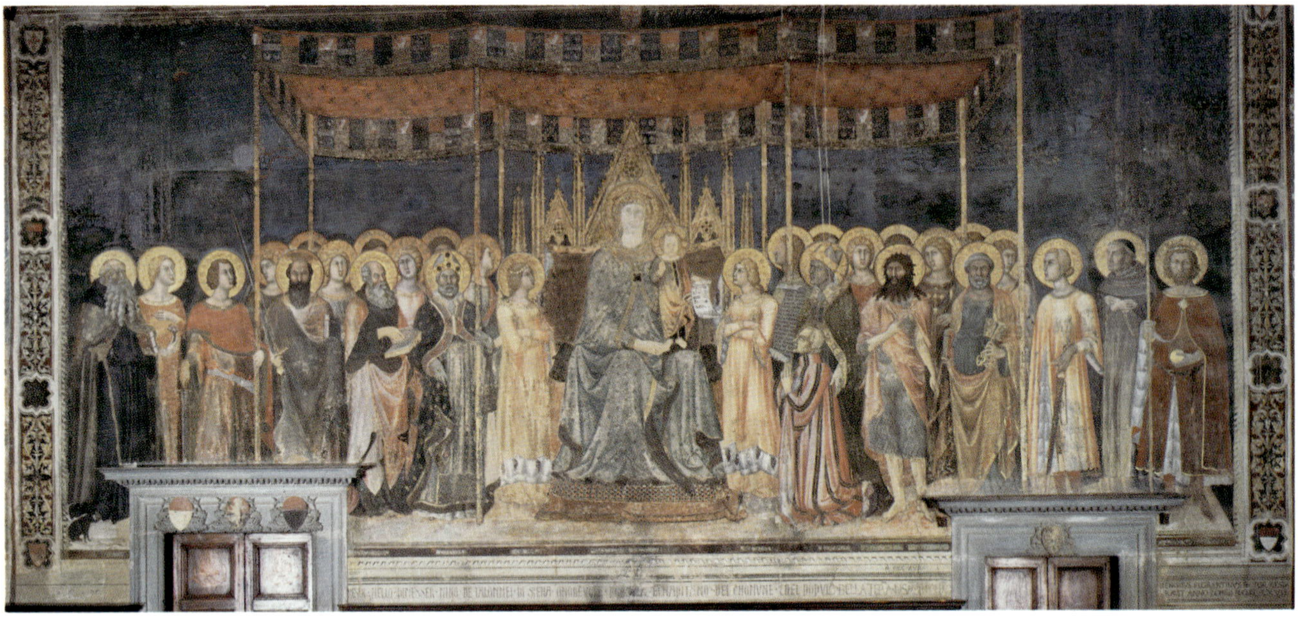

Plate 2. Lippo Memmi, *Maestà*, 1317, San Gimignano, Palazzo Comunale (Scala/Art Resource, N.Y.)

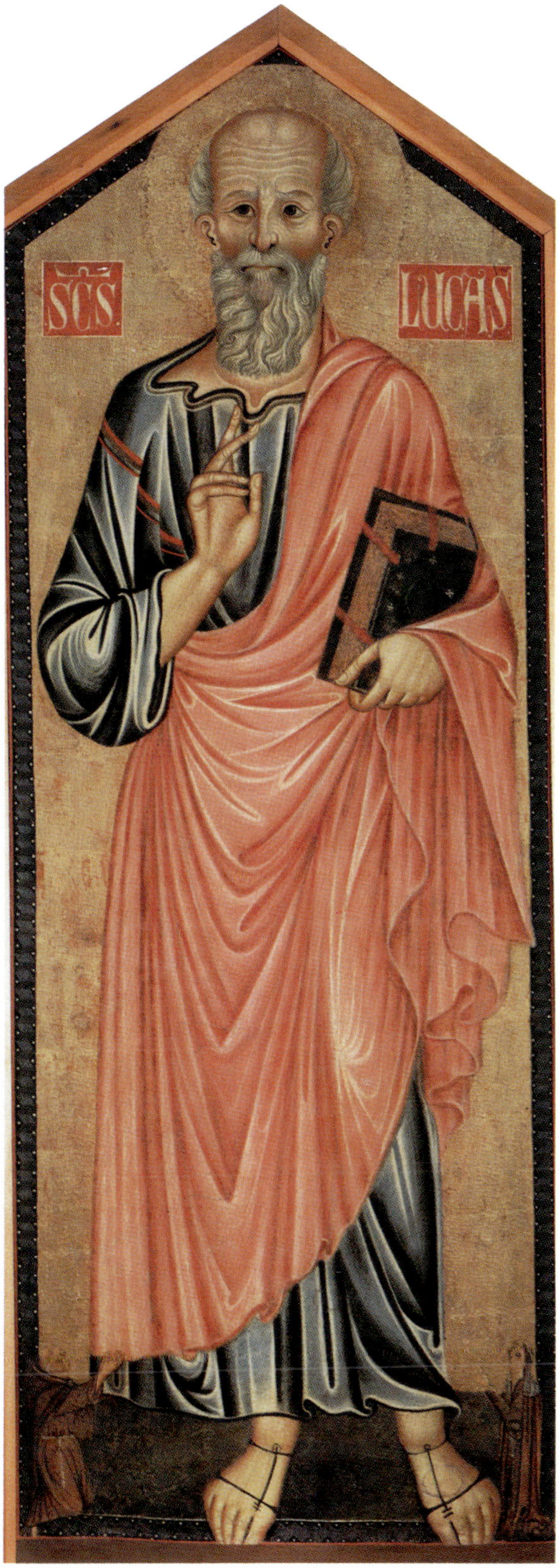

Plate 3. Magdalen Master,
St. Luke, c. 1275–85, Florence,
Uffizi (Scala/Art Resource, N.Y.)

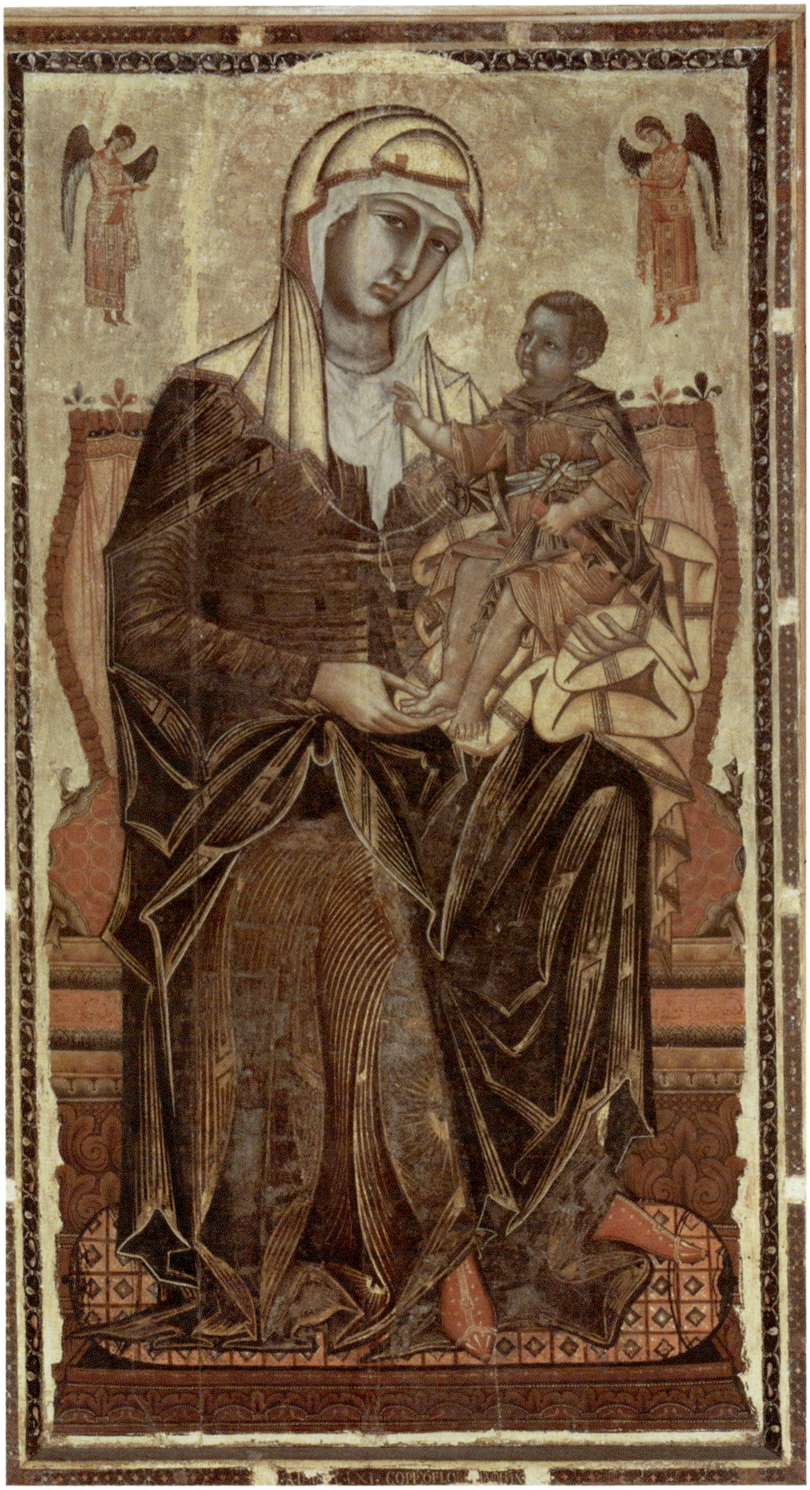

Plate 4. Coppo di Marcovaldo, *Madonna del Bordone*, 1261, Siena, Sta. Maria dei Servi (Scala/Art Resource, N.Y.)

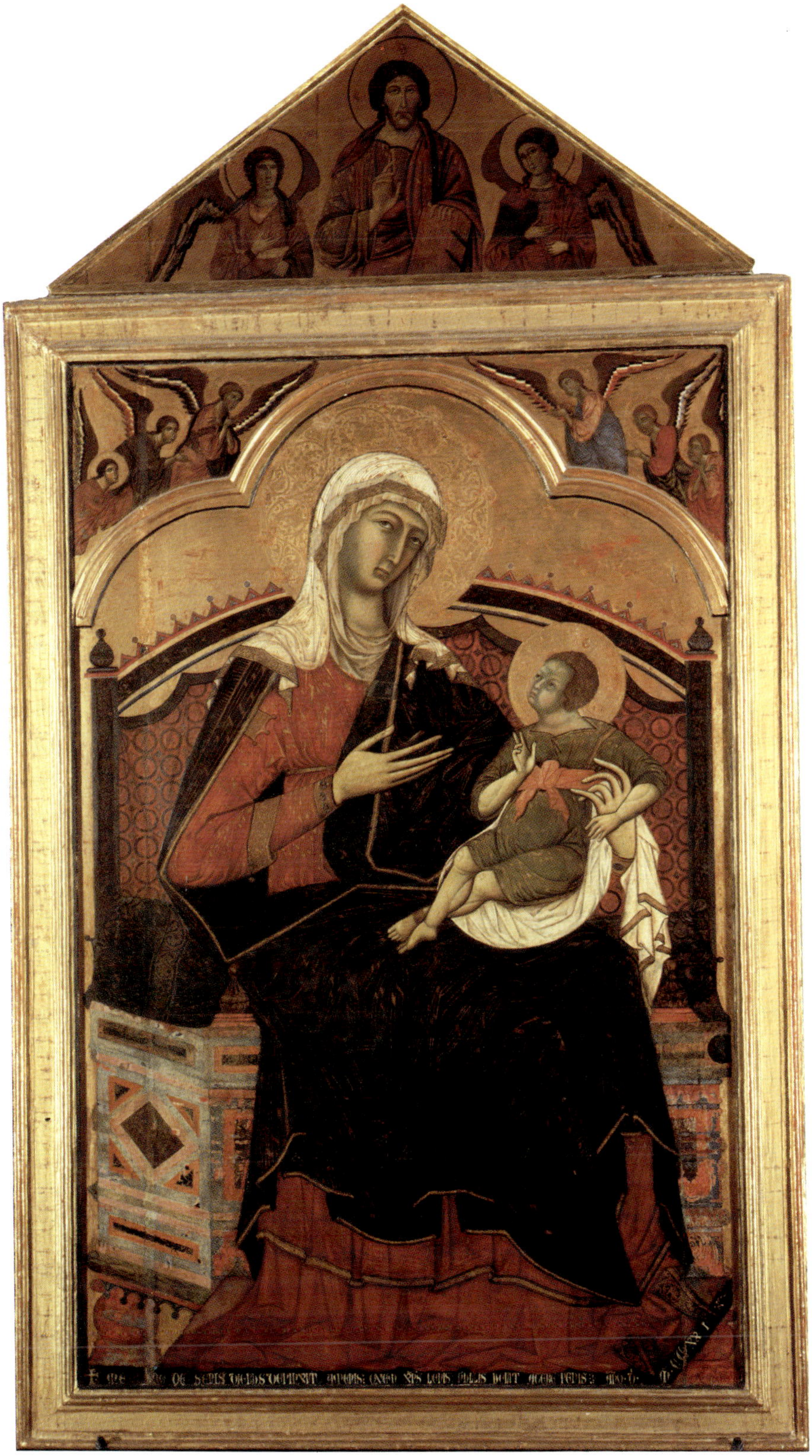

Plate 5. Guido da Siena, *Palazzo Pubblico Maestà*, c. 1270–80, Siena, Palazzo Pubblico (Fotografia di Fabio Lensini, Siena, Italy)

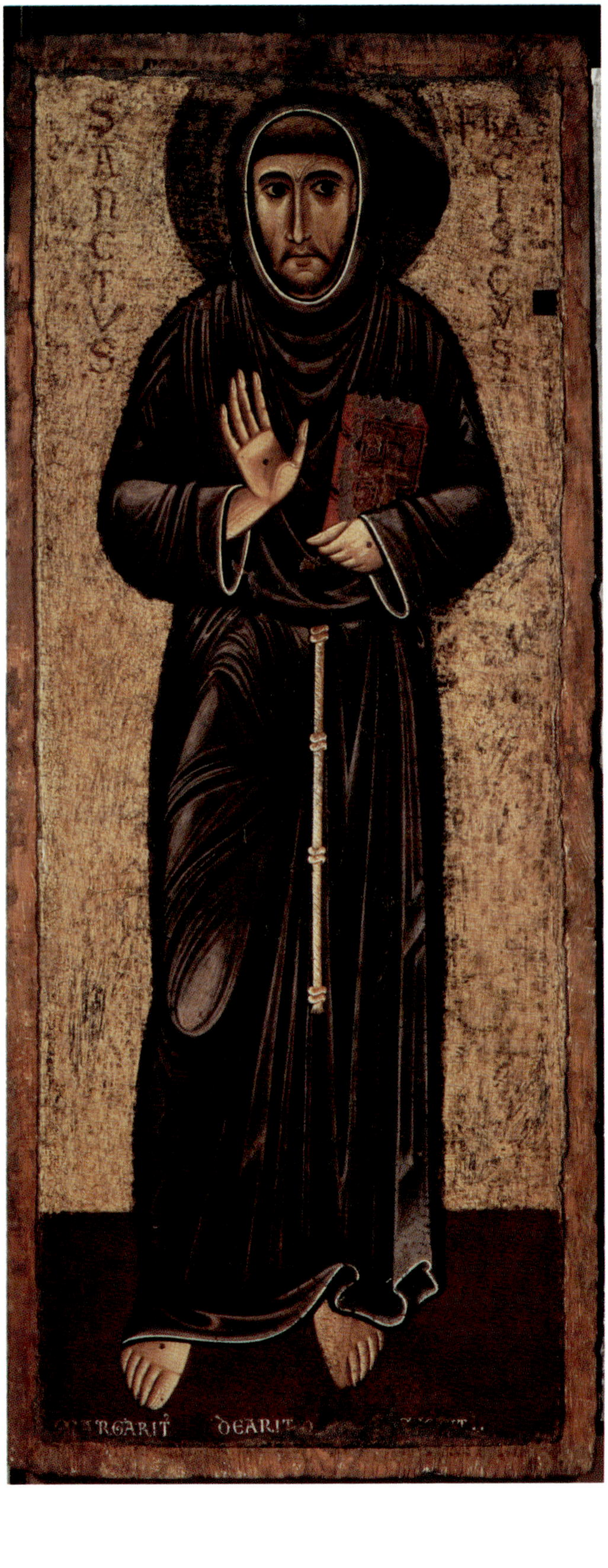

Plate 6. Margarito d'Arezzo, *St. Francis*, c. 1260, Arezzo, Museo Medievale e Moderno (Scala/Art Resource, N.Y.)

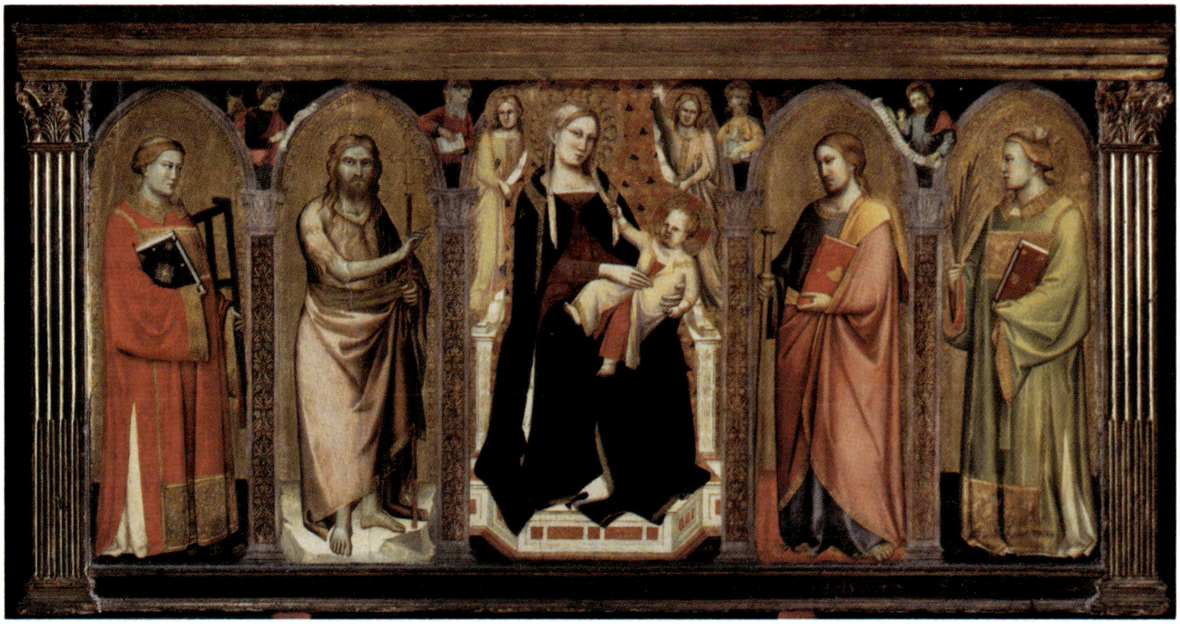

Plate 7. Taddeo Gaddi, *Madonna and Child with Four Saints*, c. 1340–5, New York, Metropolitan Museum of Art (Metropolitan Museum of Art, New York)

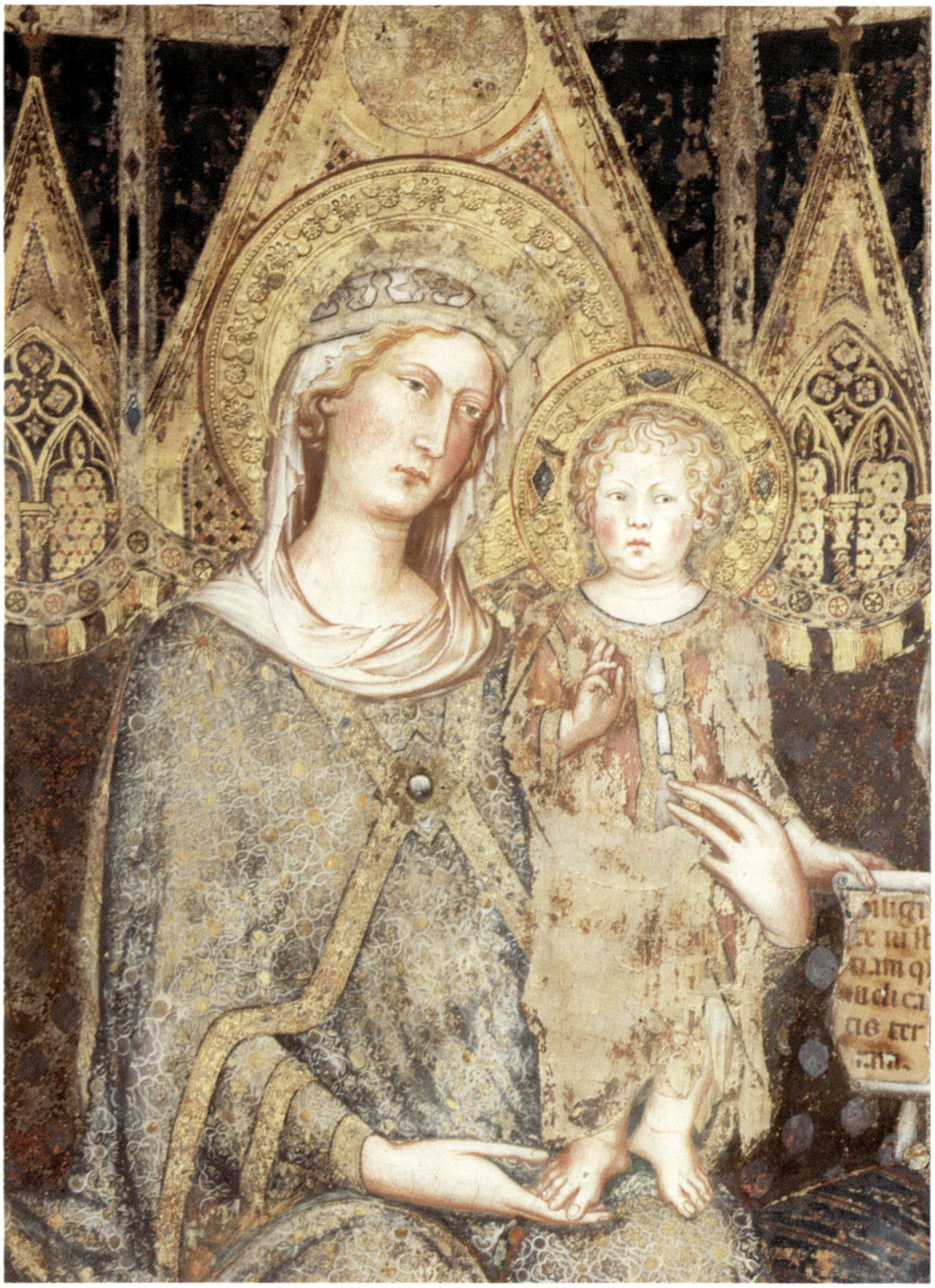

Plate 8. Simone Martini, *Maestà*, 1315–16, detail, Siena, Palazzo Pubblico (Fotographia di Fabio Lensini, Siena, Italy)

CHAPTER 1

Introduction: The Prestige of the Original

This book will focus on the phenomenon in early Italian art of paintings that were transformed from their original states relatively soon after their conception. The transformations were achieved by altering the surface through repainting, by updating the shape through reframing, or by embedding the remains of an old painting within the larger structure of a new one. Paintings of this kind are full of meaning for historians; every added component of their physical structure tells a story. They are objects that show the physical evidence of having been actively used and having elicited reactions over a period of time. They provide valuable insight into the life of images within society.

A substantial group of such hybrid images has come to light in the past hundred years or so, exciting interest in their physical constructions and the motivations underlying the transformations. Some of the hybrids are easily detected by those familiar with basic period-style characteristics. For example, altarpieces like Giotto's *Baroncelli Polyptych*, which was produced at the height of the Italian Gothic style in the early fourteenth century and then radically reframed according to Renaissance tastes in the late fifteenth century, can be readily identified as the products of two distinct periods and aesthetics (Fig. 1). Other hybrids, however, have only been recognized by the perceptive eyes of accomplished connoisseurs. To cite just one instance, the compound nature of the frescoed *Madonna in Glory* at San Lorenzo in Ponte, in San Gimignano, was provisionally identified first in the late nineteenth century by the art connoisseur and historian G. B. Cavalcaselle (Fig. 2). As he perceived, the head of the Madonna shows stylistic features close to Duccio, whereas the rest of the composition is later and Florentine in

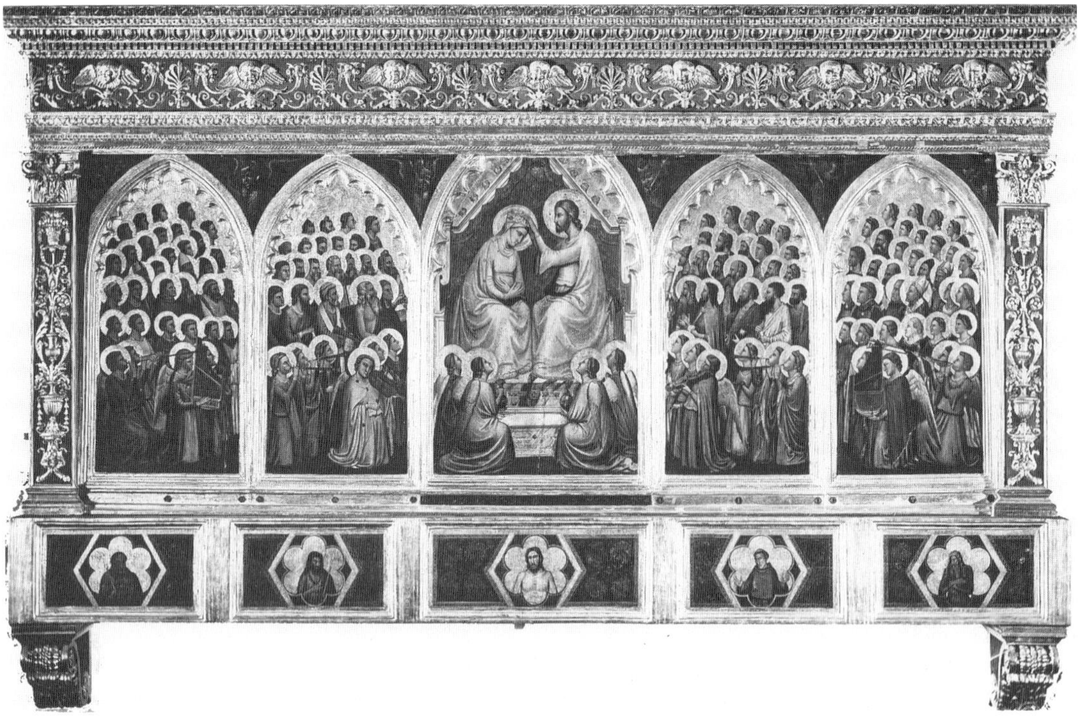

Figure 1. Giotto and his workshop, *Baroncelli Altarpiece*, c. 1330, Florence, Sta. Croce (Alinari/Art Resource, N.Y.)

flavor.[1] More recently, the extensive repainting has been attributed securely to a little known follower of Agnolo Gaddi, Cenni di Francesco di Ser Cenni, as a result of detailed stylistic comparisons.

Other transformed images have only been fully recognized due to a combination of stylistic investigations and technical examinations by painting conservators. One example of how this process of discovery works involves the cropped panel-painting of St. Dominic in the Fogg Art Museum in Cambridge, Massachusetts (Pl. 1). Formerly attributed to the School of Guido da Siena and dated c. 1280, the stratified nature of the image was recognized by Harvard University art history students in 1955 from stylistic observations. After studying x-radiographs of the painting with the assistance of conservators, seminar members arrived at a fresh interpretation of the evidence. The x-radiographs were read as indication that the saint's face had been repainted twice, and the layers were dated within a period of about forty years on the basis of stylistic features.[2]

A second example of the recognition and identification of a transformed image draws attention to the primary importance of the art restorer. Lippo Memmi's *Maestà* fresco in the town hall of San Gimignano was recognized early on as an extensively repainted work (Pl. 2). At the beginning of this

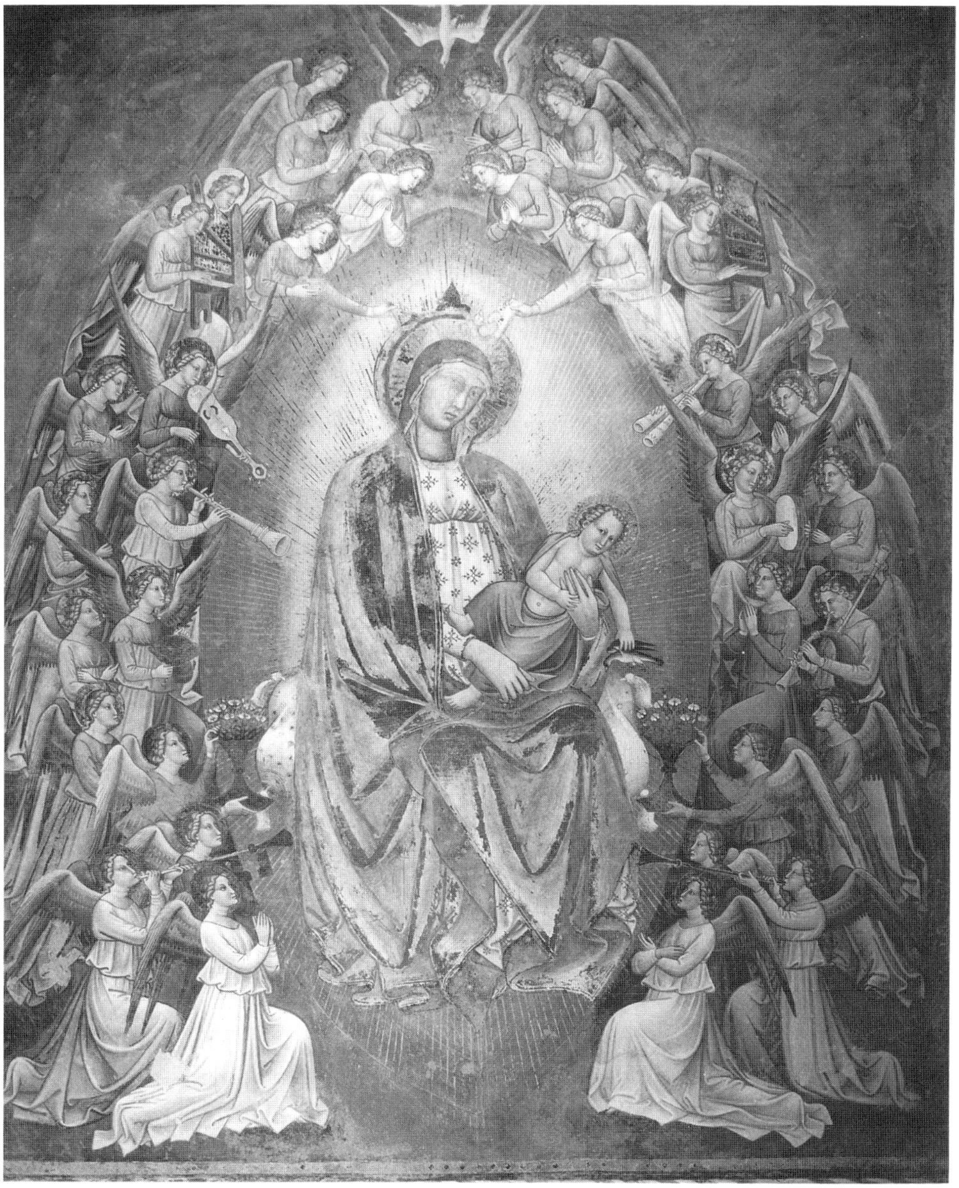

Figure 2. Cenni di Francesco di Ser Cenni, *Madonna in Glory*, c. 1413, San Gimignano, S. Lorenzo in Ponte (Foto Soprintendenza per i Beni Artistici e Storici di Siena, Italy)

century J. A. Crowe and G. B. Cavalcaselle attributed the additions as an entirety to Benozzo Gozzoli on the basis of documentary and stylistic evidence.[3] However, these views have been revised as a result of a recent technical study and restoration of the structure, and it is now believed that the fresco was repainted and expanded already in the late fourteenth century and only retouched and repaired by Benozzo Gozzoli in the 1460s.[4]

Clearly, without the perceptions of style-based art historians and the skills of modern restorers, few examples of transformed images like this one would be recognized.

Nevertheless, little interest has been shown in the historical potential of such discoveries. Rather, the approach of connoisseurship, with its stress on the prestige of the original, has encouraged concentration on the initial, creative statement embodied in a work of art whereas later alterations have been neglected and often removed. This way of thinking is reflected in how hybrid works of art are usually exhibited in museums and treated by art conservators.

Indeed, most major art galleries display their early paintings in a manner that reflects these conceptions. According to the tradition of connoisseurship, each painting embodies the artistic personality of the master or workshop that initially produced it and is thus seen as illustrative of one and only one particular stylistic period. The original form of the painting is privileged, and efforts concentrate on retrieving and conserving the work in the original state. For example, at the Uffizi gallery in Florence, which houses the richest collection of Medieval and Renaissance Tuscan painting in the world, the works are arranged in a sequence of rooms proceeding chronologically and divided according to stylistic schools. In the first room, where the earliest panels are hung, each painting is displayed in a certain amount of isolation, and generally in as close to its original form as possible with all the later accretions removed.[5] They stand as representatives of the original artists' styles and techniques. No attempt is made to communicate the other, complex historical dimensions that some of these paintings formerly possessed.[6]

One early Italian panel in the Uffizi that exemplifies the gallery's general approach is the full-length portrait of St. Luke (Pl. 3). The painting is presented in a condition close to its original form without mention of its eventful, later history. The panel was originally executed in Florence in the last quarter of the thirteenth century and has been attributed to the Magdalen Master. However, in the early part of the fourteenth century, the face of St. Luke was repainted and replaced by the likeness of St. Francis with the object of completely transforming the identity of the holy person portrayed (Fig. 3).[7] This was probably done for devotional reasons when new patrons who inherited or appropriated the panel required the mediation of St. Francis rather than St. Luke.[8] Much later, in the eighteenth century, the entire figure was repainted in oil, this time to return to the identity of St. Luke (Fig. 4). In 1935, however, the layers of repaint were removed from the panel to retrieve the sought-after original and, as displayed in the Uffizi today, the painting evidences no sign of its later history.[9] Although the recovery of such a rare example of Dugento painting has brought immense

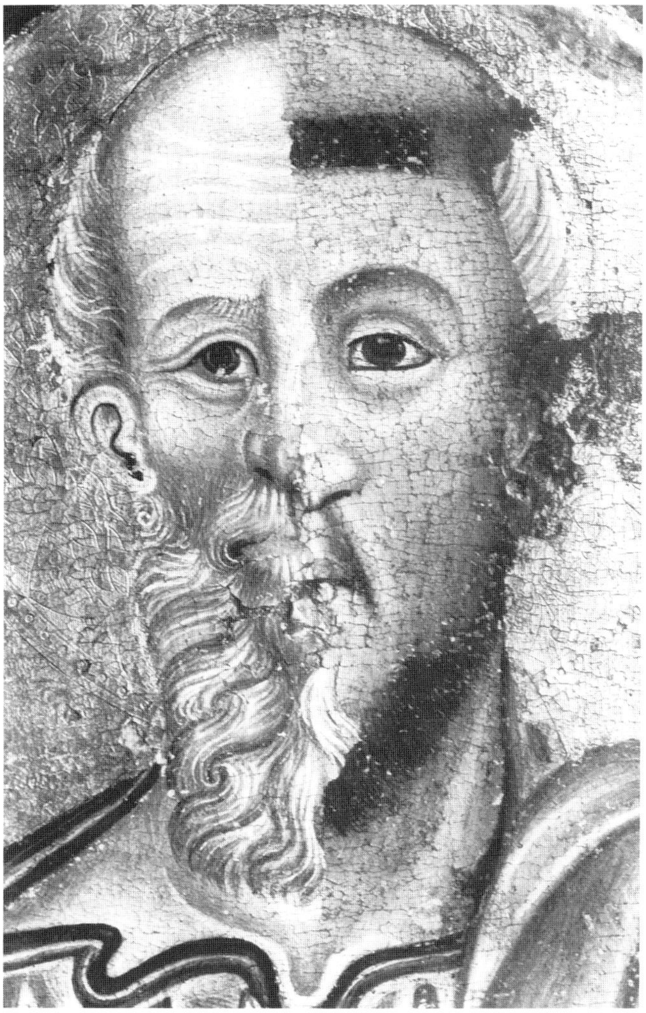

Figure 3. Magdalen Master, *St. Luke*, c. 1275–85, detail, during restoration of 1935, Florence, Uffizi (Opificio delle Pietre Dure di Firenze, Italy)

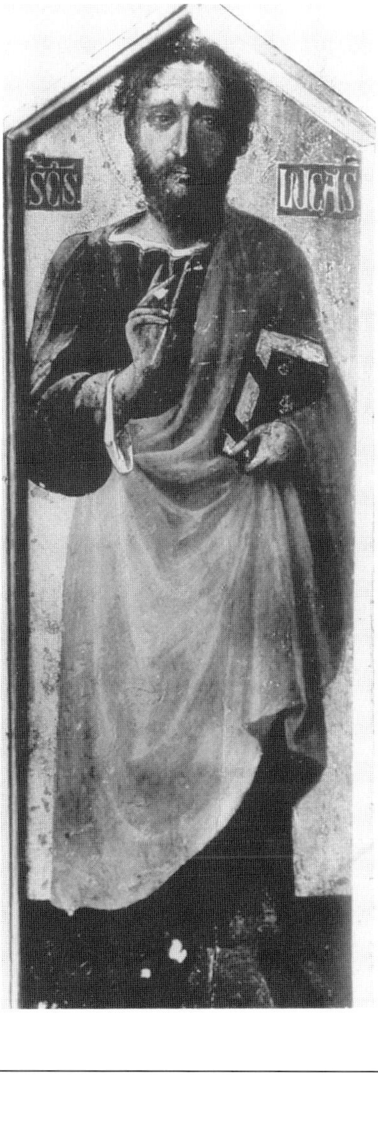

Figure 4. Magdalen Master, *St. Luke,* before restoration of 1935 (Opificio delle Pietre Dure di Firenze, Italy)

pleasure to many early Italian specialists, a more contextually oriented art historian might still question why no effort has been made to publicize the curious and fascinating sequence of transformations that the image underwent. In the case of an image created initially for a devotional purpose, which maintained its pious function over an extended period of centuries, can we without question ignore the religious context and treat the image as a purely aesthetic object whose only valued dimension is the style and quality of its earliest layer? Further, on a more public level, a display chronicling the renovations carried out on the *St. Luke* and the reasons behind them might be just the kind of thing to excite interest in the personality and history of an image that, as it stands, only attracts the gaze of a few trained eyes.

The approach taken to a second altarpiece in the Uffizi, Giotto's *Badia Polyptych*, provides further evidence of the gallery's response to hybrid images (Figs. 5 and 6). Originally painted in the early fourteenth century, Giotto's altarpiece was reframed in the years 1451–3 in Florence. Triangular pieces of wood were added to the original Gothic frame to update the old-fashioned shape of the altarpiece, and cherubs were painted on the new wooden pieces between the cusps of the old frame. But in a modern restoration campaign, between 1957 and 1958, these Renaissance additions were removed to free the painting from its later accretions. As the Florentine restorer Umberto Baldini subsequently explained, the decision to remove the Quattrocento additions was taken because of the simplicity of the procedure and in order to regain the original proportional relation between Giotto's figures and their framing architecture: "the Renaissance intervention in the structure of the polyptych had taken Giotto's figures into a new dimensional relationship; the figures were inserted into a space which was much too large and they consequently lost much of their expressive force."[10] Although many might agree with this response, it has to be understood for what it is: a modern aesthetic judgment sympathetic to the creative statement of the original artist and not to the later fabric of the image's history. No value is given to the fact that to Renaissance taste, the new dimensional relationship between the Gothic figures and their classically inspired framing was attractive. Nor are the social reasons for adding the framing elements considered. As I will argue in Chapter 5, hybrid Gothic/Renaissance altarpieces of this kind are typically the result of renovations carried out by prominent Florentine families on their private chapels and altarpieces for reasons of piety, status, and taste.

Baldini also justified the removal of the later framing elements from the *Badia Polyptych* with the argument that the process was reversible. Preserved in storage, at a later date, the extra pieces could be attached again if so wished.[11] And yet the fact remains that these pieces are sequestered

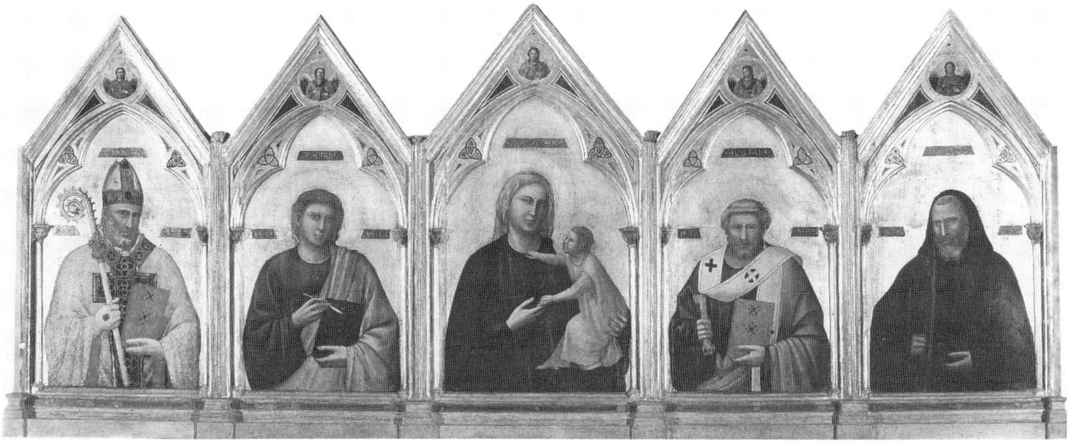

Figure 5. Giotto, *Badia Polyptych*, c. 1301–2, Florence, Uffizi (Alinari/Art Resource, N.Y.)

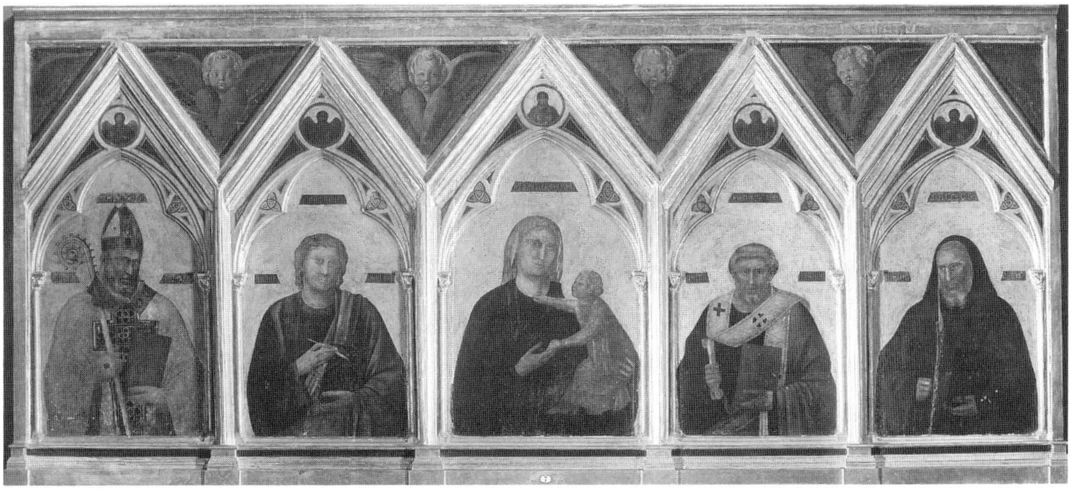

Figure 6. Giotto, *Badia Polyptych*, before restoration of 1957–8, Florence, Sta. Croce (Alinari/Art Resource, N.Y.)

away, and the painting is exhibited in its original, unadulterated state with no reference to its later history. To learn about the later dimension of the painting's life, one must turn to old, prerestoration photographs or restoration reports.

In North America, evidence of the consequences of such an approach can be seen perhaps most vividly at the Yale University Art Gallery, which houses an important group of early Italian paintings assembled primarily by the nineteenth-century collector and educator, James Jackson Jarves.

Several of the paintings in this collection were radically cleaned in the years between 1950 and 1971 to remove anything that was not part of the original works.[12] In several cases, losses of metal leaf or paint have not been repaired and, consequently, panels are displayed with large areas of bare gesso ground or wood support left exposed. One example is the fragment from an altarpiece of c. 1390 representing Saints Julian, James, and Michael, attributed to Agnolo Gaddi. The panel was cleaned in 1958 and in the process additions of nonoriginal gesso and gilding were removed.[13] As a result, there are disturbing losses all over the panel, including a particularly extensive one obscuring a large part of the mantle of St. James. Although such works provide an authentic study collection for those interested in the styles and techniques of early masters, one cannot help wondering whether, in the cleaning program, historically important, later layers may have been lost.

A similar desire to free original works of art from subsequent layers of paint or added structural components has fueled other restoration projects in Europe and North America. One of the most important centers of restoration activity in Italy has been Florence since the establishment of a state restoration laboratory there in 1932. Further, the gallery administration in Florence has sponsored a sequence of exhibitions to celebrate the results of restoration campaigns. Significantly, for the most momentous of these exhibitions, *Firenze Restaura 1972*, the startling, partially cleaned, stratified image of a *Madonna and Child* was selected as the symbol (Fig. 7). This *Madonna* was originally created in the second half of the thirteenth century in Florence by the Magdalen Master, but was subsequently repainted twice in the eighteenth or nineteenth centuries.[14] With the original layer revealed only in part, in a tantalizing way, the *Madonna* was intended to publicize the remarkable feats of modern, scientifically based cleaning procedures, but also to stand as an exemplum of the interesting aspects of old restorations, namely, changes motivated by reasons of taste and cult. Although the compound structure was dramatically spotlighted, in practice, however, little emphasis was placed on the social motivations underlying the alterations. Although repaintings like this one were explained generally as occasioned by the cult needs of devotees for a stylistically up-to-date image that spoke to them in their own language, specific historical and social circumstances were not explored.

Another complex hybrid image highlighted by the 1972 exhibition reveals in more detail the primary aims underlying the Florentine restoration program. This image began as an early Florentine *Crucifix* from the midthirteenth century, attributed to the Bardi St. Francis Master (Fig. 8). About forty years later, however, the surface was completely repainted by an unknown Florentine artist (Fig. 9). Then much later, perhaps as late as the

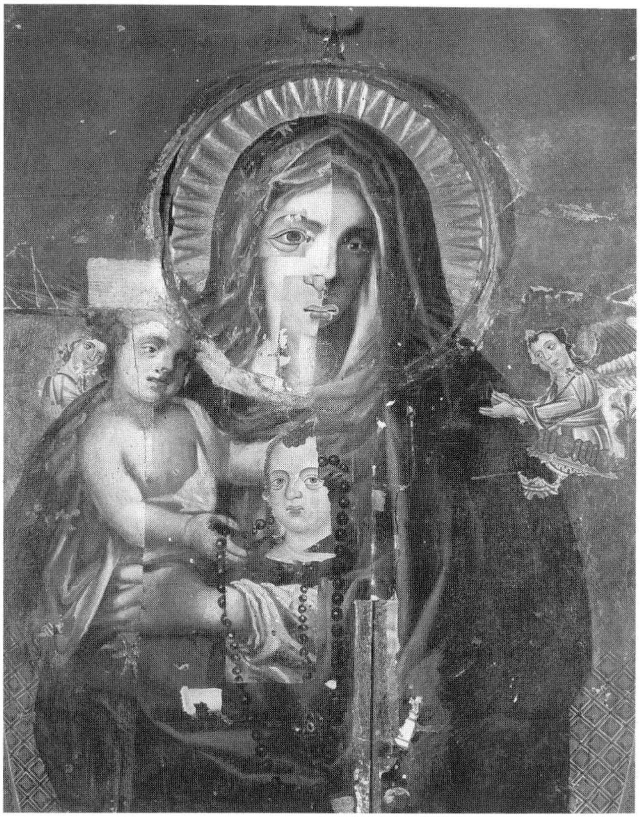

Figure 7. Magdalen Master, *Madonna and Child*, c. 1275–80, during restoration of 1947–8, Florence, Uffizi (Opificio delle Pietre Dure di Firenze, Italy)

eighteenth century, the image was again totally repainted, and, either at this time or somewhat later still, the *Crucifix* was set into a larger wooden panel to form the central section of a triptych together with two panels of saints that were derived ultimately from an altarpiece by the early Quattrocento Florentine artist, Lorenzo di Bicci (Fig. 10). In this curiously hybrid form, the painting was deposited, until the early 1950s, in the Museo Bandini in Fiesole.

In 1952, the Crucifix triptych was selected for restoration. As a first stage, the triptych complex was dismantled and the lateral panels were reunited with two similar saints by Lorenzo di Bicci, believed to originate ultimately from the same altarpiece. In this way, steps were taken to return the components to their original, disparate contexts. Left on its own, the *Crucifix* panel was described as "of little account" and "vulgar" as it stood; and yet it was deemed to be potentially of great interest because the apron form of the panel suggested an underlying structure dating from the thirteenth century.[15] Accordingly, the heavy overpainting was removed to re-

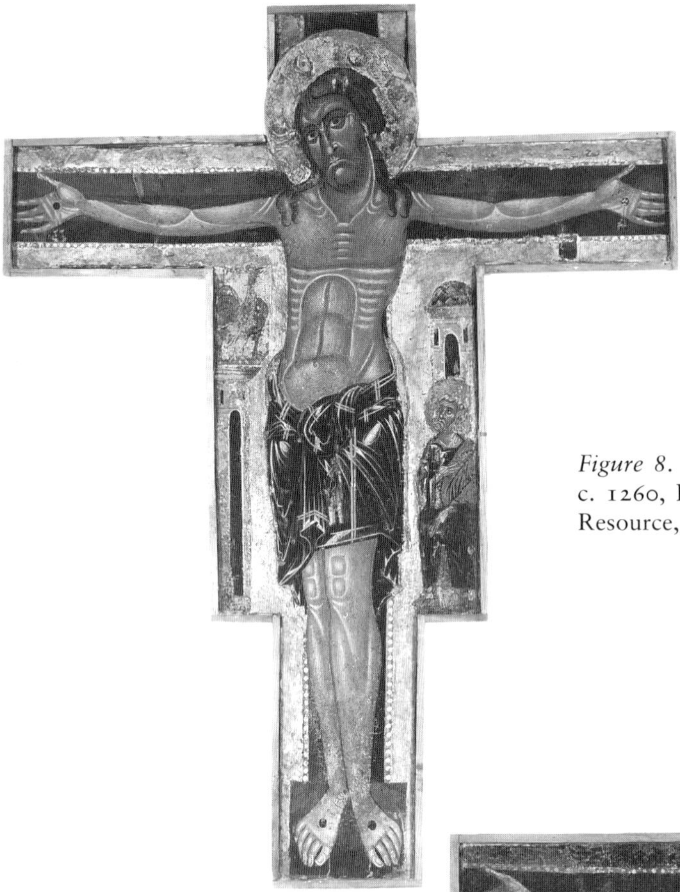

Figure 8. Bardi St. Francis Master, *Crucifix*, c. 1260, Fiesole, Museo Bandini (Alinari/Art Resource, N.Y.)

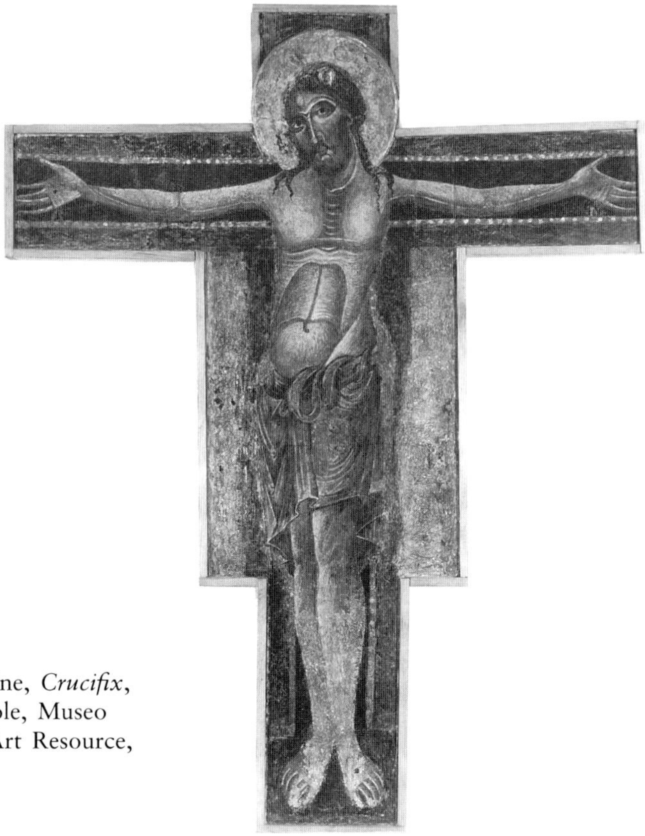

Figure 9. Florentine, *Crucifix*, late 13th c., Fiesole, Museo Bandini (Alinari/Art Resource, N.Y.)

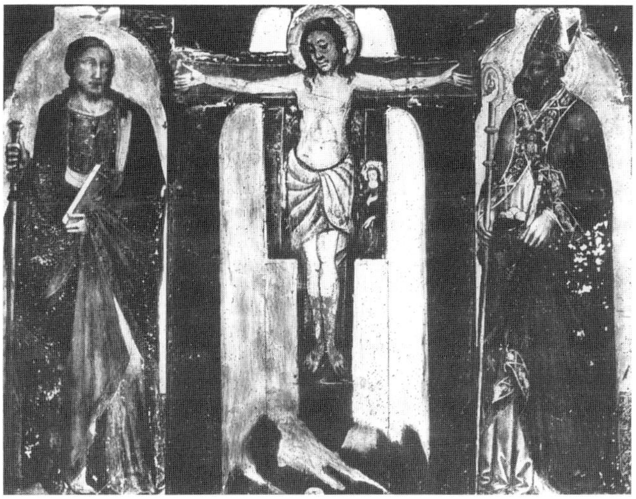

Figure 10. Crucifix and Saints, before restoration of 1952, Fiesole, Museo Bandini (Opificio delle Pietre Dure di Firenze, Italy)

veal a late thirteenth-century image, as suspected, but only one of moderate quality.[16] However, the restorers' eyes were quickly attracted to holes in the paint surface due to the flaking of paint, probably occasioned by extended exposure to heat from candles. These losses revealed the presence of an even earlier layer of paint beneath. After x-radiographs confirmed the existence of an underlying image, the decision was taken to remove the top surface using the latest methods. The presence of an intermediary varnish layer permitted the separation of the two paint strata using the solvent piridine at a temperature of 50–60 degrees Celsius, which was sufficient to dissolve the varnish without affecting either of the two tempera layers. The overlying image was detached from the original and mounted onto a separate support.

A look at photographs of the *Crucifix* in its heavily repainted, eighteenth-century condition discourages one from condemning the Florentine restorers for their desire to clean away the overlying layers. After all, they did reveal an important, midthirteenth-century painting beneath, as well as an intermediate layer of much interest. Moreover, without their excavations, we would have little knowledge of the sequence of transformations that the painting underwent. Nevertheless, the manner in which the hybrid object was treated and discussed reveals a narrow focus on the aesthetic and stylistic qualities of the earliest layers.

There is, first of all, the lack of respect for any later additions to the work of art; only the original deserves reverence. In this specific case, the attitude was rationalized: removal of poor-quality additions in order to reveal a high-quality painting beneath. Indeed, at one point, Ugo Procacci, the curator and art historian who supervised the project, remarked: "In such instances it is almost, how shall I put it, a work of charity, to destroy the ignoble repainting in order to succeed in recovering the concealed original."[17]

Secondly, there is the somewhat ahistorical and potentially misleading manner in which the separated layers are now displayed in the Museo Bandini in Fiesole. The earliest layer on its original panel and the second layer on a new support hang side by side in a corner area of the first large room of the gallery. Although tiny, brief captions summarize their relationship and the process of discovery, it would be easy to mistake the images for independent works illustrating the history of the development of the Crucifix form. I am sure that most visitors leave the museum believing that they are two separate, late Medieval panel-paintings – as I initially did myself. Further, no obvious attempt is made to publicize the later, eighteenth-century history of the object; in the caption, the later repainting is referred to only as "coarse" and the physical evidence of this dimension of the painting's life has, of course, been destroyed.

There are reasons for pressing this point. The approach of connoisseurship with its emphasis on the sanctity of the original and its evaluations based on aesthetic quality is prone to exclude the appreciation of more historical dimensions of works of art; and, consequently, when it is adopted as the rationale governing restoration decisions, historically valuable layers may be lost. Perhaps we should take a lesson from the overly eager excavations of early archaeologists like Schliemann, who in the 1870s and 1880s in attempting to uncover the lost ancient city of Troy as evoked by Homer, destroyed parts of the historical record of the area, including, ironically, portions of the layer containing Homer's Troy itself.

Some conservators today, in reaction to the invasive techniques of previous generations, are approaching works of art with greater caution and humility. In a number of major conservation schools, restorers are taught to interfere as little as possible in the fabric of the works and only to strive to halt deterioration and stabilize condition. This movement in conservation comes hand in hand with a more general intellectual sensitivity to the layered structure of the past and its rich and changing meanings.[18] And yet, despite heightened awareness of and appreciation for the hybrid structures produced by history, in many art circles, the search for the original or for the highest-quality layer in a work continues. In the restoration completed in 1989 of Gentile da Fabriano's *Madonna and Child Enthroned* of 1425 in Orvieto Cathedral, for example, a historically significant dimension of the fresco was removed in pursuit of the original layers (Figs. 11 and 12). In the late sixteenth century, a large figure of St. Catherine of Alexandria

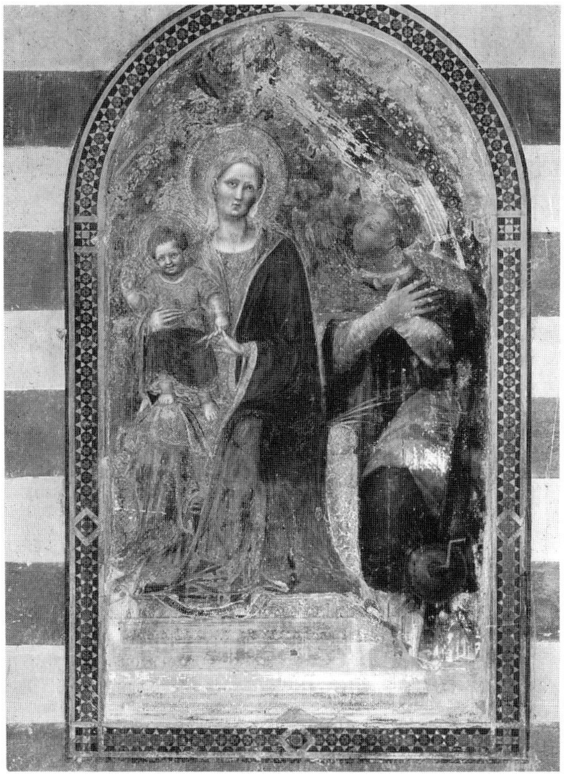

Figure 11. Gentile da Fabriano, *Madonna and Child Enthroned*, 1425, before restoration completed 1989, Orvieto Cathedral (Foto Rizzi, Rome)

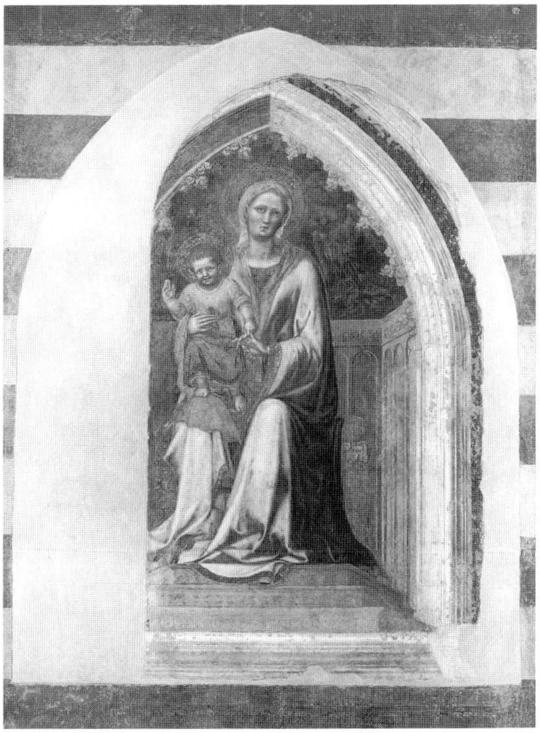

Figure 12. Gentile da Fabriano, *Madonna and Child Enthroned*, after restoration, Orvieto Cathedral (Foto Rizzi, Rome)

had been added to the right portion of the fresco by Giovanni Battista Ragazzini da Ravenna, surely for pious reasons.[19] By the sixteenth century, the fresco seems to have gained a considerable reputation as a votive image, and in the early eighteenth century, the thaumaturgic powers of the Virgin are commented upon and St. Catherine's adoring role is mentioned with appreciation.[20] During the recent cleaning, however, the repainted layers, including St. Catherine, were taken off the wall in an attempt to regain the original proportional feeling of the work and to expose the underlying surface. Although the recovery of the perspectively rendered framing niche, still partially preserved, enriches our understanding of Gentile da Fabriano's stylistic development in important ways, the attempt to retrieve the work in its original form despite the ravages of time reveals an emphasis on traditional aesthetics rather than contextual history. And although most of the figure of St. Catherine was salvaged on a layer of Japanese paper, the critical disdain for it as a component of the painting's history remains typical. As one respected reviewer added when explaining that part of the St. Catherine has actually been preserved: "at least as much of it as anyone will ever care to see."[21] Though it may be difficult for many modern viewers to understand how a late sixteenth-century artist could have been allowed to cover over part of Gentile's masterpiece with an ugly figure of St. Catherine, it seems clear that either late Cinquecento tastes were markedly different from our own or else pious aims outweighed taste in this case. Such issues merit investigation.

The recent cleaning of the *Feast of the Gods* at the National Gallery in Washington represents a similar case as purely aesthetic appraisals were involved in the discussion of the layered structure and its restoration. During the scientific examination prior to cleaning, the gallery staff discovered that the landscape background in the painting had been substantially altered not just once, but twice, after Giovanni Bellini completed it in 1514. Within the space of fifteen years, it was transformed first by the Ferrarese court artist Dosso Dossi and then by Titian. We can deduce that both changes were made at Alfonso d'Este's request, for the sake of aesthetic coherence, when he altered the pictorial decoration of his Camerino d'Alabastro in the ducal residence at Ferrara by acquiring new works by different artists. Nevertheless, the gallery's decision to save Titian's repaint during the recent restoration was justified in terms of the artist's great reputation, whereas Dosso Dossi's early additions were slighted though not removed.[22]

Two contrasting approaches to similar cleaning situations may serve to conclude this preliminary discussion of modern attitudes toward the layered structures of early images. The works involved are two important Tuscan Romanesque cult images of the Virgin – the *Madonna del Bordone* by Coppo di Marcovaldo and the *Palazzo Pubblico Maestà* by Guido da

Siena. As will be discussed in greater detail in Chapter 2, both were repainted in Siena in the early fourteenth century for devotional reasons related to the Byzantine tradition of selectively repainting miracle-working icons. In the case of the *Madonna del Bordone*, the faces of the Virgin and Child were reworked on top of the thirteenth-century originals, but no other portions of the composition were touched (Pl. 4). In the *Palazzo Pubblico Maestà*, a Gothic artist close in style to Duccio repainted the face of the Virgin, the entire body of the Christ Child, as well as the lower part of the throne (Fig. 13). However, he first did away with portions of the original paint layer and ground, making some of the changes on a fresh gesso layer.

When both images were restored in the late 1940s at the Istituto Centrale del Restauro in Rome, the responses to their historically valuable repaintings were significantly different. The *Palazzo Pubblico Maestà* was restored under the direction of Enzo Carli and the staff of the Siena Soprintendenza. As x-radiographs taken of the panel revealed that the original faces and the throne on the left side had been scraped off before repainting, conservators had little choice but to leave most of the Gothic additions. Nevertheless, the decision was taken to remove the layers of Gothic repainting from the right-hand side of the throne, from the Virgin's headcloth and from her right hand where the original still survived (Figs. 14 and 15).[23] By performing a selective removal to reveal small portions of the original, they created an image that as a totality – it hardly needs saying – reflects neither its original Dugento nor its transformed early Trecento state. Art lovers of future centuries may look upon it rather as a structure characteristic of midtwentieth-century values.

In contrast, the reaction to Coppo's *Madonna del Bordone* was more considered and cautious. When it was restored in 1948 under Cesare Brandi, the decision was made not to remove any of the Gothic repainting, even though, in this case, the original lay preserved underneath. As Brandi explained in his account of the project: "the work of art has two aspects, historical and aesthetic, and one cannot be sacrificed for the sake of the other" – a judgment worth remembering.[24]

Yet, as this introduction has stressed, in the discussion and treatment of renovated works of art, aesthetic and historical aspects have often, inevitably, come into conflict. Traditionally, the aesthetic concerns of the connoisseur for the initial creative statement have influenced restoration procedures and led to the removal of "accretions" in the attempt to recover the image in close to its earliest state, and many prominent galleries have supported such an approach. My purpose is not to quarrel with an aim that places a high value on the integrity and quality of an original master's work, but to draw attention to what is sacrificed because of the one-sided

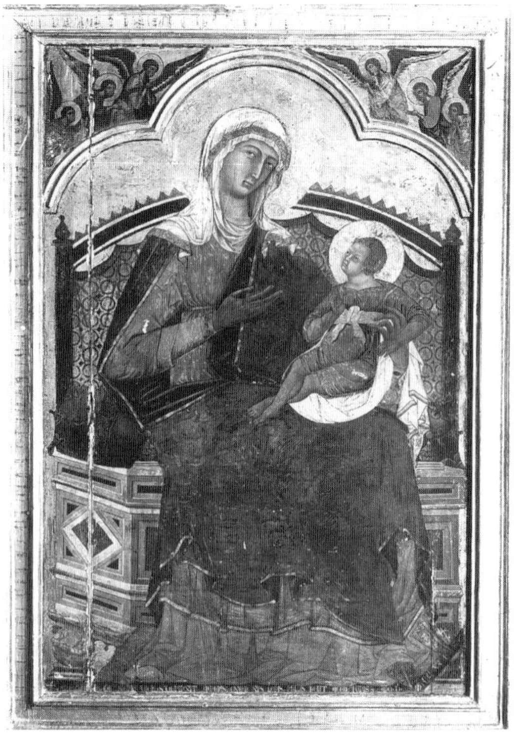

Figure 13. Guido da Siena, *Palazzo Pubblico Maestà*, c. 1270–80, before restoration of 1948–50, Siena, Palazzo Pubblico (Fotografia di Fabio Lensini, Siena, Italy)

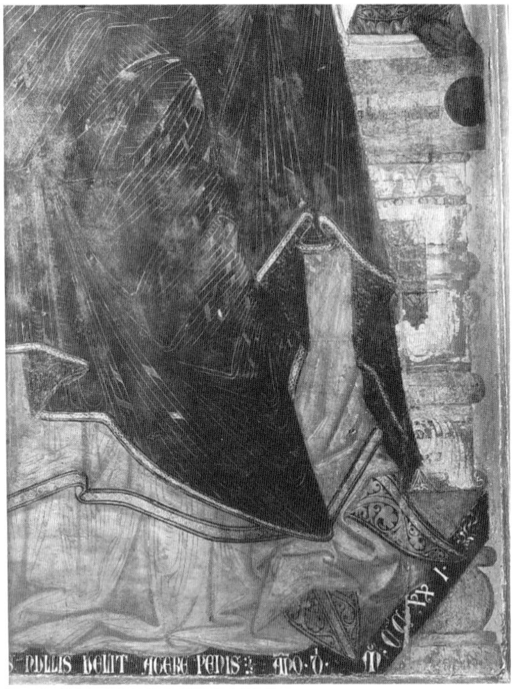

Figure 14. Guido da Siena, *Palazzo Pubblico Maestà*, detail of right-hand side of throne, during restoration of 1948–50, Siena, Palazzo Pubblico (Fotografia di Fabio Lensini, Siena, Italy)

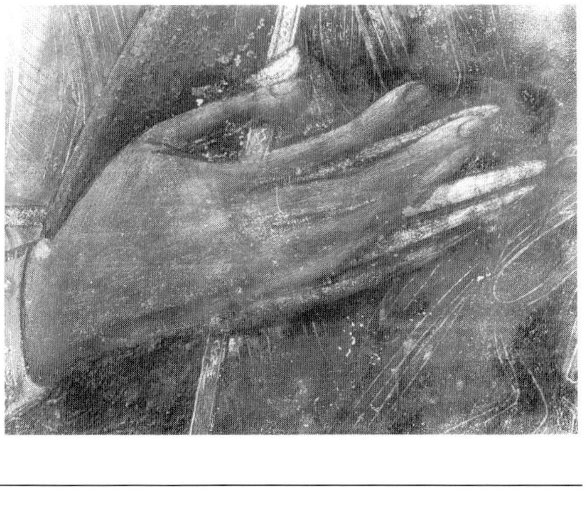

Figure 15. Guido da Siena, *Palazzo Pubblico Maestà*, detail of Virgin's right hand showing repainting, during restoration of 1948–50, Siena, Palazzo Pubblico (Fotografia di Fabio Lensini, Siena, Italy)

prevalence of aesthetic concerns. So the emphasis in this book falls on the historical significance of layered works of art. It attempts to resurrect meaningful additions where now lost, and to publicize those still preserved. Social contexts for the early "renovations" or transformations of paintings are introduced that help explain why certain images were reworked and how the added layers carry meaning. Finally, questions are raised and some answers suggested as to how a meaningful compromise sometimes can be achieved that respects both aesthetic and historical concerns.

The book concentrates on restoration in Tuscany between 1250 and 1500 for more than one reason. These two and a half centuries, spanning as they do the Late Romanesque, Gothic, and Early Renaissance styles, comprise a period when numerous earlier paintings were renovated for reasons of cult or taste. Also, modern Italian restorers happen to have been exceptionally active in Tuscany, so that as a consequence, a relatively large number of reworked images have been identified and some of them examined in detail from a technical point of view. For the sake of focus, the concentration on one chief area of artistic activity in Italy is desirable. But when available and relevant, comparative materials from other Italian regions, particularly Rome and Naples, are introduced for the sake of conveying some idea of how widespread were certain types of renovation activity.

My study is not intended to be a general survey of what happened in Italy or even in Tuscany alone. During this period, restoration was a multifaceted practice. A wide range of procedures were performed and the motivations underlying them were equally various and complex. Then as today, damage was a major cause of restoration. Paintings were frequently reworked for purely practical reasons. The surface of a panel burnt and blistered by candle flames might be brought in for repainting, or a mural deteriorating from the effects of moisture could be retouched with the simple purpose of restoring its original color and legibility. Straightforward restorations of this kind do not form the subject of this book.

A second motivation underlying many renovations is that of stylistic improvement. With shifts in aesthetic taste, paintings were often reworked to bring them up to date. Although this facet of restoration will be considered in several chapters of the book, it does not constitute the primary emphasis.

Still other restorations were accomplished for less easily fathomable reasons. One little-known example is the small Florentine *Madonna and Child with Saints and Angels* in the Worcester Art Museum, which can be attributed to Lippus di Benivieni (Figs. 16 and 17). The conservator Norman Muller discovered when he cleaned the panel in 1980 that the early Trecento work had been selectively repainted twice before about 1450. The original azurite mantle of the Virgin, subtly modeled with white in the highlights, was initially painted over with a solid azurite blue mantle decorated with a delicate gold tracery hem perhaps to give added emphasis to the figure. Then the mantle was repainted a second time with an azurite blue in egg tempera applied over a grey isolating layer.[25] As the original layer was found to be in excellent condition, these renovations could not have been initiated to repair damage. Nor can they be explained in terms of a simple updating because the original mantle was more fully and illusionistically modeled. In this case, the repaintings may reflect the peculiar whims of successive owners. Clearly, restorations were carried out during the period for a variety of reasons.

This study deals in depth with only certain more specific types of renovation applied to a select number of highly revered religious images. The book focuses on a small group of important late Medieval and Renaissance renovations, with the aim of uncovering what, on the basis of such evidence, appear to be prevailing practices, motivations, and attitudes. The renovations are initially examined from a technical point of view in order to determine exactly what was done and how the transformations were carried out. Because, however, the primary aim of the study is to set these practices within a historical and social context, I then investigate them in relation to contemporary religious and social traditions and practices, such as the expression of popular piety, the cult of images, and the church environment as a theater for the manifestation of more secular and civic concerns. The question of late Medieval and early Renaissance attitudes toward religious images from the past needs also to be considered in light of the contemporary conflict between the values of a traditional spirituality and the material concern with changes in fashion and taste.

The five central chapters of the book treat, in turn, five distinct types of renovation carried out for the purpose of spiritual enhancement. I begin with a chapter (Chapter 2) discussing the selective repainting of two famous late Dugento Tuscan Madonnas by Coppo di Marcovaldo and Guido da Siena in the context of the Byzantine tradition of refreshing devotional icons. The repaintings are considered as instances of what was a more widespread trend of Orthodox influence in Trecento Tuscany. Chapter 3 considers a related devotional phenomenon, the practice of rehousing fragments of revered images within new paintings. Two examples are discussed in which the head from an old, highly revered painting of the Madonna is enshrined inside a newly created image of the Virgin, and one where an early Madonna and Child is rehoused in several stages as the central panel of a devotional altarpiece.

The fourth chapter, on patron saints and their portraits, deals with two thirteenth-century panels of saints that were repainted relatively soon after

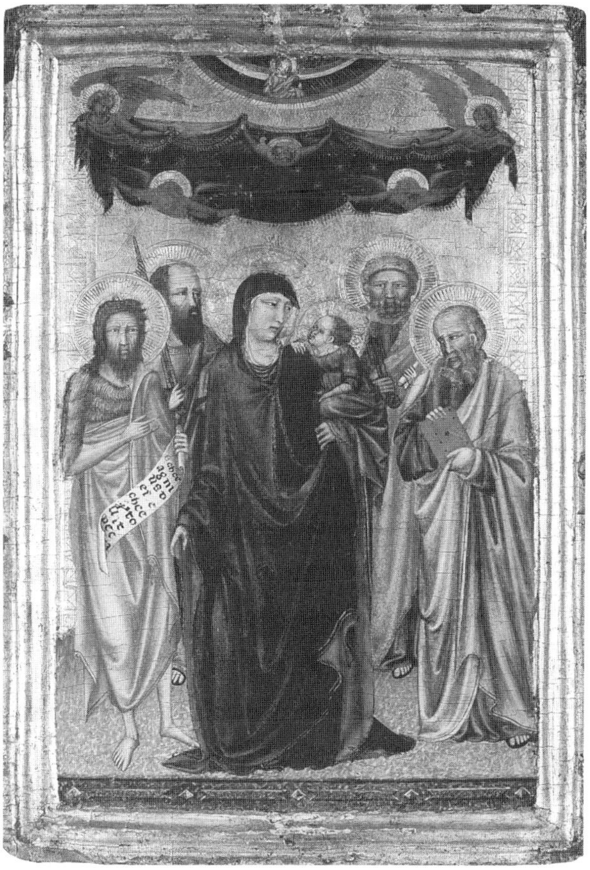

Figure 16. Lippus di Benivieni, *Madonna and Child with Saints and Angels*, c. 1330, after restoration, Worcester, Mass., Worcester Art Museum (Worcester Art Museum, Worcester, Mass.)

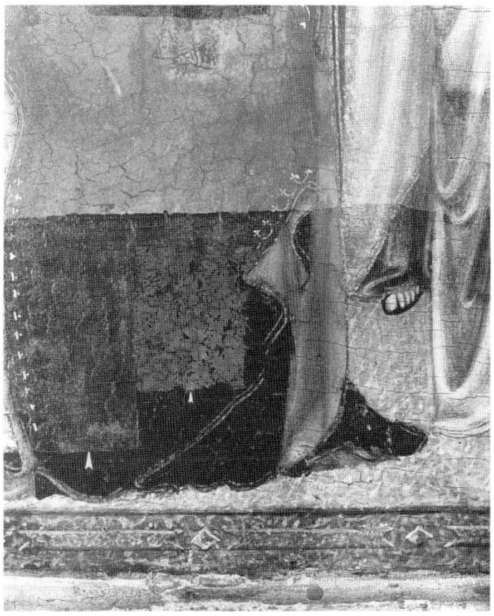

Figure 17. Lippus di Benivieni, *Madonna and Child with Saints and Angels*, detail of Virgin's mantle showing two stages of repainting, during restoration of 1980, Worcester, Mass., Worcester Art Museum (Worcester Art Museum, Worcester, Mass.)

they had been made. These renovations are treated in relation to the spiritual role played by such images in late Medieval Italy. Chapter 5 focuses on the Renaissance practice of radically reframing Gothic altarpieces. I explain that reframings of this kind were usually carried out on treasured family altarpieces destined to be enshrined in recently renovated chapel spaces. Just as such chapel renovations reflect both the public expression of family status and the more private display of religious piety, so the reframings must also be seen in relation to interacting secular and sacred concerns.

The final type of renovation considered is the repainting of murals. In Chapter 6, the renovations of two important early Trecento wall-paintings, the two *Maestà* by Simone Martini and Lippo Memmi, are discussed. As both murals decorate the interiors of major public buildings in Tuscany, I interpret their renovations in relation to their civic functions.

CHAPTER 2

The Repainting of Two *Maestà* Altarpieces

Two extremely important Tuscan Romanesque images of the Virgin were repainted in Siena in the early fourteenth century. From the point of view of physical presence alone, these paintings – Coppo di Marcovaldo's *Madonna del Bordone* and Guido da Siena's *Palazzo Pubblico Maestà* – represent two of the largest and most magnificent altarpieces of the Madonna Enthroned surviving from the late thirteenth century, when this iconography and physical format was so popular. It is thus a matter of some interest that in the second decade of the fourteenth century, about forty to fifty years after they were originally made, both images were selectively repainted by contemporary Sienese artists.[1] The *Madonna del Bordone*, originally painted in 1261 by the Florentine master, Coppo di Marcovaldo, was renovated in about 1315 by a Gothic artist close to Duccio (Pl. 4 and Fig. 18). As the conservators at the Istituto Centrale del Restauro in Rome confirmed when the painting was examined and cleaned in 1948, in the early Trecento, the faces of the Virgin and Child were repainted in the Gothic style directly over the thirteenth-century originals, and at the same time an underveil was added to the headdress of the Virgin to soften the outline of her face. The draperies of the Virgin and Child were, however, left in their Dugento form.[2] In an x-radiograph made of the face of the Madonna, the early Trecento repainting is almost completely penetrated, and a ghostly image of the original underlying structure appears (Fig. 19). The repainted face, very thinly executed, but opaque enough to block out the image underneath, is virtually transparent to x-rays. Only the new underveil in lead white shows up faintly on the radiograph. Consequently, what we see is evidence of the technique used in the original face. It is

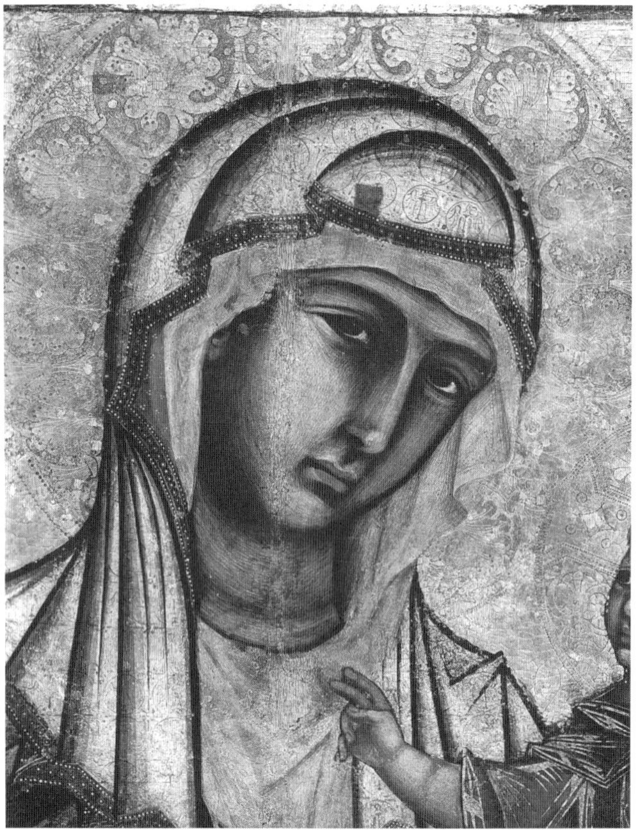

Figure 18. Coppo di Marcovaldo, *Madonna del Bordone*, 1261, detail of Virgin's face, Siena, Sta. Maria dei Servi (Roma, Istituto Centrale per il Restauro – Archivio fotografico)

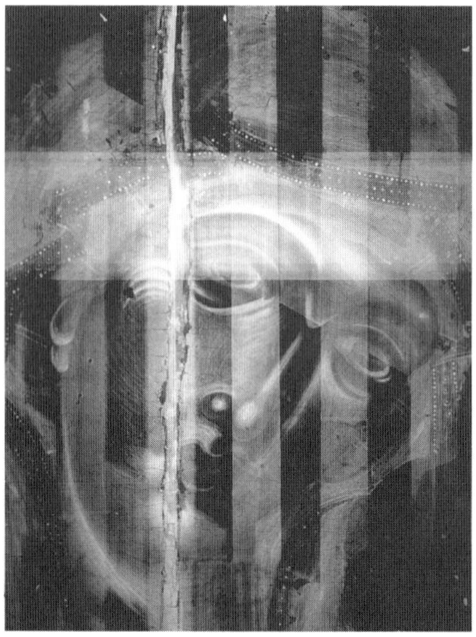

Figure 19. Coppo di Marcovaldo, *Madonna del Bordone*, x-radiograph of Virgin's face (Ing. Maurizio Seracini, EDITECH, Firenze)

apparent that in the fashion typical of the Tuscan Romanesque, Coppo di Marcovaldo used the opaque, lead white pigment much more thickly, so as to outline and highlight the facial features emphatically.

Guido da Siena's signed *Palazzo Pubblico Maestà* of about 1270–80 was refashioned in a similar way (Pl. 5 and Fig. 20). A Gothic artist in Duccio's circle repainted the face of the Virgin and added a new light-colored veil. At the same time, the Ducciesque master also repainted the flesh areas of the Christ Child, the faces of the two angels in the gable, and the lower part of the throne as well. But as conservators at the restoration laboratory of the Pinacoteca in Siena determined when the painting was examined in 1948–50, none of the draperies, including the cloth-of-honor, the green and gold robe of the Christ Child, and the pink underdress of the Virgin, was retouched in the early fourteenth century. The heavy repainting on the Virgin's blue mantle was estimated to date from the sixteenth century.

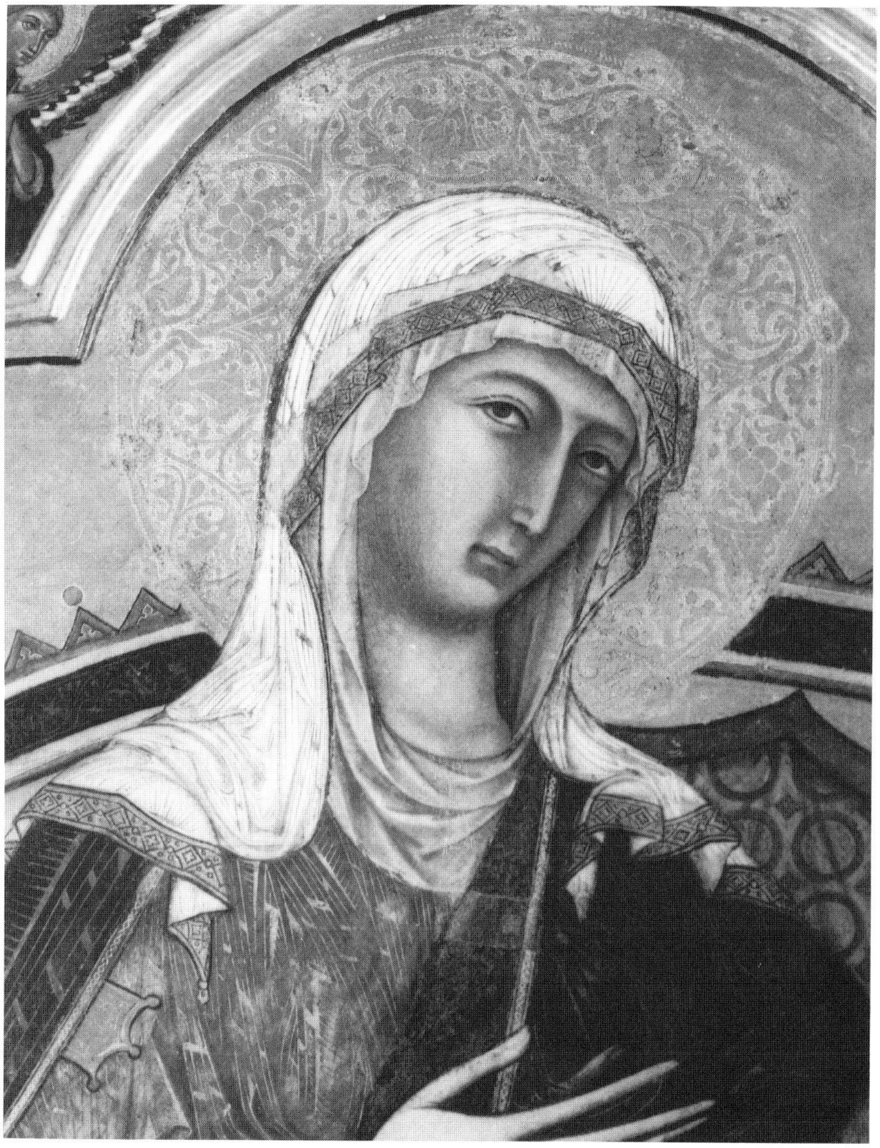

Figure 20. Guido da Siena, *Palazzo Pubblico Maestà*, c. 1270–80, detail of Virgin's face, Siena, Palazzo Pubblico (Foto Soprintendenza per i Beni Artistici e Storici di Siena, Italy)

Investigative studies involving x-radiographs also revealed that the early Trecento artist, before making his changes, scraped off the original paint layer and ground. He began his additions on a new gesso preparation, and in some areas, such as the neckline of the Virgin, the boundary between the original and the repainted areas can be relatively easily detected because the new ground was not always smoothly joined to the original gesso.[3] The face of the Palazzo Pubblico Virgin, originally strongly modeled in the style familiar from contemporary works by Guido da Siena such as the Virgin in *Dossal no.* 7 (Siena, Pinacoteca) datable c. 1271–9 (Fig. 21), now resembles the early Trecento face of the Virgin in Duccio's famous Siena cathedral *Maestà* (Fig. 22).

A CHANGE IN TASTE?

The traditional interpretation of these transformations explains the repaintings in terms of a change in taste.[4] It is argued that in the Siena of Duccio's time, the taste for things Gothic created an environment in which Romanesque works were renovated to bring them up to date. It is further argued that the repaintings provide evidence of an acute stylistic awareness on the part of patrons around 1315, and a marked preference for the new Gothic mode. However, this interpretation fails to explain why in each case the repainting was selective, focusing on the faces of the Virgin and Child and other flesh areas. It is true that portions of the throne in Guido da Siena's *Palazzo Pubblico Maestà* were modernized; however, in each of the altarpieces, the Romanesque draperies, which could have appeared equally out of date, were left untouched.

This is not to say that the repaintings are totally unrelated to Duccio's new Gothic mode, but rather that the relationship may be a less secular

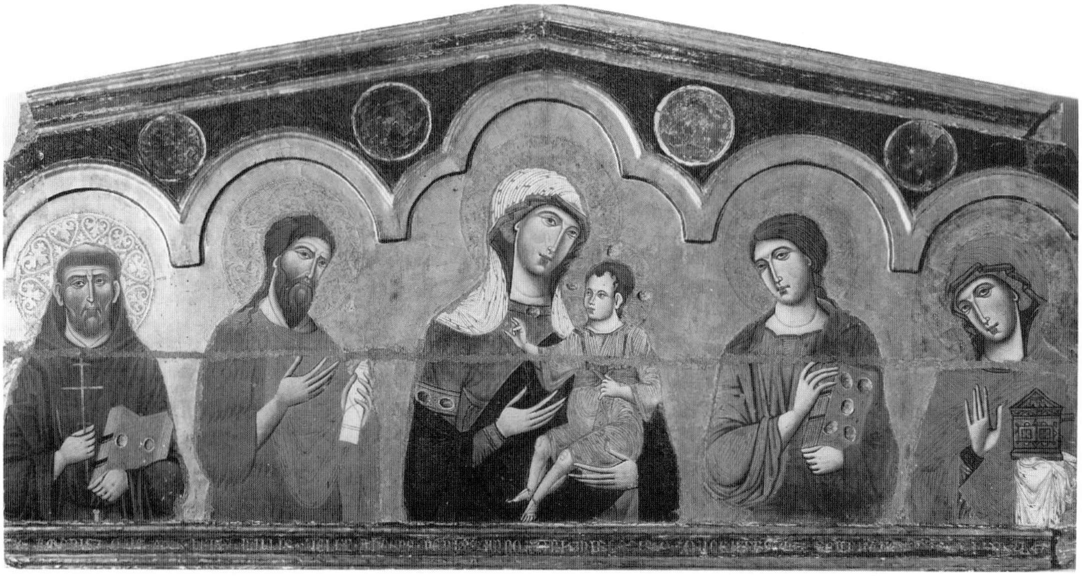

Figure 21. Guido da Siena, *Dossal no.* 7, c. 1271–9, Siena, Pinacoteca Nazionale (Foto Soprintendenza per i Beni Artistici e Storici di Siena, Italy)

one. Indeed, it is impossible to divorce the decision to repaint both images at this moment from one immensely significant event in contemporary civic history, the installation of Duccio's *Maestà* (Fig. 23). Chroniclers record how, on July 9, 1311, Duccio's recently completed, huge, double-sided altarpiece of the Virgin Enthroned with Saints, was carried in an elaborate devotional and civic procession through the streets of Siena to its destination on the high altar of the cathedral. To quote a familiar description of the festivities from the fifteenth-century chronicle history of Siena traditionally attributed to Agnolo di Tura:

the Sienese bore [Duccio's Maestà] to the cathedral on Wednesday, the ninth day of June, with great devotions and processions; with the bishop of Siena, all of the cathedral clergy . . . the city governors and officials, and all of the most worthy citizens in order, lighted lamps in their hands. And thus afterward the women and children went in procession through Siena around the Campo, all the bells sounding a gloria. And all this day the shops remained closed for devotion, and throughout Siena many alms were given to poor people, with many orations and prayers to God and to his Mother, Madonna always Virgin Mary, that she might aid,

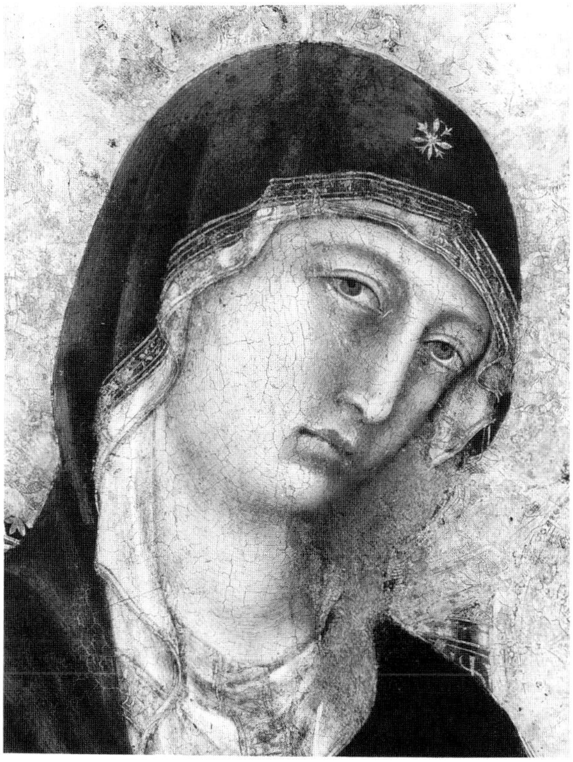

Figure 22. Duccio, *Maestà*, 1308–11, face of Virgin, Siena, Museo dell'Opera del Duomo (Foto Soprintendenza per i Beni Artistici e Storici di Siena, Italy)

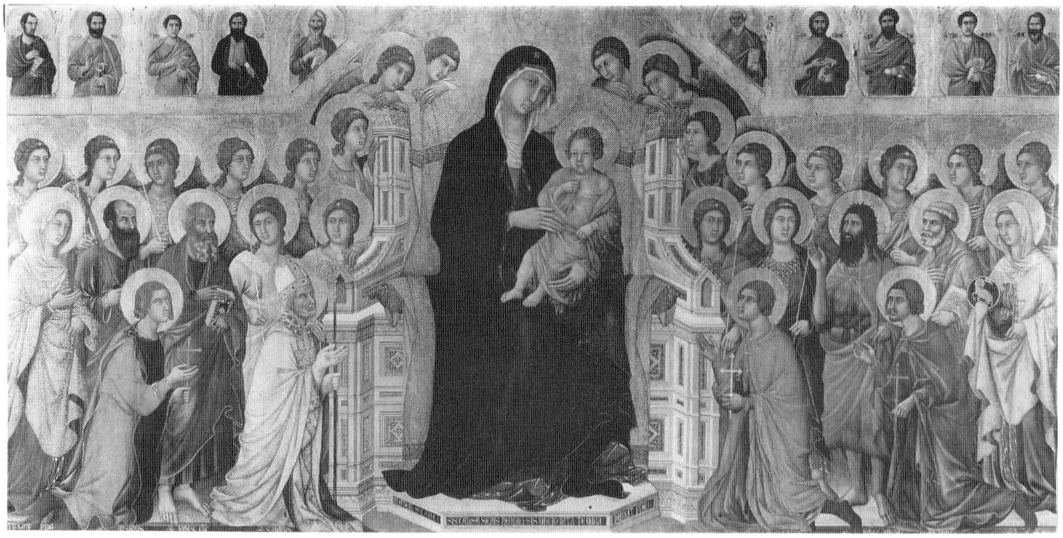

Figure 23. Duccio, *Maestà*, 1308–11, front, Siena, Museo dell'Opera del Duomo (Foto Soprintendenza per i Beni Artistici e Storici di Siena, Italy)

conserve and increase the city of Siena and its jurisdiction in peace and in a good state, as the advocate and protectress of this city and save it from every peril and every evil act against it. And thus was this painting placed in the cathedral on the high altar.[5]

Duccio's *Maestà* immediately became the most important religious image in Siena. And it is likely that as a result, his style was seen not only as the height of artistic fashion, but also became associated with religious efficacy. Duccio came to be considered the artist most able to express the divine in material form. When the two Romanesque paintings of the Virgin Enthroned were repainted in his style, they, by proxy, acquired some of the same power.[6]

And yet, in order to comprehend more fully what was taking place when these two Dugento *Maestà* were repainted, we need, initially, to extend our investigation beyond the narrow confines of Siena and its late Medieval artistic and civic atmosphere, for the practice of repainting was not limited to Siena or to the early fourteenth century. The repainting of these two Tuscan Madonnas has to be considered in the light of a much broader tradition.

A BROADER TRADITION

Similar practices of selective repainting can be identified elsewhere in Italy. One particularly relevant example is the Florentine Dugento *Madonna and Child Enthroned with the Annunciation* (Florence, Uffizi; from Villa in

Casale, nr. Greve in Chianti) by the so-called Greve Master (Figs. 24 and 25). When restorers in Florence in 1984–6 cleaned the altarpiece of its twentieth-century and extensive eighteenth-century repaint, they discovered that the Dugento faces of the Madonna and Child had also been retouched much earlier in tempera during the first decades of the Trecento by a minor Florentine artist. The Dugento face tints had been remodeled in the Tuscan Gothic style with a foundation of the green-colored "verdaccio" and overlying layers in lead white and vermilion. An intervening varnish layer helped to preserve the originals bcncath.[7]

Repaintings from later periods are also known. Duccio's *Perugia Madonna and Child*, the central panel of a polyptych probably commissioned

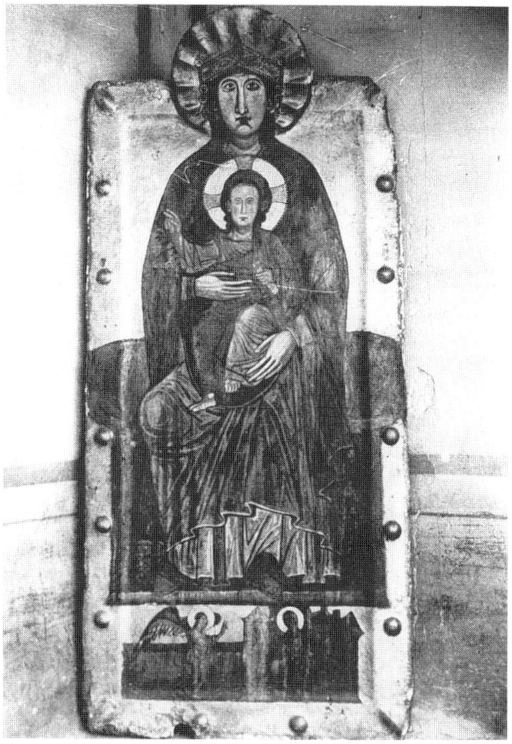

Figure 24. Greve Master, *Madonna and Child Enthroned with the Annunciation*, c. 1270–80, before restoration of 1984–6, Florence, Uffizi (Opificio delle Pietre Dure di Firenze, Italy)

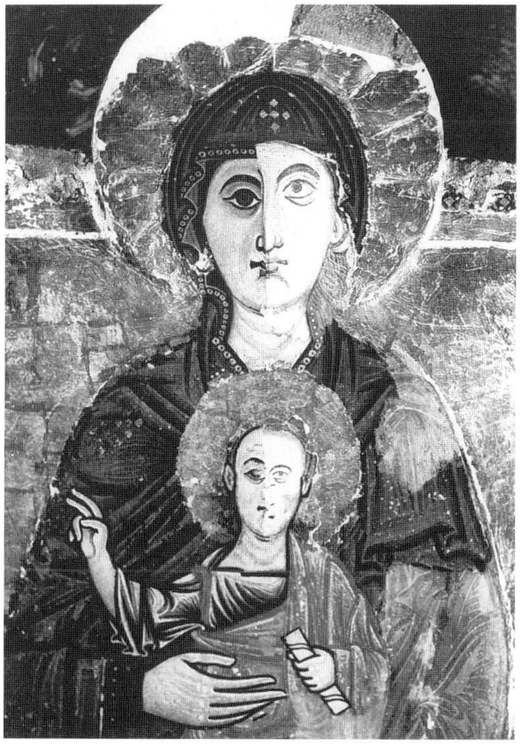

Figure 25. Greve Master, *Madonna and Child Enthroned with the Annunciation*, detail of Virgin's face showing partial removal of early 14th-c. repaint, during restoration of 1984–6, Florence, Uffizi (Opificio delle Pietre Dure di Firenze, Italy)

for the church of San Domenico in Perugia, was repainted in the late fifteenth century (Fig. 26). An Umbrian artist, usually identified as Benedetto Bonfigli, was responsible for repainting the faces and hands of the Virgin and Child, as well as the feet of the Child. These additions were removed in 1919 when the panel was restored and are thus no longer apparent.[8]

But in search of the origins of this tradition in Italy of selectively repainting portions of an image of the Madonna and Child, one is led away from Tuscany and Umbria to Rome. For the earliest example in Italy, with which I am familiar, is the *Madonna di San Luca* in the church of Sta. Francesca Romana in Rome (Fig. 27). Up until 1950, this iconic image of the Virgin and Child was generally held to be, in essence, a thirteenth-century Roman product.[9] The fact that the image had been heavily repainted was well known, and the most recent instance of these attentions was documented

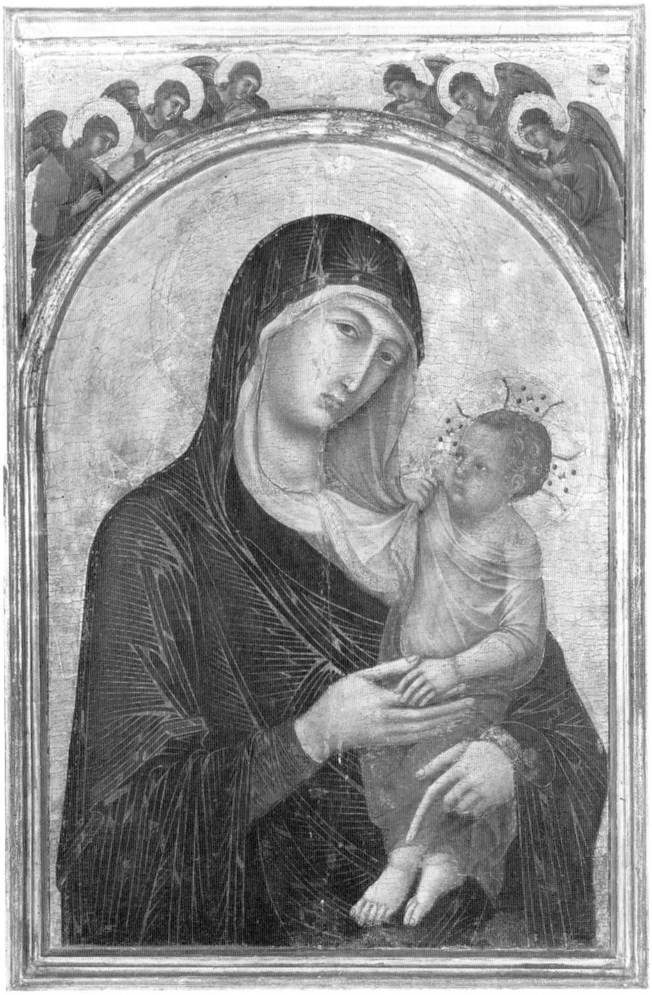

Figure 26. Duccio, *Perugia Madonna and Child*, c. 1310–15, Perugia, Galleria Nazionale dell'Umbria (Alinari/Art Resource, N.Y.)

by an inscription on the back of the panel: "Peter the German restored this panel in 1805 – pray for him."[10] But it was not until Pico Cellini restored the painting in the early 1950s that the truly compound nature of the image was uncovered. Cellini, by cleaning off overpaint, first revealed a thirteenth-century paint layer (Fig. 28), and then succeeded in removing this layer from what was an even earlier icon beneath, consisting of two pieces of linen painted in encaustic and depicting the heads of the Virgin and Child (Fig. 29). These linen pieces represent fragments of an image of somewhat larger scale dating from about the seventh century and of Roman workmanship. In the thirteenth century, they had been glued to a wooden panel and repainted.[11]

BYZANTINE ROOTS

In actual fact, however, this variety of restoration, practiced in Rome as early as the thirteenth century, represents a form of devotional repainting inherited from the Byzantine tradition. And it seems to have been in the early thirteenth century that the practice was introduced to Italy as part of the wave of Byzantine influence following the conquest of Constantinople by the armies of the Fourth Crusade in 1204. We have the *maniera greca* style and iconography of thirteenth-century panel-paintings from several main centers in Italy as an indication of the strength of this Eastern impulse. Indeed, it has long been suspected that the influence came not only indirectly, through the importation of icons from the East, brought back by crusaders, merchants, and diplomats, but also directly with the migration of artists themselves.[12] Recently, the *Kahn Madonna* in the National Gallery in Washington has been put forward as the evidence of a Byzantine artist working in Tuscany in about 1280 (Fig. 30). Although fundamentally Byzantine in style and technique, the painting betrays its Tuscan place of origin in minor details, including the incised floral designs of the halo and the blessing gesture of the Christ Child, but most notably in its overall format, that of a typical Tuscan altar panel.[13] Whether via Rome or into Tuscany directly, it must have been with this immigration of Byzantine icon painters in the thirteenth century that the technique of repainting devotional images was introduced to Italy.

The traditional Byzantine practice of repainting new images over old has been effectively documented this century in the process of modern restorations of icons. In 1967, Tasso Margaritoff, a conservator at the Byzantine Museum in Athens, drew attention to several examples in an article on a new method for detaching the successive overlying paint layers, one from the other. As one instance, he presented an Athenian icon of the twelfth or thirteenth century, which was repainted twice, once during the early

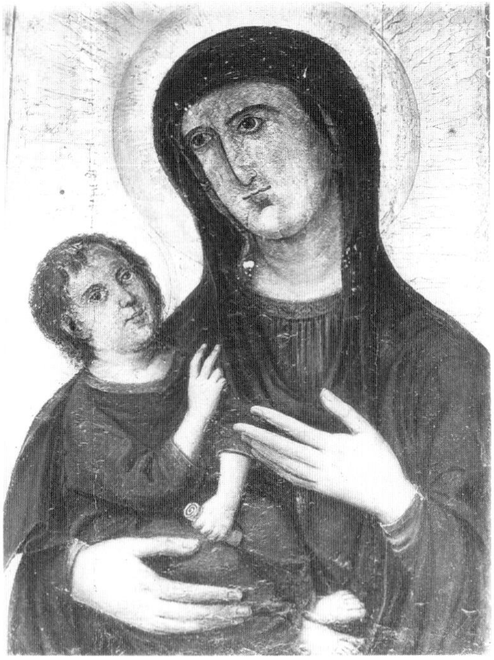

Figure 27. Madonna di San Luca, before restoration of c. 1950, Rome, Sta. Francesca Romana (la fotografia proprietà dell'Istituto Centrale per il Catalogo e la Documentazione, Roma, E20150)

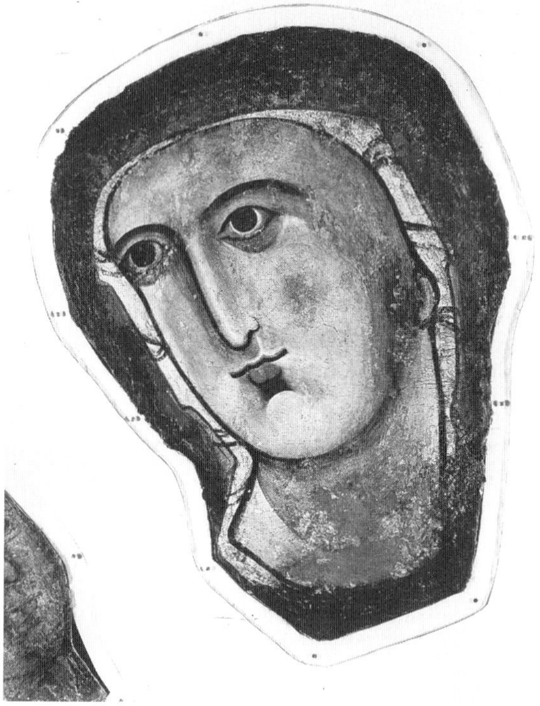

Figure 28. Madonna di San Luca, 13th-c. paint layer by a Roman artist, detached during restoration c. 1950 (la fotografia proprietà dell'Istituto Centrale per il Catalogo e la Documentazione, Roma, E28261)

seventeenth century and once, quite recently, in this century. Another is a sixteenth-century Athenian icon of the Virgin and Child, which though of high quality and good condition, was replaced in about 1710 by another version of the Virgin and Child composition.[14] Earlier examples can also be cited, such as a double-sided icon in the Byzantine Museum in Athens, with the Virgin Hodeghetria on the front and the Crucifixion on the reverse. Although the icon of the Virgin dates as late as the sixteenth century, the Crucifixion icon represents three earlier periods. The composition was first painted in the eleventh century, a background with stars and inscriptions was added a little later, and, finally, in the thirteenth century, a highly

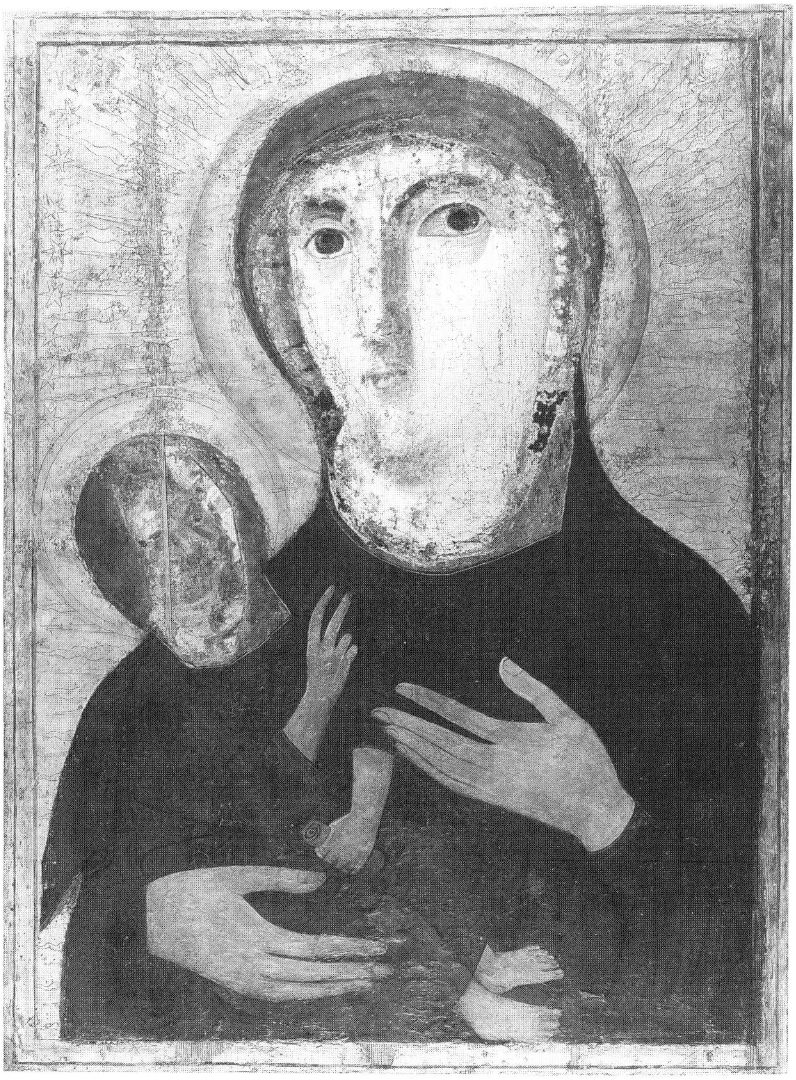

Figure 29. Roman, 7th c., *Madonna di San Luca*, after restoration of c. 1950 (la fotografia proprietà dell'Istituto Centrale per il Catalogo e la Documentazione, Roma, E47388)

skilled artist repainted the head of Christ and the figures of the Virgin and St. John.[15]

Modern icon restorers, by revealing well-preserved underlying layers, have deduced that the Byzantine practice of repainting cannot be always explained as motivated by a need to correct damage or to refresh the colors of an icon covered with darkened varnish and candle soot.[16] It has been suggested instead that repainting with a closely corresponding image had religious overtones in Byzantine societies.[17] Indeed, inscriptions painted on

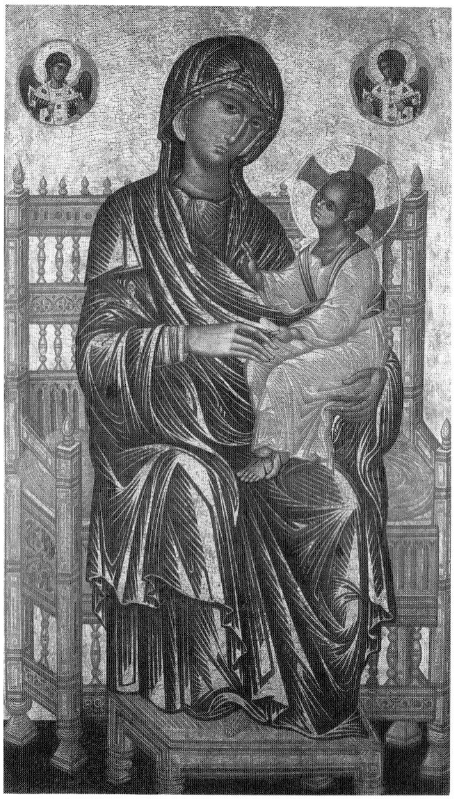

Figure 30. Byzantine, *Kahn Madonna,* 13th c., Gift of Mrs. Otto H. Kahn, Washington, National Gallery of Art (© 199: National Gallery of Art, Washington)

restored icons often refer to the restoration process in terms of a "renewal," thereby suggesting that the primary concern was to bring the image to new spiritual life by the application of a fresh coat of paint and a new material face.[18]

This Byzantine practice and its significance can be fully appreciated only in the context of the special role played by religious icons within the Orthodox church and for Orthodox worshipers more generally. Since the early Middle Ages, Latin and Greek theologians differed fundamentally in their understanding of the meaning and purpose of the icon within the church. In the West, the image of a divine person or event was considered primarily as a vehicle for instruction; religious paintings were not held to be revelations of a divine reality. As a corollary, artists were relatively free to represent sacred subjects according to their own interpretations. In contrast, in the Eastern church, the icon was interpreted metaphysically and played an extremely vital role. As a Christian image, it was held to represent an extension of the divine incarnation, and was therefore connected in an essential way to the core concept of Christianity. In an analogous way to the word of scripture, the word that in Christ was made flesh, the icon was believed to communicate to the faithful silently through representation. Through the power of the icon, the holy person or episode was made present in a mystical way.[19] For example, within the liturgy, an icon of Christ would have been considered Christ Himself, and similarly, an icon of the Virgin would have been believed to possess within itself the power and grace particular to the Virgin.[20] However, this was only true of the icon painted in the traditional manner by a fully sanctioned and inspired icon painter. Following in the footsteps of the apostle Luke, who was believed to have painted three images of the Virgin after Pentecost when he was in a state of illumination, the icon painter preserved in his image a direct, living link with the person represented by continuing sacred prototypes established in earlier authentic icons and recorded in manuals. Icon painting was a highly traditional and exact practice.[21]

Because of the Orthodox belief that the icon was a kind of incarnation of the holy person represented, the icon itself, in place of the holy person, could serve as the archetype for a new painted image. In the Byzantine tradition, new icons were often produced as copies of old images, particularly in the case of the so-called "wonder-working icons," and the fresh painting acquired all the powers of the old.[22] One of the most famous of these wonder-working icons is the *Virgin of Vladimir* painted in Constantinople in the early twelfth century and brought to Russia almost immediately. By the midtwelfth century, it was already extremely highly esteemed in Russia, being generally regarded as the protecting spirit of the country. Numerous copies were made, including the early fifteenth-century one now in the Russian Museum in St. Petersburg.[23]

The devotional repainting of old icons is perhaps best understood in relation to this practice of reproduction. The old icon, or archetype of the holy person, is repainted with an image that is in all fundamental attributes identical, though stylistically speaking it may be more modern. And in this way, an essentially new icon is created, which by physical and metaphysical proximity takes on all the spiritual resonance of its model.

POPULAR PIETY

There seems to be something fundamentally human and widespread, in the Jungian sense, in the belief that by repainting an image, one reactivates its power.[24] This perhaps can help to explain why the Byzantine practice of renovating icons caught on and lasted so long in Italy, despite the absence of an Orthodox liturgy. It caught on primarily at the very broad-based and much more universal level of popular piety.

It was at the level of popular religious practices and community beliefs that Italian Catholicism, in some aspects, most closely approached Byzantine

Orthodoxy. One devotional practice from this period in Italy that illustrates the closeness well is the tradition of replacing old, religiously efficacious images with new paintings that inherit the spiritual resonances of the superseded panels. Just as in Byzantine societies copies were made of wonder-working icons that became heirs to miraculous powers, similarly in Italy, new panels took on the associations of old ones. One interesting sequence begins with the miraculous thirteenth-century *Madonna* of the grain market in Florence, Orsanmichele, which when damaged in the fire of 1304 was replaced first by an early fourteenth-century *Madonna Enthroned*, and then by Bernardo Daddi's *Maestà* of 1346–7 (Fig. 31). The cult surrounding the thirteenth-century image – which had been seen to weep and was reputed to cure blindness, drive out demons, and heal the sick – was ultimately tranferred to Daddi's grand replacement. And in turn in the 1350s, Orcagna was hired to design a lavishly sculpted and imposing tabernacle to enshrine the new venerated image.[25]

Similarly, in Siena, the powerful, early thirteenth-century image of the Virgin Enthroned (Siena, Museo dell'Opera del Duomo) (Fig. 32), which originally stood on the high altar of the cathedral and was accredited with having secured the Sienese victory over Florence at the battle of Montaperti, was replaced in about 1270 by a new painting (Guido da Siena's *Madonna del Voto* – Fig. 33) and again in 1311 by Duccio's *Maestà*. An anonymous chronicler described the replacement of 1311 as follows:

> In this time . . . they decided to have a painting made for the high altar [of the cathedral] . . . and they removed the panel called the *Madonna degli Occhi Grossi* or the *Madonna delle Grazie* which stands today on the altar of San Bonifazio. That Madonna was the one which granted victory to the Sienese people when the Florentines were at Montaperti. And in this way the painting was *promoted* because the new one [Duccio's *Maestà*] which is much more beautiful and larger, was made . . . [emphasis added].[26]

The chronicler describes the replacement of the old image by Duccio's *Maestà* in terms of a promotion. The image was promoted in the sense that its powers and associations were transferred to a more magnificent painting. The divine essence in the image was given a new and more beautiful shell.

It must, likewise, have been at this popular level of religious behavior that the Byzantine practice of repainting venerated icons was appreciated and consequently appropriated in Italy. Certainly, it cannot be mere coincidence that right from the start in Italy the paintings selected for retouching were highly revered images, sometimes with miraculous associations; in short, Italian equivalents to the Byzantine wonder-working icons.

The *Madonna di San Luca* from Sta. Francesca Romana in Rome was one such Italian miracle-working image (Fig. 29). Using literary sources,

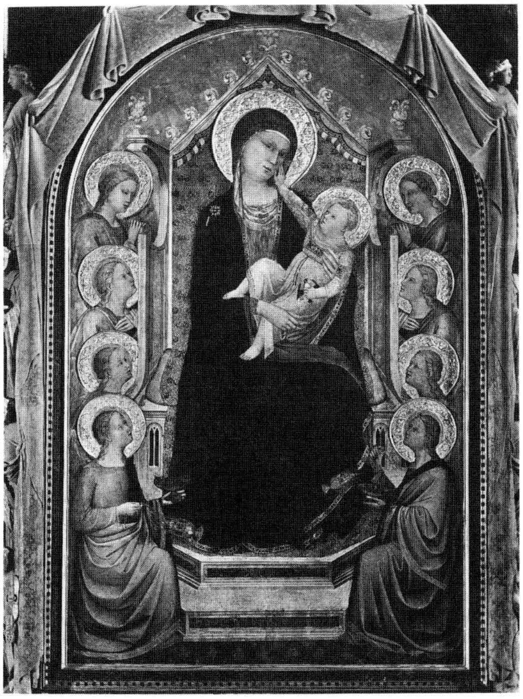

Figure 31. Bernardo Daddi, *Maestà*, 1346–7, Florence, Orsanmichele (Alinari/Art Resource, N.Y.)

Ernst Kitzinger has traced the devotional history of this image right back to the mideighth century, when an entry in the *Liber Pontificalis* records that Pope Gregory III (731–41) rewarded the icon with a heavy silver cover.[27] A second document discussed by Kitzinger and dating from the late Middle Ages describes the way in which the painting was displayed in the church, enshrined in a stone tabernacle and concealed by the silver cover donated by Gregory III.[28] Further, the document records that an inscription in silver letters on the image attested that the icon was painted in Troy by no other than St. Luke. It was believed to have been brought back to Rome and donated to the church by a crusader who had family ties to Sta. Francesca Romana. The remainder of the document, which, as Kitzinger remarks, was clearly meant to be displayed near the icon in the church, recounts the painting's marvelous history for the benefit of pilgrims and visitors. Two miracles in which the icon was involved are related. In a fire during the pontificate of Honorius III (1216–27), which partially destroyed the church (a fire that can be historically documented), the icon miraculously remained unharmed. Then, after having been removed while the church was under reconstruction, the icon returned on its own accord to its original position in the renovated building.[29]

This is the story. In reality, it must have been as a result of damage incurred during the fire that the image was repainted in the thirteenth century.[30] The fact that the faces of the Virgin and Child were, however, spared must have been considered miraculous and contributed to the image's increasing reputation. In any event, the thirteenth-century repainting can be explained as a renewal process performed on an important but damaged image, an image in need of physical and, by association, spiritual revivification. Whether the restoration was devotionally motivated, or occasioned by a propagandistic desire to make the image look as if it had miraculously survived the fire in immaculate condition, cannot be determined. What is certain, however, is that it was a strongly venerated icon with a long history of religious power that was singled out for repainting.[31]

It is, likewise, within this originally Byzantine tradition of repainting strongly venerated images that the Sienese renovations of Coppo di Marcovaldo's *Madonna del Bordone* and Guido da Siena's *Palazzo Pubblico Maestà* must be considered. For there is evidence to suggest that in each instance it was not only a civically important but also a religiously efficacious image that was selected for renovation.

In the case of Coppo's *Madonna del Bordone*, the image had auspicious origins in connection with the Sienese victory over Florence at the battle of Montaperti in 1260 (Pl. 4). The inscription on the frame records that the altarpiece was painted in 1261, soon after the date of the battle.[32] According

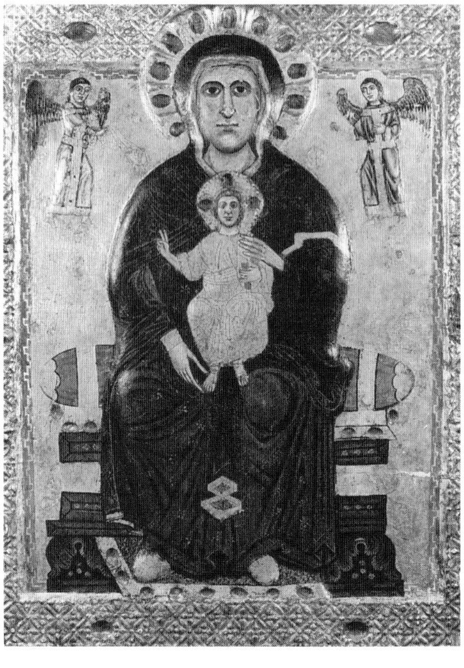

Figure 32. Tressa Master, *Madonna degli Occhi Grossi*, c. 1230–40, Siena, Museo dell'Opera del Duomo (Foto Soprintendenza per i Beni Artistici e Storici di Siena, Italy)

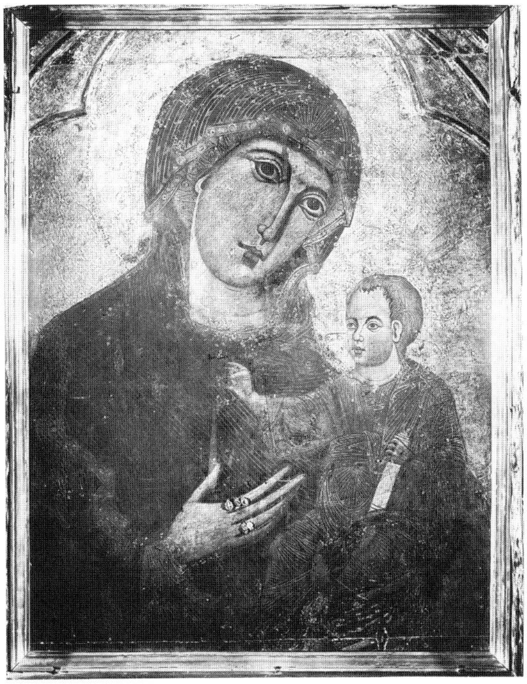

Figure 33. Guido da Siena, *Madonna del Voto*, c. 1270, Siena Cathedral (Alinari/Art Resource, N.Y.)

to a legend that can be substantiated in part, the Florentine artist, Coppo, was taken prisoner at Montaperti, but won the favor of the Sienese and his liberty by painting this masterpiece.[33] As Gertrude Coor-Achenbach discovered, a surviving list of the Florentines present at Montaperti does include one Coppo di Marcovaldo who acted as a shieldbearer.[34] That the image is intimately connected with the Sienese and Ghibelline victory over Guelph Florence has been recently underscored by Rebecca Corrie, who points to imperial references in the iconography, most significantly the repeat design of Hohenstaufen eagles on the Madonna's headscarf, as emblematic of the Virgin's loyalty to the Ghibelline cause.[35] Thus, the origins of the painting can be connected with a most significant event in the late Medieval history of Siena when the Virgin as patron saint displayed her preference for the people of Siena. As Helene Wieruszowski has recognized:

> In this period decisive events of civic history were often also landmarks in the development of relations between patron saints and their cities as indicated by the dedication of churches, sacred symbols, and paintings . . . and a considerable number of artistic representations of saints by major contemporary artists owed their origin to such historical events and the consequent commissions.[36]

For a painting like Coppo's *Madonna del Bordone*, such beginnings were auspicious, as they infused it right from the start with virtues and power through association. Coppo's image of the Virgin as Queen of Heaven, the first in a sequence of large enthroned Madonnas produced in Siena following the battle, must have become intimately connected in people's minds with the powerful Virgin who had presided at Montaperti.

The site for which the altarpiece was intended also would have enhanced the prestige of the image. Scholars are agreed that it was commissioned by the Sienese branch of the Servite order in whose church, Sta. Maria dei Servi, the panel hangs to this day. The order had been founded in Florence in 1233, and came to settle in a monastery just outside the walls of Siena on the invitation of the bishop in 1239.[37] By 1259, they had acquired a site inside the walls and were becoming increasingly prominent civically under the leadership of a Sienese prior general, Fra Jacopo da Siena.[38] They took possession of the ruinous parish church of San Clemente and began renovations that the communal government helped to fund in the years 1260 to 1262. [39] Documentary references suggest that, in accordance with Servite devotion for the Virgin, the alteration of the dedication of the church was carried out quickly, transferring the primary dedication to the Virgin while still retaining the patronage of San Clemente.[40] As has been generally assumed, Coppo's huge Madonna must have been destined to grace the main altar once the rebuilt church was ready for use.

In a shrine officially devoted to the worship of the Virgin, Coppo's *Madonna* was the original image on which these religious sentiments focused. One tradition states that the founders of the Servite monastery in Siena prayed before it.[41] But, perhaps most significantly, the *Madonna del Bordone* at some early point in its history gained the reputation of being able to work miracles. The word "bordone" means pilgrim's staff and, according to one plausible theory, the painting acquired its name from a pilgrim's staff that had been placed near the panel as an *ex voto*, a sign of gratitude for grace received.[42] A varient theory explains that the name arose because it was the custom for pilgrims to lay their staffs on the high altar just below the painting on their return from Rome.[43] An early indicator of the prestige in which the altarpiece was held are the copies that were commissioned, most notably the one made by Coppo himself for the Servites in Orvieto in about 1265–70.[44] From the seventeenth century, we have a document that shows that the painting has retained its powers and importance. In 1699, Monsignor Borgognini, the bishop of Montalcino – "moved by the greatest devotion for [this] sacred image" – purchased the chapel where the Madonna then stood with the purpose of embellishing it in honor of this Virgin.[45] It was the powerful images of the day that were enshrined or embellished, and such attentions, like the earlier repaintings, were a way of expressing devotion.

Guido da Siena's *Palazzo Pubblico Maestà* also had strong devotional credentials (Pl. 5). Like Coppo di Marcovaldo's *Madonna del Bordone*, Guido's altarpiece seems to have been commissioned to stand on the high altar of one of the major churches in Siena where it became a focus of veneration. In 1262, the Dominicans of Siena were awarded funds to complete the construction of their new church of San Domenico in its initial form, begun in 1225 on the hill of Campo Regio on a large piece of land donated by the Malavolti family. The commission of Guido's *Maestà* can be associated with the decoration of this new church.[46] However, the strongest, though at the same time the most controversial, evidence for this cult history is the inscription along the bottom front of the panel which reads: ME GUIDO DE SENIS DIEBUS DEPINXIT AMENIS: QUEM XRS LENIS NULUS VELIT AGERE PENIS ADO. D.M. CCXXI. The date of 1221 has been the source of much debate and confusion over the years as it is clearly not the date of execution, for the style of the painting indicates a date of about 1270–80.

The authenticity of the inscription has been argued for on two grounds. Firstly, as Offner and Stubblebine recognized, the text corresponds closely to the inscription running along the base of *Dossal no. 7* in the Pinacoteca in Siena, an altarpiece securely attributed to Guido da Siena and dating from the 1270s (Fig. 21).[47] Secondly, during the restoration of the painting in 1948–50, Cesare Brandi examined the inscription and confirmed that it must be contemporary with the oldest layers of paint. As Brandi pointed out, the pink of the Virgin's underdress overlaps the blue ground of the inscription in several places and one of the gilt striations from this dress runs down over the lettering. Brandi also affirmed that these overlapping areas, clearly visible in detailed photographs (Fig. 14), are portions of the original, late Dugento painting.[48]

Since 1950 and the confirmation of the inscription's originality, two alternate hypotheses have been put forward to explain the mysterious date of 1221. Enzo Carli argued that the date was inherited from an older work that Guido's *Maestà* both replaced and commemorated.[49] This theory was subsequently taken up by Hellmut Hager.[50] But the more convincing explanation was presented first, but only partially, by James Stubblebine and then developed and refined by Julian Gardner. As both scholars point out, the year 1221, the year of St. Dominic's death, was a date of great significance for the Dominican order.[51] Such a date could plausibly have been added both to emphasize the image's connection with the religious leader of the order, and thereby to give to the image added devotional force, but also to make Guido da Siena's *Palazzo Pubblico Maestà* one of the oldest and, as a consequence, one of the most efficacious altarpieces in Siena. Significantly, it was this highly revered image that was singled out for devotional repaintings alongside Coppo's *Madonna del Bordone*.

As a final point, it is tempting to speculate that the early Trecento repainting of Guido da Siena's *Maestà* was also connected with the resonant date of 1221. Perhaps the renovation of the image was ordered just prior to 1321 as a way of commemorating and celebrating the centenary of St. Dominic's death and his close affiliation with the altarpiece as recorded in its inscription.

□ □ □

It has been argued in this chapter that the selective repainting of religious images in late Medieval Italy, in particular the repainting of two Tuscan Maestà, can only be fully comprehended within the more ancient Byzantine tradition of the renewal of devotional icons. It seems to have been at this time of cross-fertilization that the Byzantine practice of repainting, along with other popular religious habits, was introduced into Italy and taken up. It is only within the context of Orthodox influence that many aspects of the initially curious phenomena of late Medieval retouching can be explained.

One more piece of evidence may act as final proof. As I remarked near the beginning of this chapter, the traditional explanation for these renovations, based on the theory of a marked change in taste c. 1315, fails to account for the selectivity of the repainting. Why, for example, were the faces of Coppo di Marcovaldo's *Madonna del Bordone* and Guido da Siena's *Palazzo Pubblico Maestà* transformed, but the draperies left with their Romanesque appearance? The context of Orthodox ideas and popular devotional practices does provide at least a partial answer. In the Eastern art of icon painting, the face, hands, and feet of the holy person, being the essential gesturing parts through which the archetype communicates with the worshiper, are considered most important. Consequently, when covered with decorative, silver-gilded plates (*riza* or *oklad*), as icons so often were in the Middle Ages, it was essential that these features be left exposed. One example is a covering for an icon of Saints Peter and Paul, dating from the first half of the twelfth century and now in the Novgorod Museum of Art and Architecture in Russia (Fig. 34). Holes were left in the covering to reveal the saints' faces, hands, and feet.[52] Selectively retouching the faces of a Virgin and Child with a new coat of paint represents an analogous devotional gesture. The most essential elements of the incarnate image were renewed in order to embellish and reactivate the whole.

Thus, renovations of the kind discussed in this chapter and exemplified specifically by Coppo di Marcovaldo's *Madonna del Bordone* and Guido da Siena's *Palazzo Pubblico Maestà* have to be interpreted within the context of popular religious practices inherited ultimately from the Byzantine

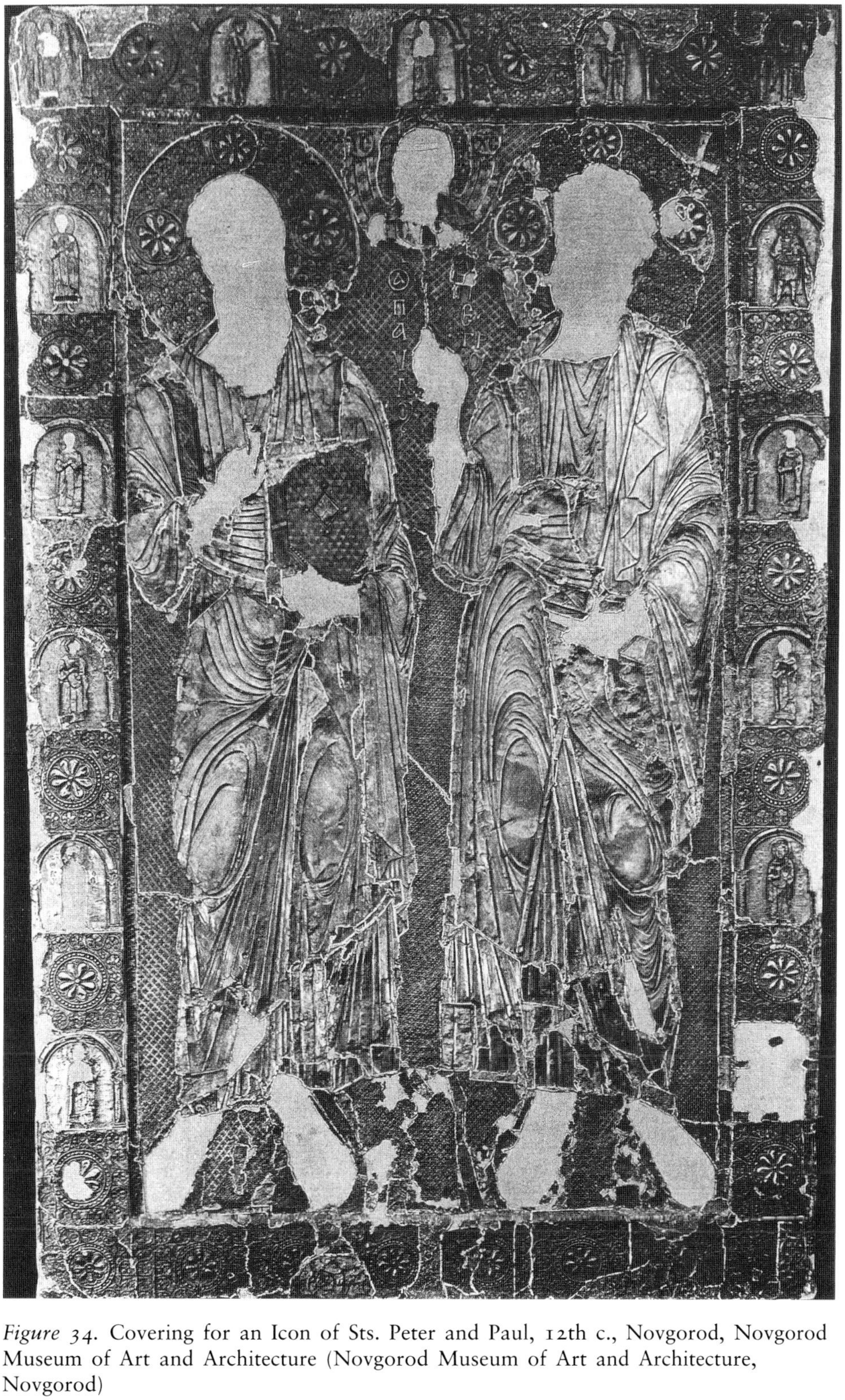

Figure 34. Covering for an Icon of Sts. Peter and Paul, 12th c., Novgorod, Novgorod Museum of Art and Architecture (Novgorod Museum of Art and Architecture, Novgorod)

tradition. Although stylistic modernization occurs – indeed, it is an inevitable part of Medieval and Renaissance repainting – updating should not be considered an end in itself. Rather, the act of modernization should be seen in a devotional light. In the case of the two Madonnas by Coppo and Guido, for example, it is likely that the up-to-date style of the repainting, in particular the renewed aspects of the faces and hands, ensured more effective communication with the contemporary worshiper. In addition, the association of this style with Duccio's *Maestà* altarpiece, the most esteemed religious image in Siena at the time, probably lent increased power. In short, when these two Tuscan Madonnas were retouched by artists close to Duccio in the early Trecento, a devotional activity was taking place. Highly revered images were given a fresh coat of paint both as a reward for past efficacy and to effect a renewal of power.

CHAPTER 3

Enshrining the Remains of Revered Images

A large number of the renovations performed in the late Gothic and early Renaissance period in Tuscany, whether they involved simple retouchings or more extensive structural procedures, were carried out on images with a strong reputation for religious efficacy and were devotionally motivated. Works of art acquired such reputations on the basis of three sets of credentials that they often possessed in combination. One was the power to work miracles, an ability often initially known only locally through stories, but later established through recorded legends and an institutionalized cult. A second was age. Very old paintings were often highly revered because of their age and authority. Finally, there was the credential of an exotic origin. Byzantine icons or even paintings resembling them were especially cherished because of their association with the concentrated and mystical spirituality of the East and because they were believed to mirror more closely the image of the divine. Even in a very fragmentary state, such highly revered works were carefully preserved just as a relic might be. And as an extension of the preservation process, images of this kind were sometimes renovated for the sake of spiritual renewal. This chapter has as its focus three revered paintings, two surviving only as fragments, that were, in each case, preserved and revitalized by enshrining the old image within a newly painted work. In the first instance, the painting was an old panel of the Virgin and Child that was rebuilt ultimately as the central portion of a Madonna and Saints altarpiece. However, in the other two examples, the renovation process was even more startling: The original images survived in fragmentary form – in each case, only the head from an old painting of the Madonna was salvaged – and the restoration process involved creating a new image of the Virgin around the preserved piece. Through renovation, the remains of old, efficacious images were given new life.

THE SELVE MADONNA

The first of these salvaged panels is preserved as part of a complex, hybrid altarpiece housed in the church of SS. Filippo e Giacomo at Lecceto near Malmantile just west of Florence (Figs. 35 and 36). The altarpiece, representing the Madonna and Child Enthroned in the central panel and to the sides Sts. Catherine of Alexandria, Gregory the Great, Dominic and Catherine of Siena with the Annunciation above, now takes the form of a Renaissance pala set in a classicizing architectural frame. However, close scrutiny reveals that the tripartite composition has actually been assembled from diverse elements. The central Madonna and Child is painted on panel apparently in the style of the prolific mid-Quattrocento Florentine artist Neri di Bicci, as seen most obviously in the characteristically chubby face of the Christ Child with his turned-up nose. In contrast, the lateral portions, painted originally on panel but later transferred to canvas, can be attributed to the circle of Biagio d'Antonio, a later Quattrocento master who collaborated during the early 1480s with Domenico Ghirlandaio and then set up a workshop in Faenza.[1] Stylistic comparisons can be drawn between the standing saints in the lateral portions of the Lecceto triptych, with their typically large, low foreheads, long noses, and intensely staring eyes, and the saints in Biagio d'Antonio's *Faenza Altarpiece* (Faenza, Pinacoteca Comunale) of 1483–4 (Fig. 37).[2] But this triptych format with stylistically diverse central and lateral panels was evidently not the original structure, for it is apparent that the top of the central panel in the Lecceto triptych has been cut, leaving little space for the Madonna's halo; and this must have been done in order to align the three compartments when the side panels were added and the pala created. Formerly, the central *maestà* image either stood on its own as an independent altarpiece or functioned as the central panel of an earlier work.

Furthermore, by focusing on the central Madonna panel alone, it becomes clear that it, too, is a complex, renovated structure. Initially, one is puzzled by the stylistic inconsistencies in the image, particularly in the area of the Virgin's face. How in a mid-Quattrocento Madonna can one account for the retarditaire appearance of the slit eyes, a characteristic usually associated with Gothic works, as well as the use of stippled gilding to decorate the Virgin's halo and the border of her mantle? An even more obvious archaic element is the raised disc on which the Virgin's head and halo are represented, a feature reminiscent of Dugento works.

In fact, the central panel of the Lecceto triptych seems to have been

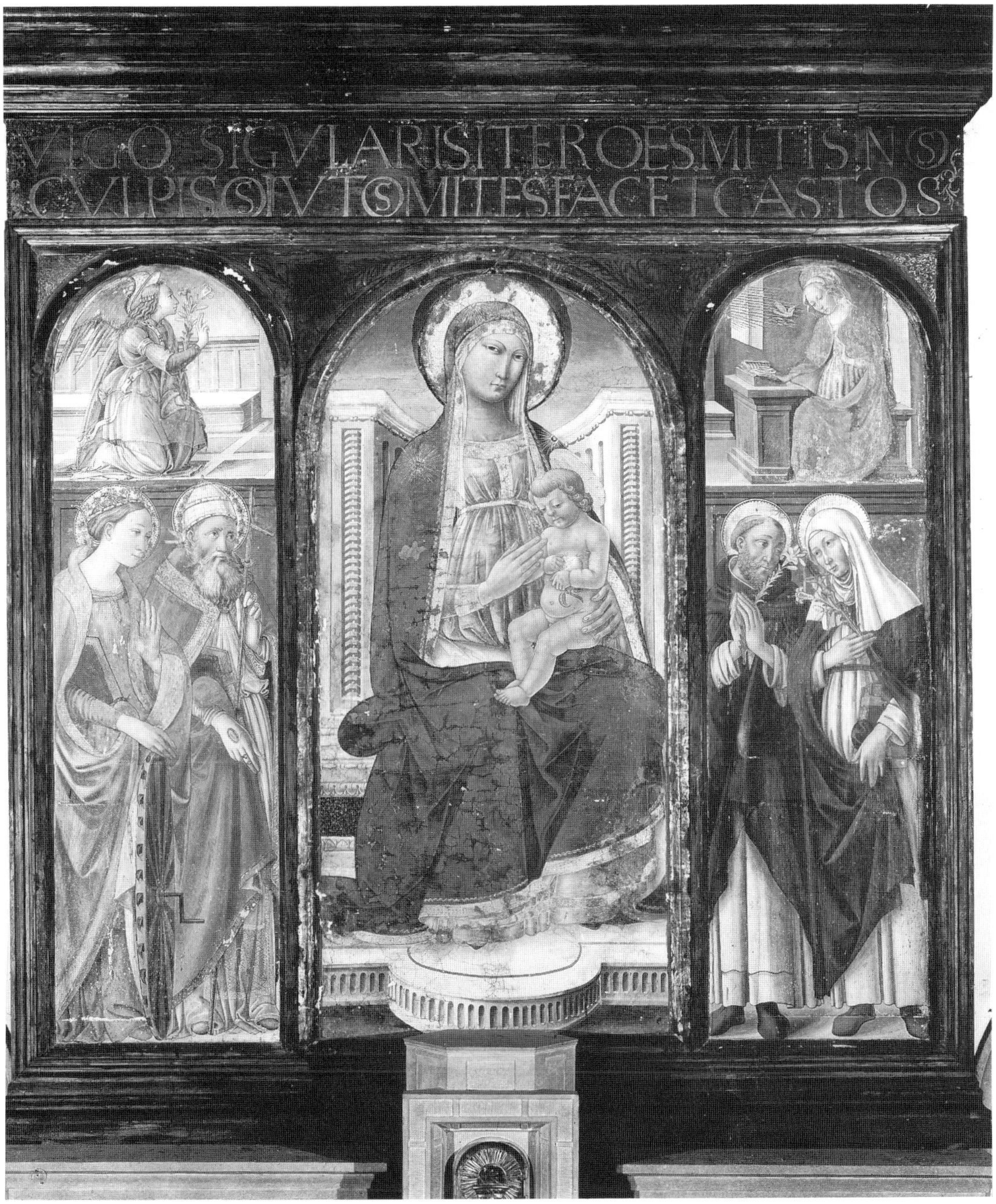

Figure 35. Neri di Bicci, *Selve Madonna*, c. 1482, Lecceto, SS. Filippo e Giacomo (Archivio Fotografico Soprintendenza per i Beni Artistici e Storici di Firenze, n. 159415)

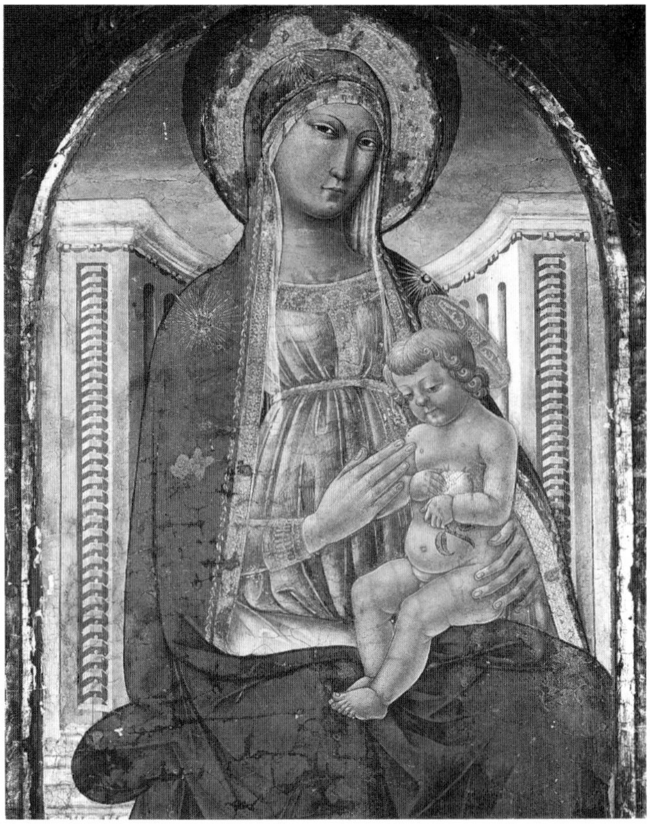

Figure 36. Neri di Bicci, *Selve Madonna*, c. 1482, detail of Virgin's face, Lecceto, SS. Filippo e Giacomo (Archivio Fotografico Soprintendenza per i Beni Artistici e Storici di Firenze, n. 159416)

renovated on two, or perhaps even three, separate occasions before being joined to the lateral panels with side saints to form a Renaissance pala (Fig. 38). Deep fissures running horizontally from either side of the Madonna panel at the level of the Virgin's neck, which reach the head disc at about one-third of its height, provide the clue to the earlier construction of the work. It took the form of an "articulated rectangle," that is, a rectangular panel with a disc of wood wedged into the center of its short, upper side. This was a variety of panel-painting construction popular in the Dugento particularly for altarpieces of the Virgin and Child enthroned; indeed, Edward Garrison includes thirty examples in his catalogue of Italian Romanesque panels.[3] Thus, the central Madonna panel must date back to the Dugento. We can imagine how it consisted of an image of the Virgin and Child enthroned in which the body of the Virgin and the entire figure of the Christ Child were represented on the rectangular portion of the panel, but

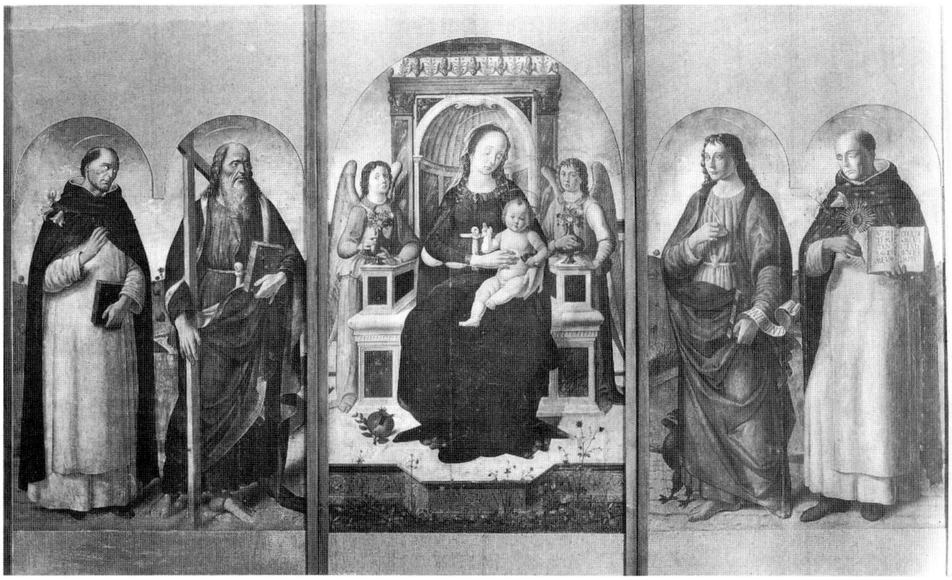

Figure 37. Biagio d'Antonio, *Faenza Altarpiece*, 1483–4, Faenza, Pinacoteca Comunale (Alinari/Art Resource, N.Y.)

the Virgin's face and halo were isolated above on the inserted disc of wood.[4] The recent discovery that the inserted disc is made of a different type of wood from the rest of the rectangular panel may suggest an even earlier origin for this important portion of the image. The fragment bearing the Virgin's face would then have been salvaged and reused in the Dugento on account of an established devotional reputation.[5]

Technical evidence also reveals that the Madonna and Child panel in its Dugento form underwent renovations in the Trecento. At this time, round-edged triangles of wood were added to either side of the circular head disc to transform the upper section of the structure into a solid arch, a shape more in line with contemporary standards of altarpiece construction. The image also seems to have been repainted; indeed, areas of the figures, most notably the red lake dress of the Virgin, still exhibit the fine, parallel brush strokes typical of the Trecento tempera modeling technique. Unfortunately, it has so far proved impossible to securely identify the master responsible for this first stage of modernization, even with the help of x-rays, as when large areas of the image were repainted again later, in the mid-Quattrocento, a dense layer, opaque to x-rays, was applied to cover the Trecento features.[6] Still, on the basis of the figures' general outlines and the visible areas of Trecento drapery, it may be possible to tentatively identify the first restorer as an early Giotto follower, perhaps Taddeo Gaddi.[7]

About a century later in the mid-Quattrocento, the next set of renovations

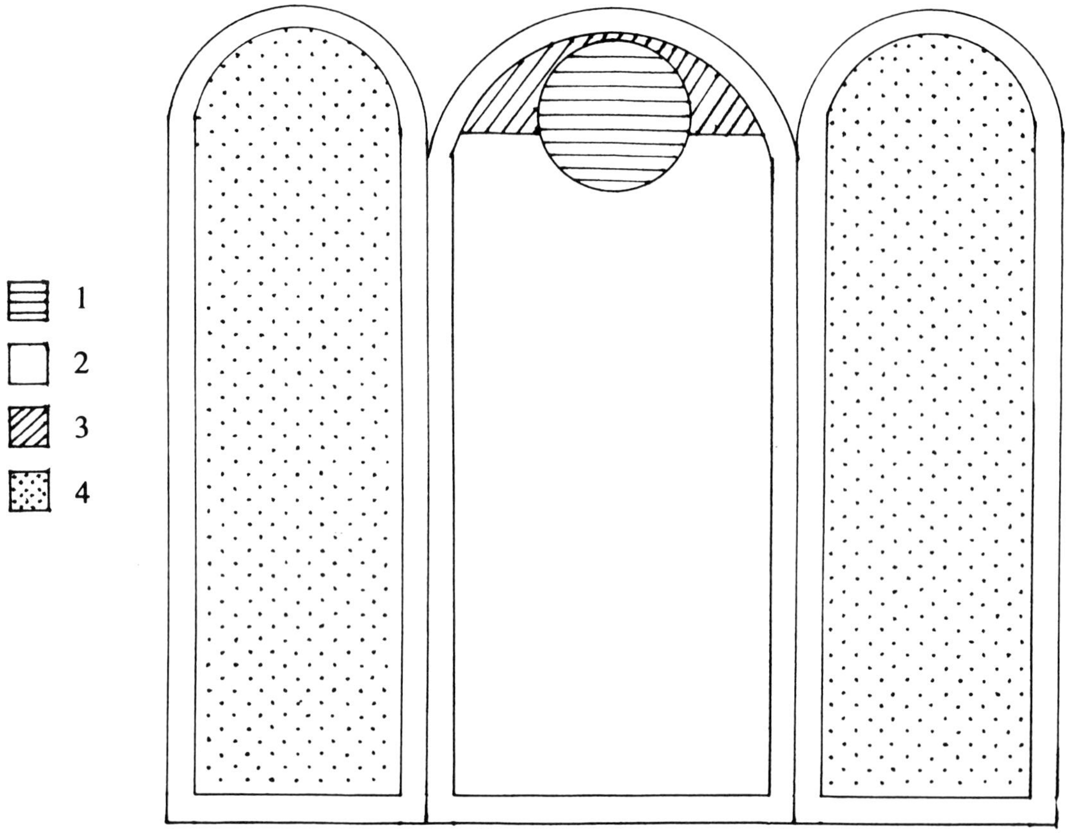

Figure 38. Stages of Construction of Selve Altarpiece: 1. head disc, Byzantine (?) or Romanesque; 2. articulated rectangle, 13th c.; 3. Madonna and Child Enthroned, 14th c., Florentine, repainted by Neri di Bicci, c. 1482; 4. side panels added and pala created, circle of Biagio d'Antonio, c. 1489 (Anne Finnessy, Kingston, Ontario, Canada)

to the central panel of the Lecceto triptych was carried out. The faces and draperies of the Virgin and Child were selectively repainted and regilded. However, in this instance, the additions were made in a manner sensitive to the Trecento layer of the altarpiece. Specifically, Neri preserved the Gothic, orientalizing appearance of the Virgin's face and attempted to duplicate the tooled gold haloes and drapery borders typical of the Tuscan Gothic style.

In summary, a careful, surface examination of the style and construction of the Lecceto triptych reveals its compound nature. The disc carrying the Virgin's head and halo may represent the oldest part of the complex, preserved in fragmentary form from an early image and subsequently incorporated into a Dugento structure. However, this hypothesis remains to be confirmed. The hybrid central panel of the Madonna and Child dates back to the Dugento and has been renovated twice, initially in the Trecento, when the shape was updated and the figures repainted, and again by Neri di Bicci in the midfifteenth century, who repainted and regilded portions of the image. Finally, it was later in the fifteenth century that the triptych was assembled by inserting the isolated Madonna panel as the central section into a Madonna and Saints altarpiece of Renaissance design. Such repeated renovations indicate a strong desire to preserve and regenerate the original Dugento Madonna or its even earlier face. In order to discover just why this was the case, we must investigate the early history of the image.

Tracing the provenance of the Dugento Madonna will help to provide clues to its origins and devotional significance. As mentioned before, at present, the triptych of which the Madonna panel forms a part is housed in the majestically austere, late Quattrocento altar-chapel of the Dominican church of SS. Filippo e Giacomo at Lecceto, a chapel erected under the patronage of the Florentine statesman Filippo Strozzi and dedicated to the Virgin (Fig. 39). However, this was most likely not the earliest traceable location of the central panel. As Eve Borsook has suggested, Strozzi probably transferred the painting of the Madonna from a nearby church, Sta. Maria delle Selve, close to the town of Lastra a Signa, where he held patronage over another chapel dedicated to the Virgin.[8]

Sta. Maria delle Selve is a church with a strong devotional history centering on the worship of the Virgin (Fig. 40). The origins of the church can be traced back to a simple oratory or small chapel on the site, where the Carmelite saint, Andrea Corsini (1301–74), is said to have had his famous vision of the Madonna. The saint's early biographers record how, in his younger years as a novitiate, Andrea went to the Selve chapel to celebrate his first mass and the Virgin appeared in the company of throngs of angels to tell Andrea that she had chosen him as her special servant.[9] Subsequently, in 1343, when the chapel and surrounding land were given to the Carmelites of Florence, they erected a new church and adjacent monastic buildings, and the chapel used by Andrea Corsini was incorporated into the structure of the church.[10] By the year 1400, the church was complete, having a central nave terminating in a choir chapel, two chapel spaces on either side of the nave with altars, and the subterranean chapel of Andrea Corsini attached by steps to the choir.[11]

Records indicate that during the late Medieval and early Renaissance period, at least three important images of the Virgin were housed at the Selve church. One was an alabaster statue that stood on the altar in the crypt chapel of Andrea Corsini. According to legend, it was this Virgin who took bodily form and spoke to Andrea.[12] A second image was the "Madonna delle Grazie," located on the first altar to the right of the nave. Already in 1390 there are accounts of the great veneration for this Madonna, with devotees coming from neighboring communes such as Pistoia

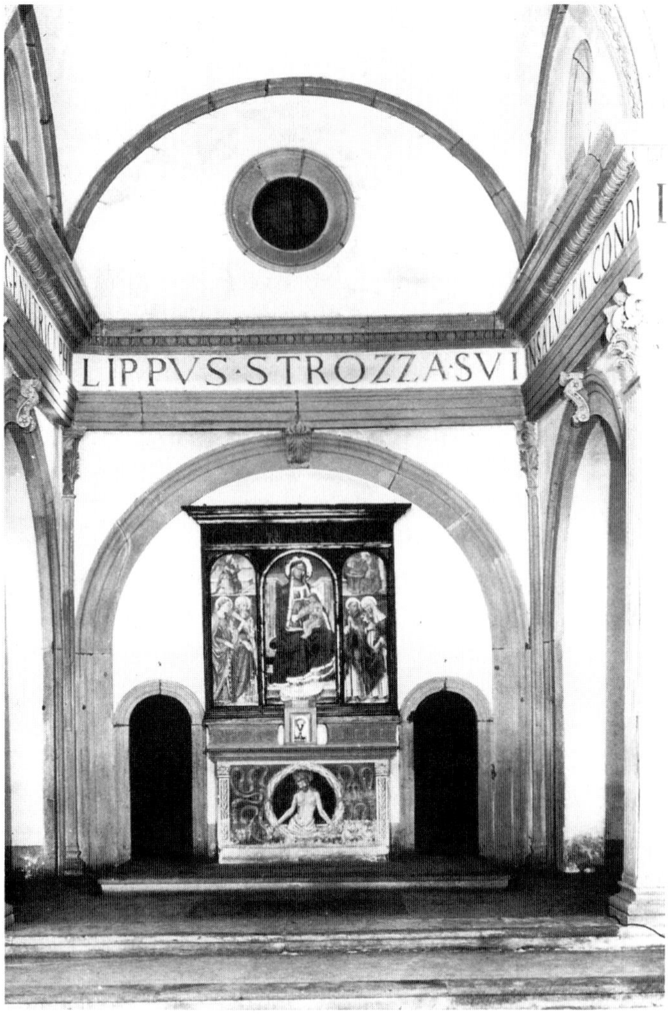

Figure 39. SS. Filippo e Giacomo, Lecceto, altar chapel (Archivio Fotografico Soprintendenza per i Beni Artistici e Storici di Firenze)

to worship at the altar.[13] During the fifteenth century, the Soderini family held patronage over the altar housing this highly revered Madonna.[14]

A renovation project undertaken by Neri di Bicci for the Soderini can be connected with the image of the *Madonna delle Grazie*. Neri di Bicci records in his work-diary entry for September 8, 1454, that at the behest of the friars of Sta. Maria delle Selve and Tommaso di Lorenzo Soderini, he painted portions of a tabernacle. According to his description, the tabernacle consisted of an old image of the Madonna and Child housed in the central compartment, new panels to either side with representations of Carmelite saints carried out by Neri himself, and, also by Neri himself, an image of God the Father in the gable above. Significantly, he describes the central Madonna as "painted in the very old Greek [Byzantine] style."[15] It seems safe to suppose that the iconlike Madonna enshrined in a tabernacle was the *Madonna delle Grazie* from the altar patronized by the Soderini. The present whereabouts of the tabernacle is unfortunately unknown, but it appears to have been in the Selve church as late as 1927, for Raimond van Marle, in his *Italian Schools of Painting*, lists among the works attributed to Neri di Bicci a "tabernacle around a Byzantine Madonna" in Sta. Maria delle Selve.[16] Guido Carocci's more detailed description of 1895 makes the correspondence even more certain: "A Madonna of the twelfth century of Byzantine style, within a tabernacle painted by Neri di Bicci."[17]

It is, however, the third image of the Virgin originally enshrined in the Selve church and a renovation project carried out on the image also by Neri di Bicci that most concern us here. This was the *Madonna del Carmine* that stood on the second altar to the right of the nave.[18] The original image is no longer in the church and no descriptions survive; however, one can perhaps gather something about its appearance on the basis of other still extant Madonnas used by neighboring Carmelite foundations.

The Carmelites typically chose representations of the Madonna that were

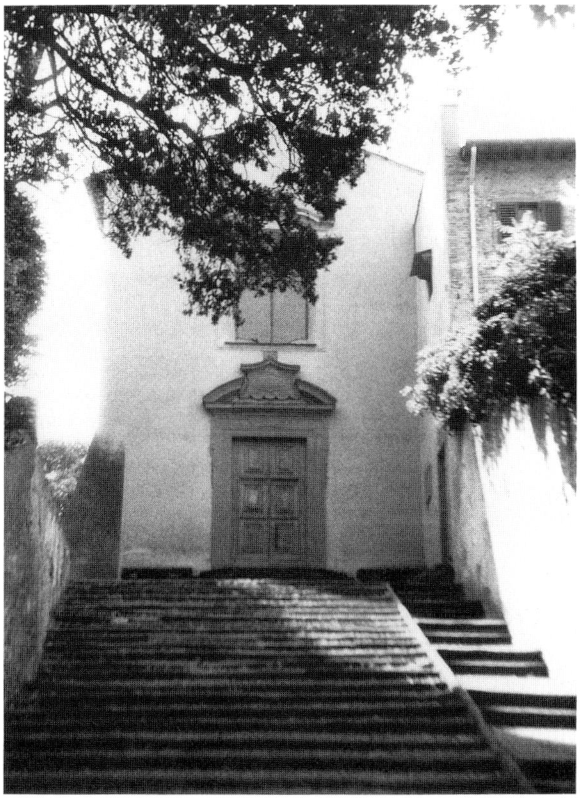

Figure 40. Sta. Maria delle Selve, nr. Lastra a Signa, facade (author)

antiquated and Byzantine in appearance. One of the most important extant is the recently cleaned *Madonna del Popolo* in the church of Sta. Maria del Carmine in Florence (Fig. 41). This large altarpiece of the Madonna and Child enthroned can be attributed to a Florentine master close to Coppo di Marcovaldo and dated about 1260.[19] The strong Italo-Byzantine flavor of the image is most apparent in the stylized poses of the Virgin and Child that follow the *Hodeghetria* type, as well as in the use of chrysography for the mantle of the Virgin and the robe of the Christ Child, a method of distinguishing divinity. In fact, in the eighteenth century, the painting was described by Giuseppe Richa as painted in the *maniera greca* and was reputed to have been "brought back from the Levant."[20] Although the exact original location within the church is unclear, documentary accounts indicate that by 1460, the altarpiece was housed within the Brancacci Chapel and strongly venerated despite its antiquated appearance.[21]

In Siena, the friars of S. Niccolò del Carmine possessed two iconic, half-length images of the Virgin. One known as the *Madonna dei Mantellini* was produced in Tuscany c. 1280 in the *maniera greca* style. The original location of this Madonna in the church is unclear.[22] But, significantly, the other revered Madonna image, displayed originally on the high altar, was

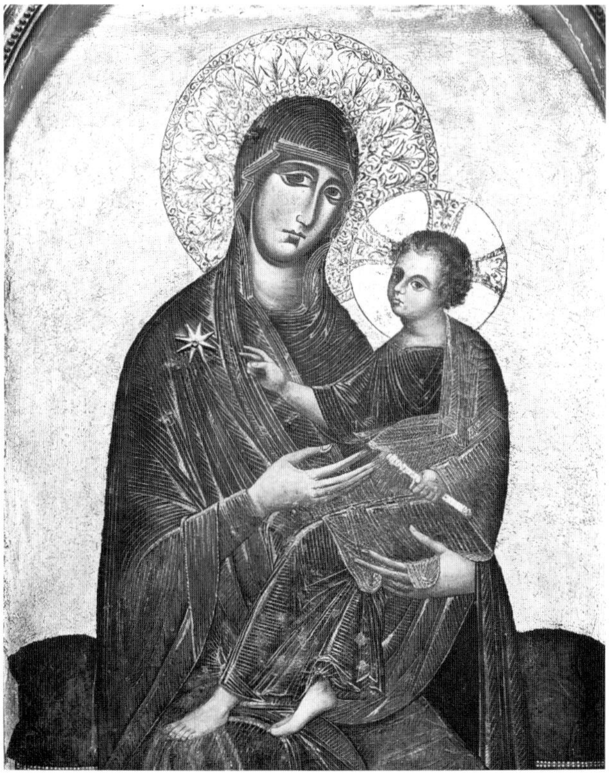

Figure 41. Close to Coppo di Marcovaldo, *Madonna del Popolo*, c. 1260, Florence, Sta. Maria del Carmine (Alinari/Art Resource, N.Y.)

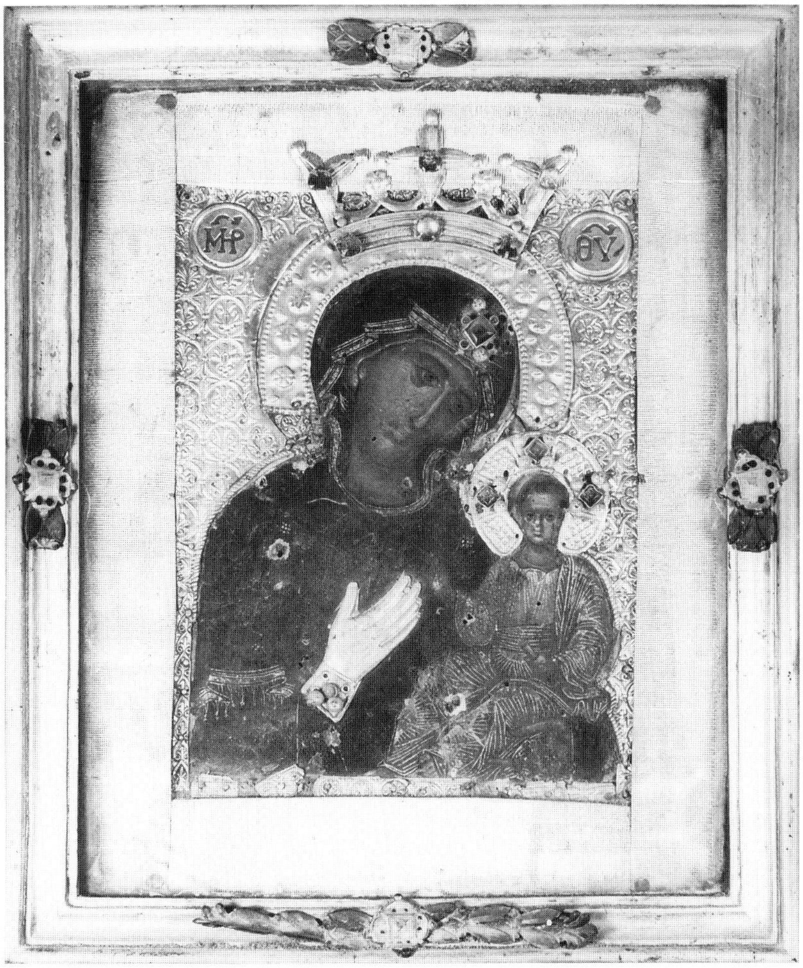

Figure 42. Byzantine, *Madonna di San Luca,* c. 1300, Siena, S. Niccolò del Carmine (Fotografia di Fabio Lensini, Siena, Italy)

actually of Byzantine manufacture, dating from about 1300 (Fig. 42). According to early Sienese accounts, this icon became the focus of cult worship, a cult fueled by legends that attributed the painting to St. Luke.[23] It was a widely held belief that St. Luke had painted several icons of the Virgin just after Pentecost; and in the minds of the Sienese of S. Niccolò del Carmine, their Byzantine Virgin was one.

Antiquated, Byzantine-style images of the Virgin were selected by the Carmelites to support the propaganda of the order. It was the platform of the Carmelites that they were not only the oldest of all the monastic orders, but also the first to focus worship on the Virgin. They asserted that the Virgin had appeared on Mount Carmel to bless their order and that in response they had erected a shrine in her honor in 83 A.D., long before any of the other orders had taken root.[24] A Byzantine-looking painting of the Virgin helped support these claims. Ancient and highly revered as the image was, many might be persuaded that it had been brought by members of the order to Italy when they came West in the years around 1240.

The *Madonna del Carmine* at Sta. Maria delle Selve may well have been similarly antiquated and Byzantine in style. And perhaps its ancient and exotic appearance helped to engender reverence and inspire devotion. Although no accounts of mass veneration of this Madonna survive, we do have evidence that her powers were esteemed by one important family. Late in 1476, Filippo Strozzi took over the patronage of two chapels in the Selve church, one being the chapel of the *Madonna del Carmine*.[25] As a document discovered by Eve Borsook reveals, about two years later in August 1478, Filippo Strozzi recorded payment for a wax image of his son and heir, the eleven-year-old Alfonso, sent to the chapel of the Virgin at Sta. Maria delle Selve.[26] The wax image must have been an *ex voto* sent to thank the Selve Virgin for her assistance in a dangerous situation involving Alfonso, probably an illness.[27] Here is suggestive evidence that as far as the Strozzi were concerned, the Carmine Madonna image had power.

After acquiring patronage over the chapel of the *Madonna del Carmine*, Filippo Strozzi naturally wished to redecorate it according to his own taste and place his stamp upon it. From a document of November 3, 1476, we learn that the friars of the Selve church agreed to allow Strozzi to adorn the chapel with the appropriate accessories and to affix his family crest.[28] But after furnishing the chapel with the ecclesiastical vestments and implements required for the celebration of Mass, Strozzi subsequently undertook still more substantial renovations. Beginning on March 11, 1482, he made a series of payments to Neri di Bicci for two images.[29] One is described simply as a "tabernacle" with no reference made to the subject presented. It is not possible to correlate the brief description with any surviving work by the artist. But the second image ordered by Strozzi and described as "a panel of Our Lady" can be identified with some certainty as the central portion of the hybrid pala now in Lecceto, the *Madonna and Child Enthroned* discussed at the outset of this section. There is, moreover, some support for the hypothesis that the Madonna panel renovated for Strozzi by Neri di Bicci was actually the *Madonna del Carmine* in the Strozzi chapel at Sta. Maria delle Selve. Indeed, the Selve *Madonna del Carmine* was most likely an old and Byzantinizing image as we have gathered based on trends in Carmelite taste; and this fits with the Madonna and Child panel from the Lecceto triptych, which, as technical examination of its structure has revealed, is Dugento and incorporates a head disc that may be even older. Further, because the *Madonna del Carmine* was in Strozzi's family chapel at Sta. Maria delle Selve, it is natural, therefore, to suppose that as part of his chapel redecorations, Strozzi would have desired to have that panel updated.

Neri di Bicci had already performed a restoration procedure on one of the Madonna images in the Selve church, as we have seen. He was commissioned by the Soderini to enshrine the *Madonna delle Grazie* within the structure of a tabernacle. In turn, Filippo Strozzi commissioned Neri to carry out a related operation on the devotional altarpiece in his family chapel, the *Madonna del Carmine*, that involved selectively repainting a powerful Madonna image that had already been renovated at least once before, in the Trecento. Neri's careful attempt to recapture some of the stylistic features of the Trecento layer in his work reflects the respect of Neri and of his patron for the valued Madonna.

Significantly, Filippo Strozzi's appreciation of the spiritual status and genealogy of the Madonna Neri had revitalized is further revealed by the way he wanted it displayed. In one of the documents recording payment to Neri for the renovated Madonna, Strozzi also paid him for repairing and painting a curtain to cover the altarpiece.[30] Curtains of this kind were designed to cover highly revered cult images. On special days, they were drawn open to reveal the image, but otherwise they acted as a protective shield, preserving the image's efficacy and shrouding it in mystery.

But what happened to the Selve Madonna in the years following 1482, and how did it come to be at Lecceto as part of a more complex Renaissance altarpiece? Quite soon after Neri di Bicci had refreshed the *Madonna del Carmine* panel, and certainly in the 1480s, Filippo Strozzi seems to have removed the image from the Selve church with the purpose of rehousing it more magnificently in his newly built chapel at Lecceto. The finishing touches were being carried out at Lecceto early in 1489 when the artist Biagio d'Antonio was paid for painting in gold an inscription in Roman letters carved along the frieze around the chapel that read: "Filippo Strozzi built [this chapel] for the Virgin Mother out of respect" (Fig. 39).[31] It must have been in these years that the Selve Madonna underwent one further renovation. Biagio d'Antonio was commissioned to transform the Gothic-style Madonna enthroned into a Renaissance pala so that it might fit more harmoniously into its new chapel space at Lecceto. A collaborator of Biagio's, perhaps the "Maestro di Marradi," produced two panels with standing saints that were added to the sides, and the new tripartite painting was set inside a heavy, classically architectural frame. Finally, to complete the process of further enshrining the sacred Selve Madonna, Strozzi chose an inscription for the frame that expressed his reverence, though it hinted also at his spiritual anxiety: "Gentle Virgin, unique among all, release us gently from our sins, make us pure."[32]

THE MONTEVERGINE *MAESTÀ*

The Benedictine monastic complex of Montevergine outside the town of Avellino east of Naples owns a highly valued cult image of the Madonna and Child enthroned with angels. Until recently, the Madonna altarpiece was housed in the old Gothic church of Santa Maria di Montevergine in the ornate Baroque "Cappella della Madonna" to the right of the nave (Fig. 43), but it can now be found in the presbitery of the adjacent, modern basilica built in the years 1952–61, where it is placed above a rich marble-encrusted throne. This huge representation of the Maestà, almost equivalent in size and monumentality to Duccio's *Rucellai Madonna* of 1285, fits stylistically with the *maniera greca* period in late Dugento Tuscan painting (Figs. 44 and 45). The pose and gestures of the enthroned Madonna, with the Christ Child balanced lightly on her left hip, recall, at some distance, the Byzantine *Hodeghetria* prototype. Strongly Byzantine in feel, the panel can be attributed to the Tuscan artist, Montano d'Arezzo, who is believed to have trained in Assisi and Rome before becoming an official painter at the Naples court in the late 1290s. The *Montevergine Maestà* is usually dated to the early years of his Neapolitan position, c. 1295–8.[33]

For centuries, the *Montevergine Maestà* has been the focus of fervent cult worship sustained primarily by legendary accounts of the origins of the miraculous image. According to the story recorded by chroniclers of Montevergine from the sixteenth century on, the head of the Virgin had an exotic genealogy. It was believed to have belonged initially to one of the Madonna icons painted by St. Luke and preserved in Constantinople in the church of Santa Maria. On the night of July 25, 1265, the head was salvaged as a relic and brought from Constantinople by the last Latin Patriarch, Baldwin II (d. 1273). In turn inherited by his grandniece, Catherine II of Valois, wife of Philip of Anjou, the head held place of honor in the royal treasury. Some years later, however, Catherine, in an act of piety, donated the cult object to the monastery at Montevergine amidst elaborate celebration. As part of the same gesture, Catherine commissioned the court artist, Montano d'Arezzo, to complete the image by reconstructing its original form as closely as possible.[34] The legend is recounted in an abbreviated form in a Latin inscription of 1776 on the funeral monument of Catherine II and her family in the church of Montevergine.[35]

This attractive story has recently been discredited on several grounds. It has been established from documentary evidence that the young Catherine II of Valois did not arrive in Naples as the new wife of Philip of Anjou until 1313, some fifteen years after the generally agreed date of Montano d'Arezzo's *Maestà*.[36] Furthermore, a review of the literary accounts has led scholars to the conclusion that the legend of Catherine II's inheritance and

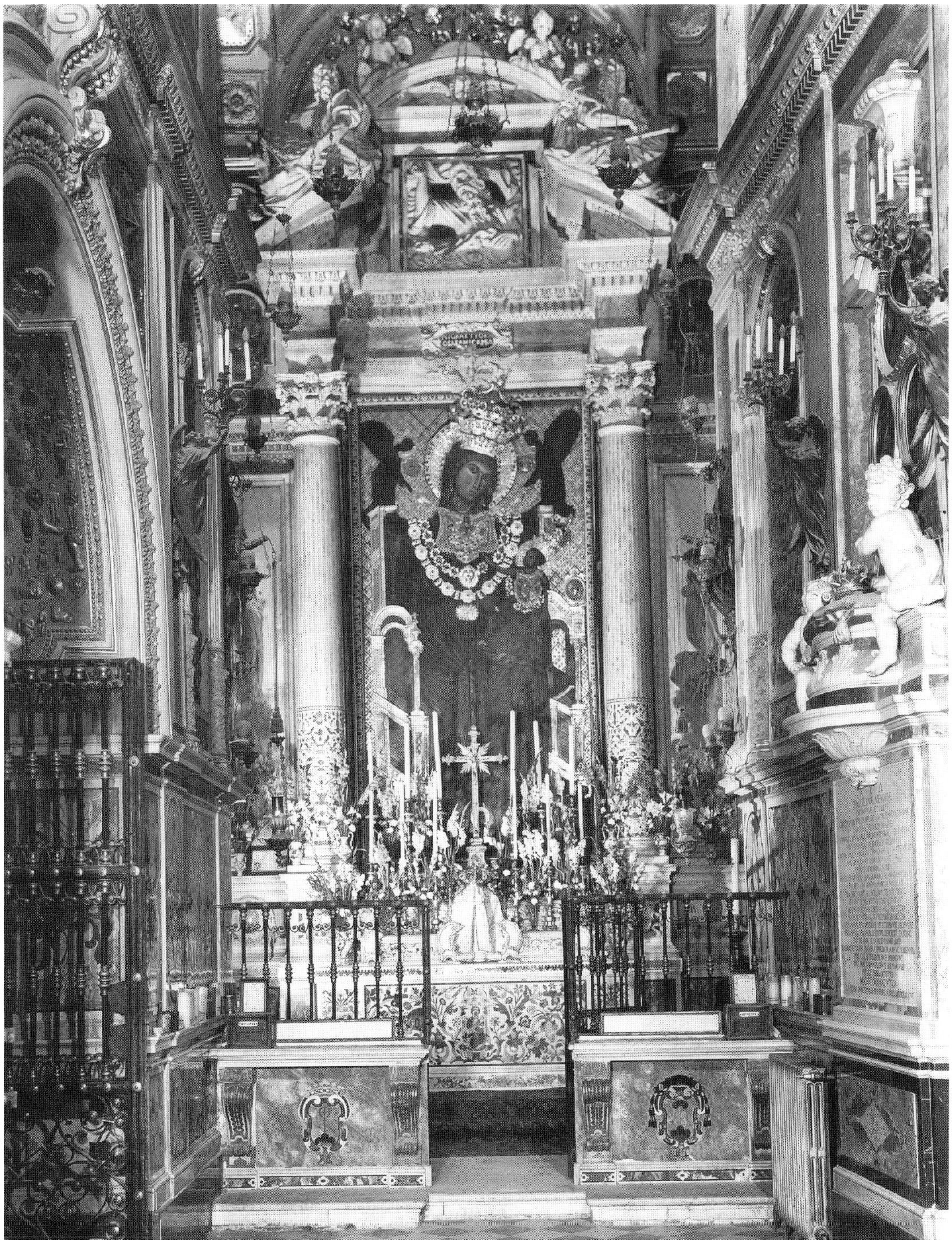

Figure 43. Sta. Maria di Montevergine, nr. Avellino, "Cappella della Madonna" (Alinari/Art Resource, N.Y.)

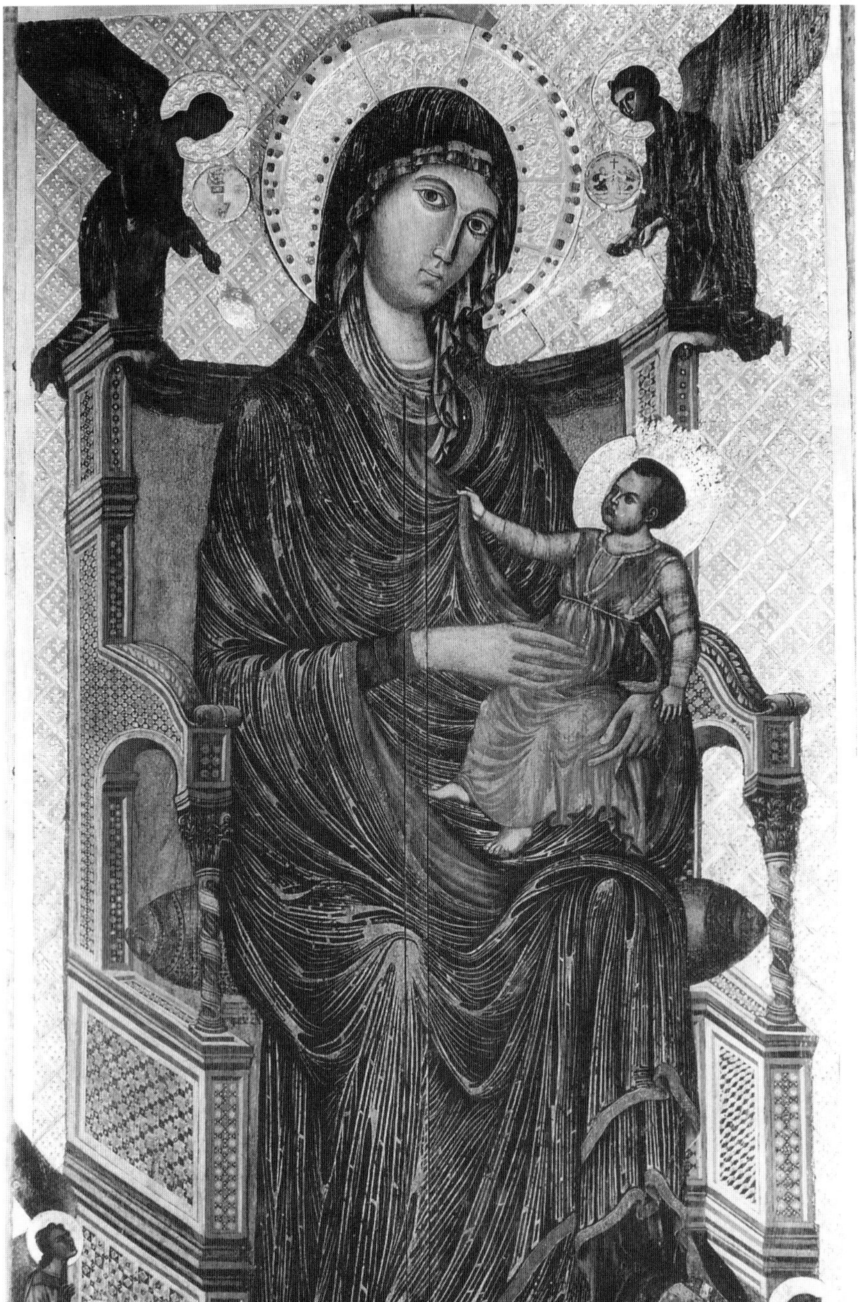

donation of the sacred head was initially concocted by heirs and subsequently embellished by chroniclers.[37]

Nevertheless, a closer, technical examination of the panel-painting itself does suggest that certain elements of the legendary history may have a foundation in reality. Most significantly, the painting is a hybrid structure composed of two distinct pieces of wood. The head and neck of the Madonna, including the halo, comprise a separate, irregularly shaped disc that is circular around the upper three-quarters of its circumference but extends out at the base in the form of a wedge. This disc, substantially thicker at its upper edge (5.5 cm) than down below (2.5 cm), has been set into an opening of uniform depth (2.5 cm) in such a way that the upper arc, with the Madonna's halo, protrudes about three centimeters, and the lower section, with the neck of the Madonna, remains flush.[38] The unusual compound structure of the *Maestà* does give some credence to the traditional

Figure 44. Montano d'Arezzo, *Montevergine Maestà*, c. 1295–8, Sta. Maria di Montevergine (Soprintendenza per i Beni Artistici e Storici, Naples, n. 31374) *facing page*

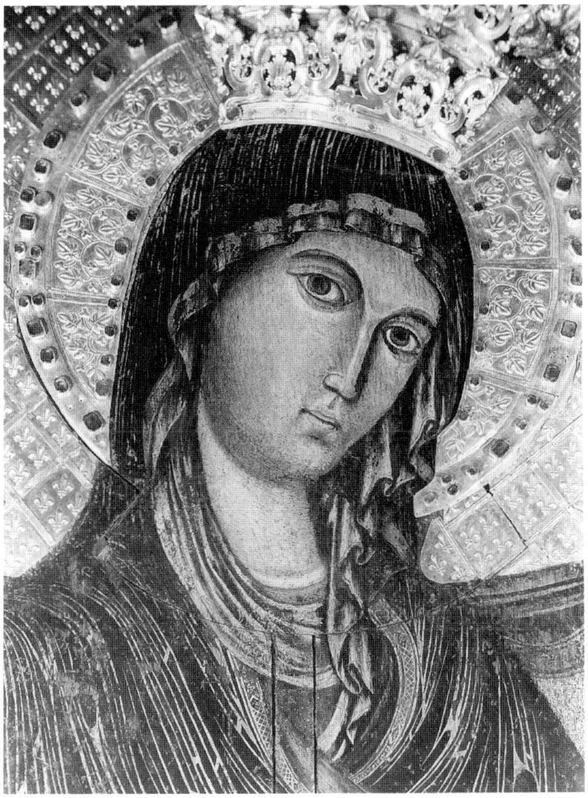

Figure 45. Montano d'Arezzo, *Montevergine Maestà*, detail of Virgin's head and neck showing separate head disc (Soprintendenza per i Beni Artistici e Storici, Naples, n. 31370)

story that the head of the Madonna was derived from an earlier image.

Having said as much, it should be pointed out that an earlier cult image of the Madonna enthroned from Montevergine, the so-called *Madonna di S. Guglielmo* (Montevergine, Museo), has a similar compound structure (Fig. 46). This panel, representing the Madonna as Queen of Heaven nursing the Christ Child, is traditionally held to have been commissioned by the founder of the monastery, San Guglielmo, in 1124, the year in which the first oratory was consecrated.[39] As the structural format the altarpiece takes is not found in Campanian art until the second half of the thirteenth century, however, the Madonna must have been ordered considerably later,

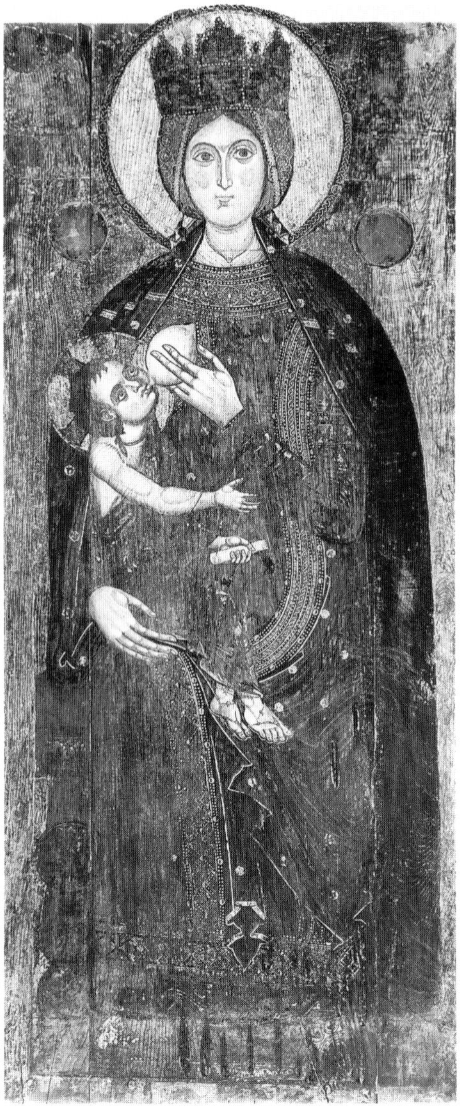

Figure 46. Campanian, *Madonna di S. Guglielmo*, c. 1270–80, Montevergine, Museo (Soprintendenza per i Beni Artistici e Storici, Naples, n. 31375)

well after the new Romanesque church had been erected on the site under Abbot Giovanni I (1172–91). Garrison suggests a date of c. 1270–80.[40] The image takes the form of an "articulated rectangle"; it is constructed in such a way that the head of the Virgin, painted on a separate disc of wood with a flattened bottom, has been inserted into the top portion of the rectangular panel carrying the rest of the composition, so that the disc sticks out a little way beyond the top of the background. In order to provide a more expressive effect, the head-disc has also been raised slightly in the upper area of the face and halo, above the level of the encasing panel. As mentioned previously, this form of panel-painting was a popular type in the Dugento. Garrison, in his catalogue of Italian Romanesque panel-paintings, provides thirty examples illustrating how the type emerged in the early thirteenth century in Florence, became very popular in Tuscany in the period 1250–75 with a few examples from Umbria, the Abruzzi and Campania, and fell out of favor by about 1300.[41] A characteristic example is Margarito d'Arezzo's *Madonna and Child Enthroned* (Arezzo, Museo Medievale e Moderno; formerly Montelungo, S. Maria) of c. 1270–80, where the head of the Virgin is painted on a separate disc of wood wedged part way into the top of the main rectangular panel (Fig. 47).

Montano's *Montevergine Maestà* may have been commissioned in part as a grand replacement for the church's earlier cult Madonna, the *Madonna di S. Guglielmo*, and Montano may have deliberately tried to echo the compound structure of the earlier Madonna in his new work. Still, this does not in any way preclude the possibility that the head-disc of Montano's *Maestà* was ultimately derived from an older image. Indeed, although Montano's *Maestà* and the earlier *Madonna di S. Guglielmo* share basic structural features, their construction is not identical. The shape of the head-disc in Montano's work, with its neck extension, is unique. Further, whereas the head-disc in the *Madonna di S. Guglielmo* protrudes beyond the limits of the main, rectangular component of the panel-painting as is usual in images of this sort, Montano's disc is fully encased within the image. These distinctive features place Montano's *Maestà* in a category all its own and leave the question of the origins of the head-disc open.

As the *Montevergine Maestà* remains an immensely popular cult image still today, the monastic authorities are loathe to have the panel taken down for technical investigation. November 1960 was the last occasion when the painting was removed for restoration and examination. Leonetto Tintori carried out the restoration procedures, which included removing substantially later layers of repainting, particularly from the area of the Virgin's face. X-radiographs were also made of the Virgin's face and neck. These reveal the subtle painting of the layer attributed to Montano d'Arezzo with fine linear brushstrokes that follow the contours of the face in a

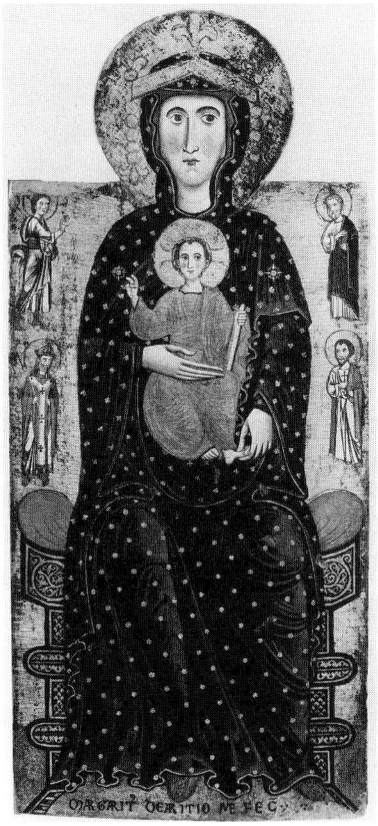

Figure 47. Margarito d'Arezzo, *Madonna and Child Enthroned*, c. 1270–80, Arezzo, Museo Medievale e Moderno (Archivio Fotografico della Soprintendenza di Arezzo – Sezione Beni Artistici e Storici)

manner typical of early Trecento tempera painting in Tuscany. The only sparse evidence of an underlying paint layer is in the area of the Virgin's left eye, where part of the pupil seems to have been repainted. There is no sign of the emphatic underlayer modeled in lead white seen in Coppo di Marcovaldo's *Madonna del Bordone*.[42]

The x-ray findings can be interpreted in two different ways. One explanation is that there is no underlying layer and never was. The legend of the earlier and exotic origins of the headpiece is purely fabricated. However, it is also possible that an underlying layer does exist but is not fully evident on the x-radiographs. Perhaps the original face was painted in such a way – thinly and without heavy undermodeling in lead white – as to make it virtually transparent to x-rays.

One expert, conversant with the technical evidence, expressed his belief in the substance of the legend. Ferdinando Bologna, who had the rare opportunity of examining the paint surface when the Madonna was in the restoration laboratory at Naples in 1960, detected under the face of the Madonna, and only in this area of the composition, traces of an earlier image. He tentatively attributed the underlying face to the early thirteenth

century, and suggested also that the archaic style of the overlying image may have been influenced by the head beneath.[43] Earlier, in 1949, the skilled connoisseur of Italian Romanesque panel-painting, Edward Garrison, had recorded a similar opinion. After examining detailed photographs of numerous examples of "articulated rectangle" Madonnas, Garrison categorized the *Montevergine Maestà* as a separate type altogether. He published his belief that the headpiece was substantially earlier, c. 1265, and Campanian in style, while conceding that the rest of the image might well be by Montano d'Arezzo and perhaps as late as 1310.[44] Together, these informed observations lend much support to the view that the head-disc of the *Maestà* came originally from an older image of the Madonna.

Further, although the legendary associations of Montano's *Maestà* with Catherine II of Valois, Philip of Anjou's wife, have had to be abandoned for reasons of chronology, historians in recent years have begun to construct a more convincing context to explain this extraordinary commission in the late 1290s. P. M. Tropeano has advanced the theory that Montano's Madonna was commissioned by Charles II of Anjou and his wife Mary of Hungary as a kind of *ex voto*, a thank you, following the release of first Charles, and later his children and collaborators, from imprisonment by the Aragonese between 1284 and 1295.[45]

Following the establishment of the royal House of Anjou in Italy in 1263, sanctioned by a legal agreement between the pope, Urban IV, and the French king, Louis IX, the Anjou were compelled to defend their territorial claims to Naples and Sicily against the Spanish with military force. This campaign was led by Charles of Salerno, heir to the throne, until June 1284, when he was taken captive in a sea battle with the Aragonese. After the death of his father, King Charles I, in 1285, Charles of Salerno's release was negotiated so that he might succeed to the throne of Naples. The provisional release was not achieved until 1289, with the terms requiring the barter of Charles' own three sons, Louis, Robert, and Raymond-Berenger, as hostages. In turn, these three were not released from imprisonment in Messina until 1295 with the Treaty of Anagni.[46]

During the extended period of imprisonment endured by Charles and his sons, the Angevin court in Naples under his wife Mary became a prayer circle. As Tropeano suggests, the shrine devoted to the Virgin at Montevergine near Naples may have provided a sanctuary for intensive supplication of the Virgin. Subsequently, when Charles and Mary's sons were released in 1295, their liberation may have been attributed, in part at least, to divine assistance mediated through the Virgin.[47] The royal couple had maintained strong ties with the monastery ever since 1271, when, as newlyweds, they spent time there.[48] In a document of 1298, written only three years after the release of his sons and in the period of the commission of Montano's

Maestà, Charles II speaks of a long-standing devotion, nourished in his younger years, for the Virgin Mary and for the sanctuary of Montevergine.[49] It may have been shortly following the release of their three sons that Charles and Mary dedicated a votive chapel there to the Virgin who had assisted them, and soon afterwards, perhaps in 1296, that they commissioned Montano to complete the devotional *Maestà* as an *ex voto* and focal point of worship.[50]

Evidence that soon after the *Montevergine Maestà* was completed facsimiles were created provides some indication of the strength of the contemporary cult surrounding the image. One of these is recorded only by tradition: Montano is believed to have produced a replica of the *Maestà* for a votive chapel in the palace of Philip of Taranto, Charles II's son, in the center of Naples. The palace chapel and a general reference to Montano's activity there are recorded in a document of 1310.[51] However, a second replica survives, albeit in poor condition, in the church of Monteverginella in the center of Naples. Located since the sixteenth century in the third chapel on the left of the nave, the image, in fresco, was originally painted over the high altar in a position of greater significance.[52] Despite the deteriorated condition and heavy repainting, one can still get a good sense of the style and format beneath. The enthroned Virgin and Child are backed by a cloth-of-honor held by angels that replaces the gilt plaquettes with fleur-de-lis in the original panel at Montevergine. Eleven angels, instead of the original eight, are positioned around the divine pair in attitudes of devotion. This frescoed substitute for the *Montevergine Maestà* must have been ordered soon after the church of Monteverginella was established in 1314. The construction of the church was financed by Bartolomeo di Capua, an important figure in the Angevin court circle, in the hope of saving the life of his sick daughter, and was dedicated "to the honor and glory of Almighty God and the Blessed Virgin Mary His Mother."[53] Presumably, the replicated *Maestà* functioned in this location as a votive image that carried with it some of the revered power of the Montevergine original. The Virgin, whose power to intercede and prevent tragedy had been recently witnessed by Charles II and Mary of Hungary and had subsequently been commemorated in the *Montevergine Maestà*, was now called upon by Bartolomeo di Capua.

This contextual information provides a satisfactory explanation for the commission of the Montevergine altarpiece, and the contemporary replication of the image yields evidence of its active cult. Nevertheless, the problem of the head and its provenance remains. Did the headpiece come originally from a revered Byzantine icon or an earlier cult image? Although the evidence provided by the x-radiographs is not sufficiently clear to arrive at a secure conclusion, there is enough other circumstantial information to present a persuasive case. First and foremost, the unique, compound structure of the image lends strong support to the theory that the headpiece has a separate and exotic provenance; and, second, the observations of Garrison and Bologna offer further support. Moreover, the technical aspects of the painting style adopted by Montano supply additional evidence that the head originated from an earlier image of Italo-Byzantine or Byzantine origin.

The panel-painting techniques employed in this instance by Montano reveal his attempt to recreate a Byzantine cult image through imitation. Just as the iconography recalls Byzantine *Hodeghetria* prototypes, so also the methods and materials replicate those used on Byzantine originals. For one thing, Montano applied gold striations to the Virgin's blue mantle, replicating the Byzantine technique of chrysography, a method used to distinguish divinity. Although this was a technique used by a number of contemporary Italian Romanesque and early Gothic artists under the influence of the Byzantine tradition, such as the Sienese master Duccio, a second method adopted by Montano is more uniquely Byzantine. Instead of covering the background of his panel with extremely thin, gold leaf laid over an adhesive layer of red bole as was traditional in Italy, Montano followed a technique familiar from Byzantine icons by applying a network of separate brass plaques for the background and for the haloes. The lozenge-shaped plaques fixed to the background are impressed with fleur-de-lis motifs, a reminder of the Angevin patrons of the image, whereas the plaques that make up the haloes of the Virgin, the Christ Child, and the angels are decorated with vine patterns and elaborate animal and bird designs.[54] That these plaques were part of Montano's original conception can be seen from an examination of the underlying panel surface, where the intended positions of the plates are marked out.[55] Clearly, Montano carried the project of Byzantine imitation one step further than his Italian contemporaries.

The reason for this, I would argue, was one of authentication. Montano's patrons, Charles II of Naples and Mary, asked their court artist to create an image worthy to house their reputedly Constantinopolitan head of the Virgin, and an image that by virtue of its Byzantine style and technique would serve to authenticate the head it enclosed. Even if the head itself was not actually of Byzantine origin, but came from an older image of more local manufacture as Garrison supposed, the royal couple took pains to present it as such.[56] For reasons of cult, the older head-disc of mysterious provenance was embedded within Montano's pseudo-Byzantine *Maestà*.

THE MADONNA OF SAN LORENZO IN PONTE

A third revered fragment is enclosed within the Madonna of the Oratory of San Lorenzo in Ponte, in San Gimignano. In its present state, the image takes the form of a Madonna and Child in Glory (Fig. 2). The Virgin is shown enthroned with the Christ Child on her knee, set within a mandorla and surrounded by two rings of angels. These angels celebrate the Virgin as mother of the divine Christ Child by crowning her, playing instruments, offering her vases of flowers, and adopting positions of devotion. Above, a descending dove signals the presence of the Holy Spirit.

Although now incorporated into the mural decoration inside the oratory, the fresco was originally on the east outside wall of the adjacent church to the right side of the portal (Fig. 48). Nevertheless, despite this earlier external location, the fresco is preserved in remarkably good condition with the exception of the Virgin's face, which is very worn. Differences in condition are also apparent in the Virgin's mantle. In the area surrounding her face, the mantle, painted originally in azurite blue, has turned green in spots, whereas the blue of the rest of the mantle is preserved in its original form.

These disparaties in condition and technique point up the hybrid nature of the image. Furthermore, such differences are also evident in the style of the composition. Indeed, as G. B. Cavalcaselle recognized already in the late nineteenth century, the qualities "in the head and neck of the Virgin can be compared with the characteristics of the Sienese school of Duccio and his followers, while it is clear that the rest of the painting belongs to another hand."[57] Despite the poor condition of the Virgin's face, one can still discern in the outlines of her features stylistic characteristics reminiscent

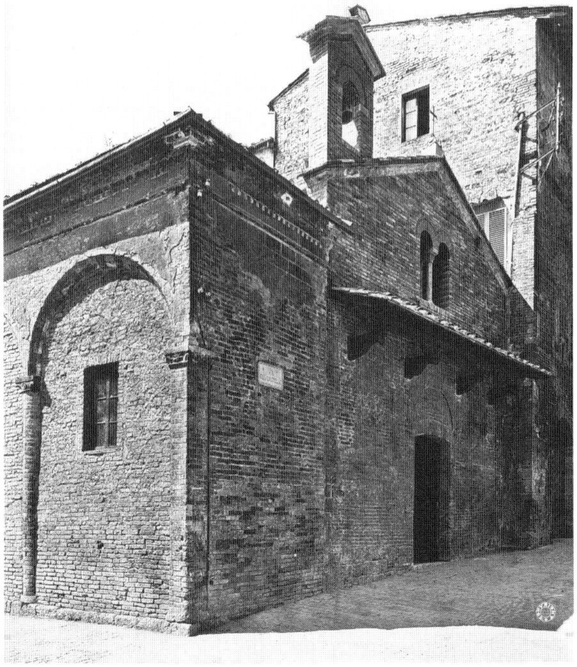

Figure 48. S. Lorenzo in Ponte, San Gimignano, exterior (Alinari/Art Resource, N.Y.)

of Sienese Gothic works: strident, sensuous features; greenish shadow tones in the skin; a white inner veil; and the face outlined and framed in a graceful way by the headdress (Fig. 49). In recent years, the head has been attributed alternately to two early Trecento Sienese artists, to Simone Martini by Enzo Carli and to Simone's father-in-law, Memmo di Filippuccio, by Miklòs Boskovits.[58] An attribution to Memmo di Filippuccio, although plausible because he spent the years 1303–17 as principal painter of San Gimignano, cannot be substantiated. There is not, as yet, an established corpus of works for this artist. On the other hand, the damaged state of the face makes comparison with secure works by Simone Martini difficult as the quality of the fresco is nearly impossible to gauge. If Simone Martini is responsible, the simple technique of the rayed halo would indicate a date of execution earlier than the completion of his *Palazzo Pubblico Maestà* (1315–16). The rayed design on the halo, traditional in fresco painting, was produced by repeatedly indenting the built-up layer of plaster with a linear, sticklike instrument. However, in the *Palazzo Pubblico Maestà*, Simone introduced a new halo-decorating technique whereby attractive natural designs – flowers, leaves, stars, and so on – were created by pressing matrices into the built-up plaster. Consequently, if the face is by Simone Martini, a date of c. 1310–14 seems likely.[59]

The rest of the *Madonna and Child in Glory* was formerly attributed by the nineteenth-century historian of San Gimignano, Luigi Pecori, and by others to Cennino Cennini of Colle Val d'Elsa, the Giottesque master best known for his treatise on artists' techniques.[60] However, the traditional assignation has been questioned more recently, and scholars today are generally agreed that the early damaged fresco was reworked by Cenni di Francesco di Ser Cenni, who was responsible in 1413 for other frescoes in the oratory and adjacent church.[61] Little known except to specialists in late Gothic Tuscan painting, Cenni di Francesco matriculated in the painters' guild in Florence in 1369 and was active in the area around Florence and in western Tuscany until about 1415. His best known work is the fresco cycle of the Legend of the True Cross in San Francesco in Volterra, which he signed and dated in 1410. In style, these frescoes reveal Cenni as a follower and imitator of Agnolo Gaddi.[62] The *Madonna and Child in Glory* at San Lorenzo in Ponte exhibits the Gaddiesque characteristics typical of Cenni's work and finds close stylistic parallels in other works attributed to the artist. In Cenni di Francesco's fresco of the *Madonna Lactans* in the Palazzo Comunale at San Miniato al Tedesco near Empoli, dated 1393, the Virgin is clothed in a similarly patterned, high-waisted dress, and her pointed facial features and exposed wavey hair closely resemble the features of the angels seen in profile in the San Lorenzo in Ponte mural (Fig. 50).

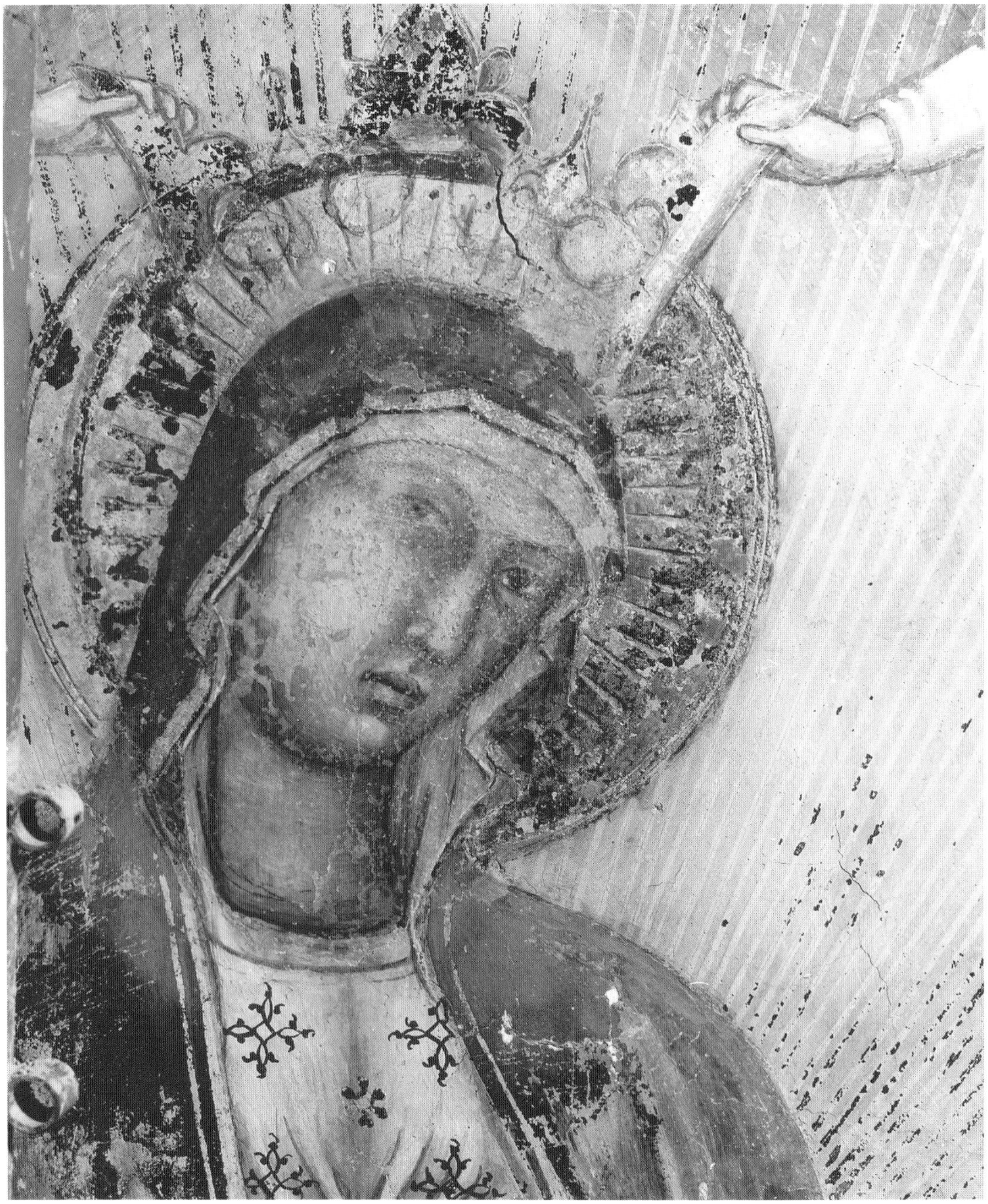

Figure 49. Simone Martini (?) and Cenni di Francesco di Ser Cenni, *Madonna in Glory*, detail of Virgin's face, c. 1310–14, San Gimignano, S. Lorenzo in Ponte (Foto Soprintendenza per i Beni Artistici e Storici di Siena, Italy)

But our primary concern is to discover why Cenni di Francesco was hired to renovate the Madonna of San Lorenzo in Ponte – which had presumably originally taken the form of a Madonna and Child enthroned – while leaving the original face intact. According to legend, the Virgin's face had been miraculously preserved from damage despite the exposure suffered by the rest of the fresco in its location on the outside wall of the church. Consequently, when Cenni was commissioned to restore the damaged but greatly venerated image in the early fifteenth century, he was instructed to leave the miraculous face untouched while creating around it a joyous new image of the Madonna and Child in Glory.[63] An investigation of the immediate historical context may help to reveal more completely the motivations underlying this renovation.

The renovation performed by Cenni di Francesco seems to have been only one part of a larger redecoration program for the Romanesque church of San Lorenzo in Ponte and its oratory. For in 1413, Cenni executed a number of frescoes in the church interior, including a majestic mural of *Christ and the Virgin Enthroned in Judgment* on the altar wall, the *Inferno* on the left wall of the nave, and a corresponding image of *Paradise* on the

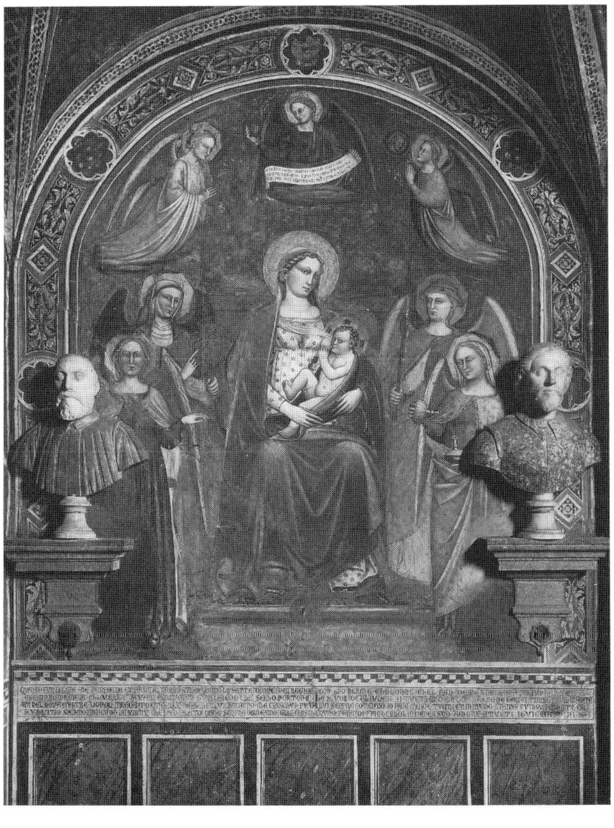

Figure 50. Cenni di Francesco di Ser Cenni, *Madonna Lactans*, 1393, San Miniato al Tedesco nr. Empoli, Palazzo Comunale (Alinari/Art Resource, N.Y.)

right wall of the nave (Fig. 51). In addition, Cenni carried out fresco decorations on the interior of the oratory, including *San Lorenzo and Saints* on the entrance wall, and a *Triumph of Death* in fragmentary condition on the end wall. It must have been as part of this extensive campaign that Cenni repainted the Madonna on the outside wall of the church.

Programs of church redecoration of this kind were usually financed by wealthy patrician families from the neighborhood as a gesture of piety. The situation at San Lorenzo in Ponte was no exception. The church seems to have been patronized by the prominent Salvucci family. One of the most important families in San Gimignano, both socially and economically, the Salvucci achieved great wealth and prestige during the period of communal growth in the first half of the fourteenth century.[64] They lived originally in the Contrada di Piazza with impressive towered palaces across from the Collegiata, but in 1332 moved their primary family residence to the via del Castello, the street onto which San Lorenzo in Ponte faces.[65] San Lorenzo in Ponte became their neighborhood church and received the consequent financial benefits.

The connection was fused even more strongly when a Salvucci son, Niccolò Salvucci, became rector of the parish church. Indeed, it was during Niccolò's tenure in 1413 that the redecoration program was carried out, presumably with the easily garnered support of the Salvucci.[66] Furthermore, as part of the program Cenni di Francesco was commissioned to fresco an image of the Crucifixion with a portrait of a young, male donor, kneeling (Fig. 52). The young man can only be Niccolò Salvucci.

This votive image of the Crucifixion provides a major clue to understanding the renovations carried out at San Lorenzo in Ponte c. 1413, including the repainting of the Madonna. Although it is now incorporated into the mural decoration of the interior of the oratory, before it was moved in 1516, the *Crucifixion* was painted on the outside north wall of a loggia attached to the east side of the church in close proximity to the *Madonna in Glory*.[67] Positioned so prominently on what became essentially an extension to the facade of the church, the fresco announced through its iconography important religious themes of the institution. In the image, two dolorous angels collect the blood from Christ's wounds in cups, while the Virgin, John, and Mary Magdalen gesture in despair. The male donor, Niccolò Salvucci, participates in the event through devotional contemplation. Eucharistic symbolism and the theme of salvation through Christ are both emphatically present. The fresco seems to offer this advice: By following the model set by Niccolò Salvucci and participating as fully as possible in the sacrifice of Christ through the vehicle of the Eucharist, salvation can be achieved.

The image of the *Crucifixion*, however, was only part of an iconographic

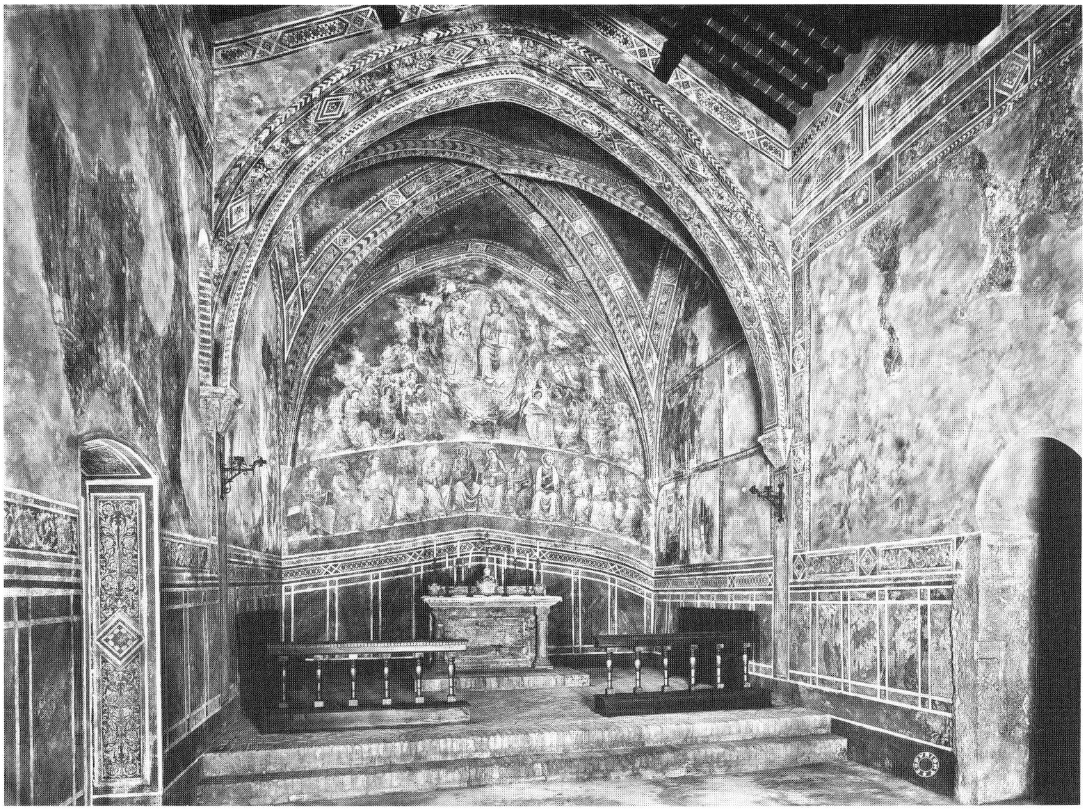

Figure 51. S. Lorenzo in Ponte, San Gimignano, interior showing frescoes by Cenni di Francesco di Ser Cenni, 1413 (Alinari/Art Resource, N.Y.)

story that can be pieced together from the decoration of the church, beginning with the *Madonna in Glory* formerly nearby on the outside east wall. In this fresco, the Virgin was glorified as the vehicle through whom the Christ Child and future savior of humankind was given birth. The culminating scene in the sequence was represented in full above the altar in the church where the Christian's devotional journey also reached its climax. Christ as Judge and the Virgin on His left were enthroned in a mandorla and surrounded by music-making angels. They presided in a court of law with the twelve apostles as the jury below them, on the Day of Judgment, the day when mens' fates would be decided.

The prominence of the Virgin in this sequence can be partially explained, in the most general way, as a manifestation of the cult of the Virgin, a cult that was very strong during this period throughout the Italian peninsula. But the more particular explanation is more persuasive. The presence at San Lorenzo in Ponte of an important devotional image of the Virgin,

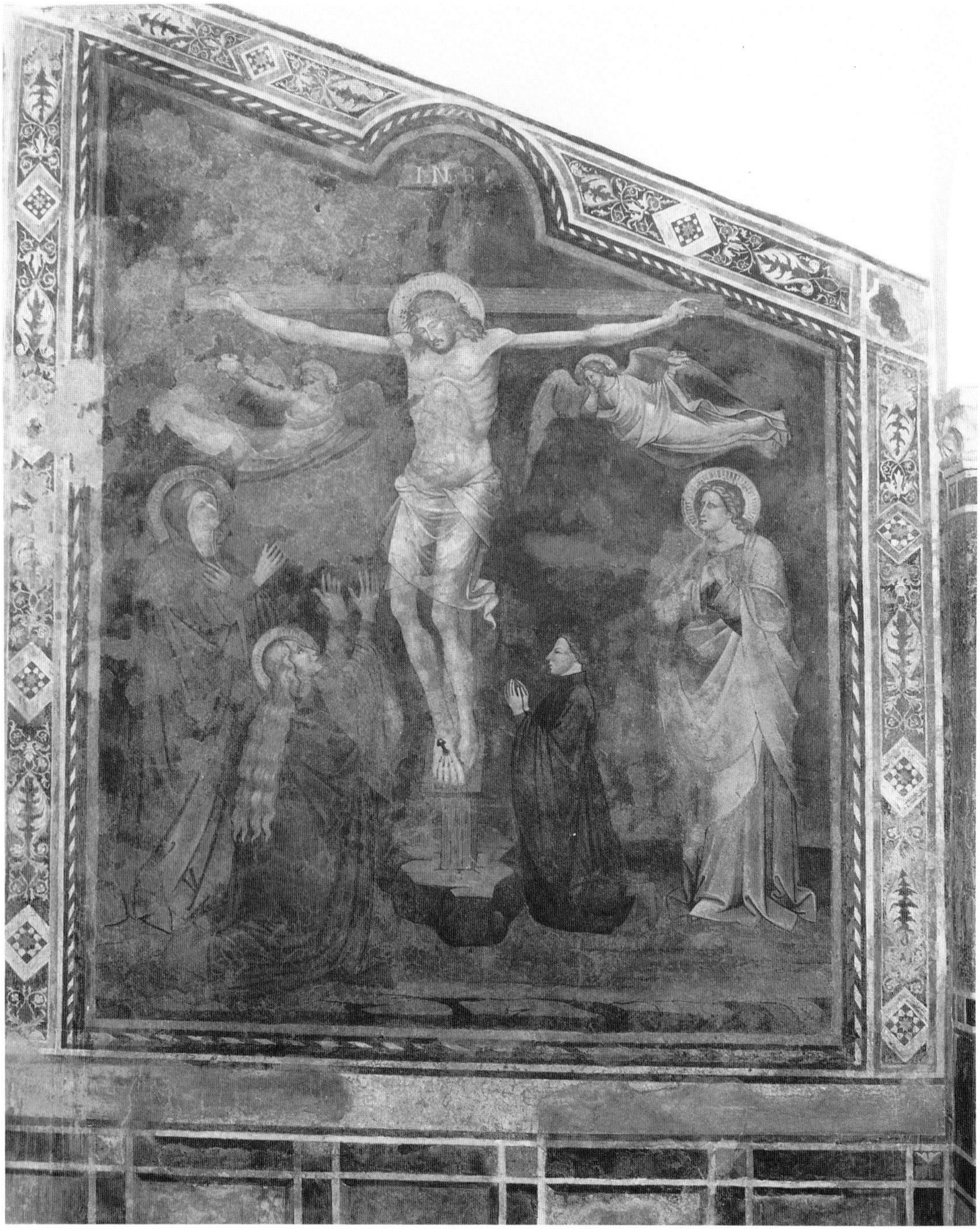

Figure 52. Cenni di Francesco di Ser Cenni, *Crucifixion*, 1413, San Gimignano, S. Lorenzo in Ponte (Foto Soprintendenza per i Beni Artistici e Storici di Siena, Italy)

preserved in fragmentary form, provided the occasion for the celebration of the Virgin's cult on a local level and the occasion for the commission of a number of frescoes, loosely sequential, in which her role was monumentalized.

The active part played by Niccolò Salvucci in these redecorations is recorded by his presence as donor in the *Crucifixion* fresco near the entrance to the church. It is most likely that as part of the same pious project, Salvucci and his family instigated Cenni di Francesco's renovation of the adjacent Madonna image. In fact, the early Sienese Madonna may have had special family associations. An investigation of family trees indicates that both artists to whom the Madonna's head has been attributed had connections through marriage with the Salvucci family. A sister of Simone Martini must have married a Salvucci because two of Simone's nieces are recorded in his will of 1344 as "born Salvucci." The Martinis and the Salvuccis were in-laws.[68] Moreover, Memmo di Filippuccio became Simone's father-in-law in 1324, and thus through Simone, he established links with the Salvucci family in turn.[69] Connections of this kind could have infused the sacred head with particular relevance, especially the close familial link between the Salvucci and Simone Martini.

But more important still were the devotional associations of the original image of the Virgin. Although no reliable accounts enumerating these survive, the Madonna's reputed power must have been considerable. After all, the Salvucci were persuaded to preserve the cult for future generations by extensively renovating the image while carefully salvaging its essential core.

SACRED REMAINS

This chapter has focused on three renovations involving old, revered images or fragments of images.[70] In each instance, the old image or fragment was given new life by enshrining it within a new painting. Significantly, this process of revitalization has analogies in the cult of relics and in Byzantine icon worship. From early on, the Christian church promulgated the belief that the fragmentary remains of the Saints, as well as clothing and other sacred objects associated with them and with Christ and the Virgin, possessed the miraculous and intercessory powers of the divine person. And subsequently, to protect them and to enhance their religious value, these holy objects were encased in expensively crafted reliquaries.[71] In a similar way it seems, old cult images of the Virgin, whether intact or in fragmentary form, were held to possess the spiritual power of the Madonna herself. These remains were set into new altarpieces or frescoed images to increase their devotional value and to reactivate their stored potential.

Furthermore, certain fragments of these cult Madonna images were believed to carry the power of the original in a particularly concentrated form. Indeed, in two, if not all three, of the examples discussed in this chapter, the concern to preserve and enshrine the head-disc from a miracle-working Madonna image suggests the head was considered the most important and spiritually potent part of the work. This logical belief – logical in that the face of the intercessor naturally becomes the focus of supplication – has roots in the Byzantine tradition.

Legendary accounts relate how the first icon in Byzantium was one of Christ's face, which Christ fashioned Himself by pressing a damp linen cloth against His face, and gave to the king of Edessa as a curative substitute for His presence.[72] The iconographic counterpart, the Virgin's face as an iconic image in its own right, appears in Western art by the early thirteenth century in German devotional psalters.[73] Soon afterwards, cult interest in the Virgin's face is manifested in Italian panel-paintings. For example, Edward Garrison draws attention to a portable Sienese triptych in Oxford, of Ducciesque style c. 1300, where the side panels are designed so that when folded across the central image of the Virgin and Child, they leave exposed and frame the Madonna's face as the focus for private prayer.[74] Concurrently, Montano d'Arezzo's renovated image of the *Montevergine Maestà* embodies a similar belief in the devotional importance of the Virgin's face. And about a century later, working with the same spiritual concept in mind, Cenni di Francesco carried on the cult practice of enclosing a powerful, painted fragment bearing the Virgin's face inside a newly composed image of the Madonna and Child in Glory.

CHAPTER 4

Revising the Portraits of Two Patron Saints

Alongside panel-paintings of Christ Crucified and the Virgin, images of patron saints became important focuses of devotion during the late Medieval period in Italy. Since early Christian times, the saints had functioned as "invisible and intimate friends" and as links with the divine.[1] Contemporary people felt comfortable seeking guidance and protection both here and for the afterlife from these spiritual mentors who had performed as model citizens during their time on earth. Initially, worship centered around the saint's grave, and relics, held to be infused with the power of the intercessor, formed a focus of supplication. Pilgrims journeyed to the grave of a favored saint, often camping there for weeks in the hope of a miraculous physical or spiritual cure. However, by the early thirteenth century in the Mediterranean world, devotion at an altar with a painted image of the saint in part supplanted graveside worship, and altarpieces of patron saints were frequently commissioned.[2]

Furthermore, during this period in Italy, just as cult images of the Virgin with the Christ Child were renovated soon after their creation for the sake of spiritual revivification, so images of patron saints were likewise subjected to similar devotional attentions. This chapter will explore the case histories of two panel-paintings of patron saints that were reworked early on in their histories: the full-length portrait of St. Francis in Arezzo by Margarito d'Arezzo and the cropped panel-painting of St. Dominic attributed to Guido da Siena, now in the Fogg Museum in Cambridge, Massachusetts. In each instance, the physical transformations carried out on the image will be described and an attempt will be made to reconstruct the devotional context in which these changes were deemed necessary and accomplished.

THE AREZZO ST. FRANCIS

St. Francis was the first patron saint to be worshiped at painted altarpieces in Italy.[3] Following the saint's death in 1226 and his canonization two years later, a number of large, historiated dossals glorifying his person and his life were produced. The earliest of these altarpieces, Bonaventura Berlinghieri's *Saint Francis Dossal* in the church of San Francesco in Pescia and dated by an inscription, 1235, shows a full-length, emblematic portrait of the friar-saint (Fig. 53). The saint is represented displaying the stigmata on his hands and feet as evidence of his closeness to Christ and power as intermediary, both factors attested to in the six scenes from his life and miracles to either side on the dossal. On the upper left part of the dossal, the first two scenes illustrate prodigious events from Francis's life: the Stigmatization and Francis preaching to the birds. In the four other scenes, miracles worked just after the saint's death and before his canonization bear witness to the power of his intercession.

As part of the spread of the cult of Francis in thirteenth-century Italy, smaller images with an isolated, full-length portrait alone were also created. Eleven of these portraits on panel from the Romanesque period are known

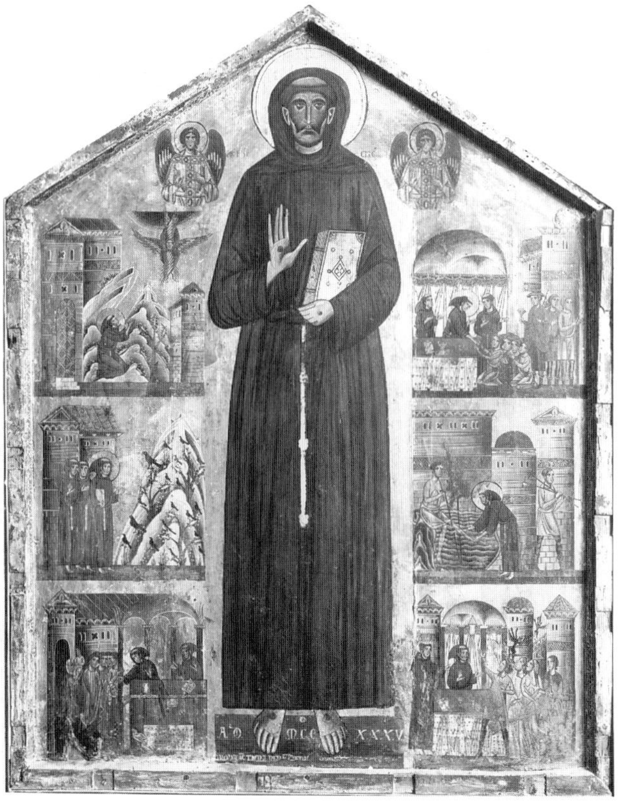

Figure 53. Bonaventura Berlinghieri, *Saint Francis Dossal*, 1235, Pescia, S. Francesco (Alinari/Art Resource, N.Y.)

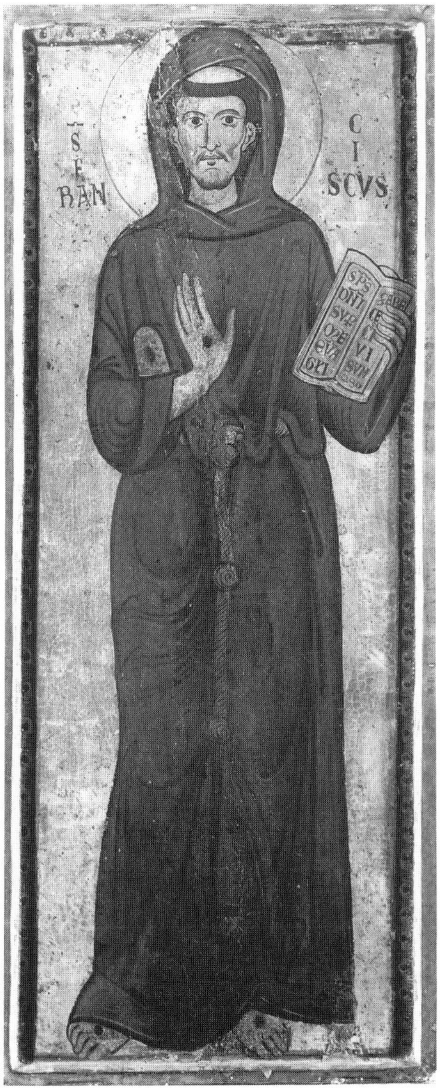

Figure 54. St. Gregory Master, *St. Francis*, c. 1230–5, Paris, Louvre (© Photo Réunion des Musées Nationaux, Paris)

to this author.[4] By far the earliest of these is the panel now in the Louvre, attributed to the Roman artist known as the St. Gregory Master and dated c. 1230–5 (Fig. 54). It is closely related to the slightly earlier frescoed portrait of Francis in the Cappella di San Gregorio of the Sacro Speco at Subiaco, probably by the same hand.[5] However, perhaps as important, because of its extensive influence, is the full-length icon in the Museo Medievale e Moderno of Arezzo. Inscribed along the base of the panel with Margarito d'Arezzo's characteristic signature, MARGARITUS DE ARITIO [ME FECI]T, the painting should probably be situated early in the artist's mature period, c. 1260 (Pl. 6).[6] It represents the first in a sequence of full-length, isolated portraitlike images of St. Francis, of varying quality, produced by Margarito and his workshop over a period of about forty years. A second example is the *St. Francis* at Castiglion Fiorentino near Arezzo, inscribed with Margarito's distinctive signature and perhaps datable as late as c. 1280–90 (Fig. 55).[7] The coarseness of the saint's features as portrayed here and the lack of subtlety in the work as a whole permit us to label it as a workshop product, modeled after and varying from the prototype in Arezzo. Indeed, Margarito's original in Arezzo must have spawned numerous replicas because as many as seven have survived the vicissitudes of time and are known to us today.[8] Of these, the *St. Francis* in the Museo Civico in Montepulciano represents a skilled and creative variation on the Arezzo formula (Fig. 56), whereas several of the other panels, including the portraits in Castiglion Fiorentino, in the Museo Diocesano in Arezzo, and in the Pinacoteca in Siena, take the form of simplified copies.

The tall, rectangular panel of St. Francis in Arezzo depicts the saint full-length and full-face, silhouetted against a heavily abraded silver background. He is shown dressed as a Franciscan friar in a plain brown habit tied at the waist by the characteristic chord with three knots (not including the one at the waist) symbolizing the Franciscan vow of chastity, poverty, and obedience.[9] The top of his tonsured head is partially covered by a cowl that also encircles and frames his face, emphasizing Francis's facial features (Fig. 57). It is the intense, staring portrait of a man of God and, in broad terms, follows the type for the saint established first in Bonaventura Berlinghieri's *St. Francis Dossal* of 1235 (Fig. 53). The austere facial features of Berlinghieri's Francis, in particular his sunken cheeks, angular beard, and ears, have, however, been softened by Margarito, perhaps to render the image more palatable. The general type for the saint found first in Berlinghieri's portrait and later in the Arezzo *St. Francis* captures in visual language the appearance of St. Francis as described by Brother Thomas of Celano. Writing in 1228–9, very soon after Francis's death and with some direct knowledge of the saint, in his biography, Celano constructed a convincingly vivid portrait while relying heavily on literary prototypes.[10] Celano recounts, as if speaking from personal experience, that the saint had a longish face with black eyes, a thin, straight nose, and a black beard.[11] Later in the legend, Celano adds the interesting, if perhaps not fully trustworthy, remark that Francis had a swarthy complexion that, however, turned pale after the stigmatization.[12] In Margarito's panel, in addition to his distinctive facial features and Franciscan attire, the stigmata displayed on Francis's hands and bare feet invite viewers to meditate on his closeness to Christ and resultant importance as an intercessor. Although there can be little doubt, the saint is further identified by name on the upper portion of the panel: SANCTUS FRANCISCUS.[13]

This emblematic portrait of St. Francis was extensively repainted very

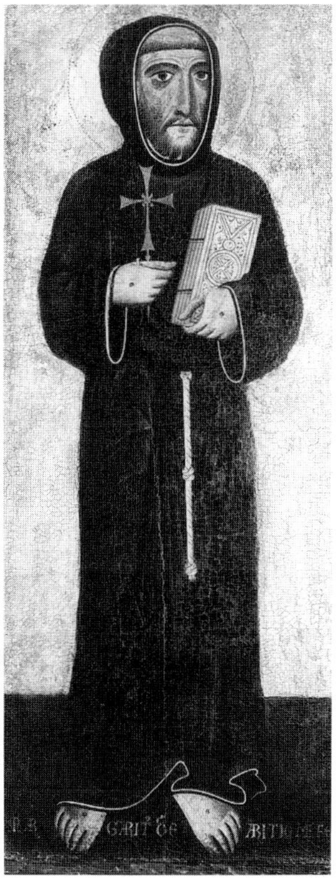

Figure 55. Margarito d'Arezzo, *St. Francis*, c. 1280–90, Castiglion Fiorentino, Museo (Archivio Fotografico della Soprintendenza di Arezzo – Sezione Beni Artistici e Storici)

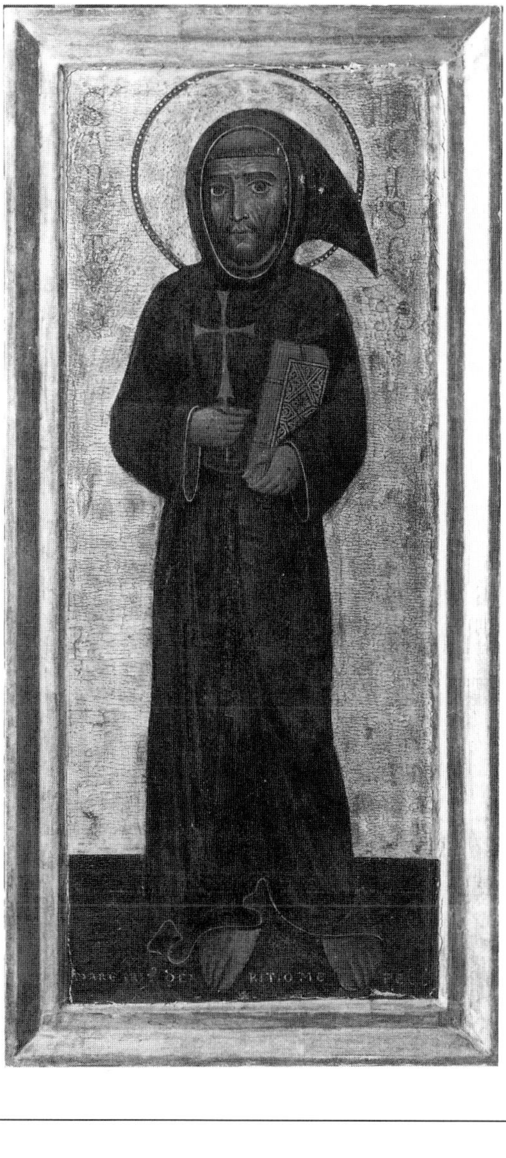

Figure 56. Margarito d'Arezzo, *St. Francis*, c. 1280, Montepulciano, Museo Civico (Foto Soprintendenza per i Beni Artistici e Storici di Siena, Italy)

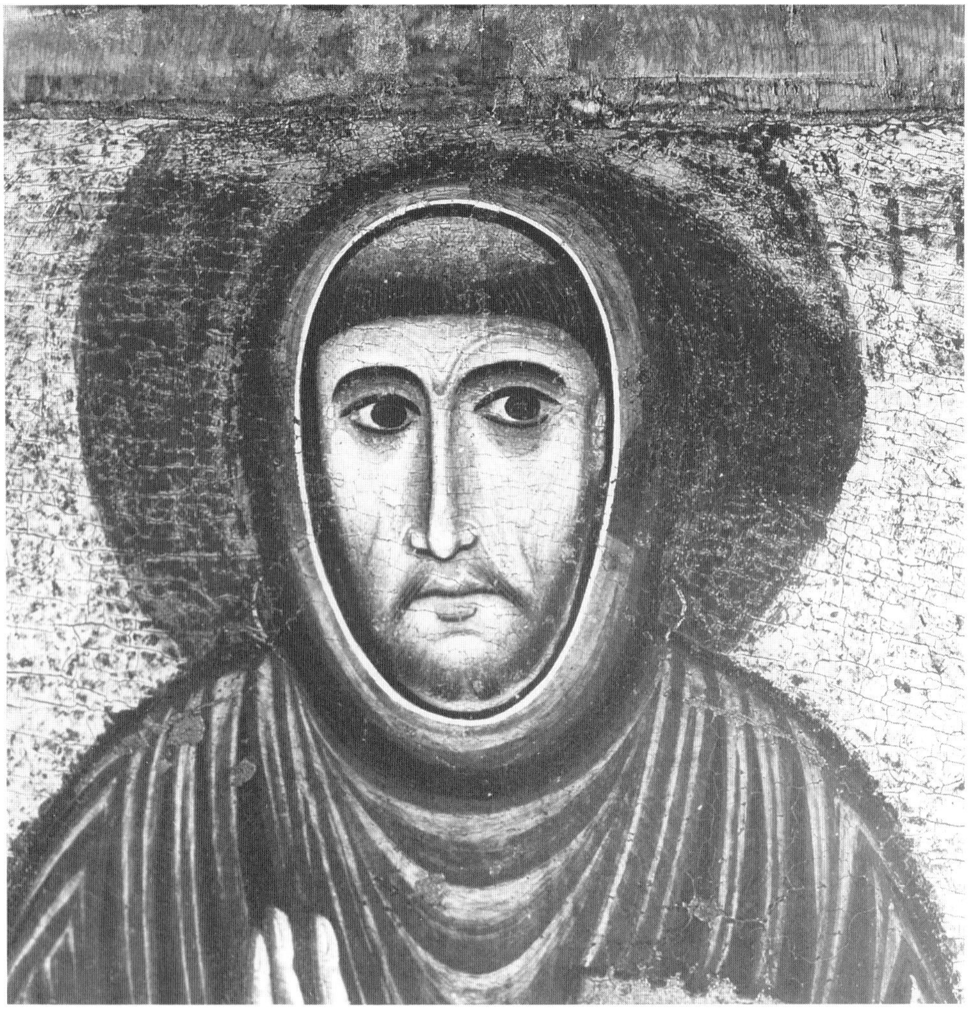

Figure 57. Margarito d'Arezzo, *St. Francis*, c. 1260, detail of face, Arezzo, Museo Medievale e Moderno (Archivio Fotografico della Soprintendenza di Arezzo – Sezione Beni Artistici e Storici)

soon after its initial creation. When the panel was restored in 1972–3 in Arezzo, it was discovered that the image of the saint had been extensively reworked at an early date, and x-radiographs taken at the Istituto Centrale del Restauro in Rome confirmed the presence of an earlier intact paint layer beneath the surface (Fig. 58). Most of the image of the saint had been retouched with the exception of his proper left hand holding the book and probably his two feet as well. The lower, ground space of the panel had also been left in its original form, including the artist's signature, which was preserved as testament to the importance of Margarito's contribution. Although microscopic examination of the paint surface and structure indicated

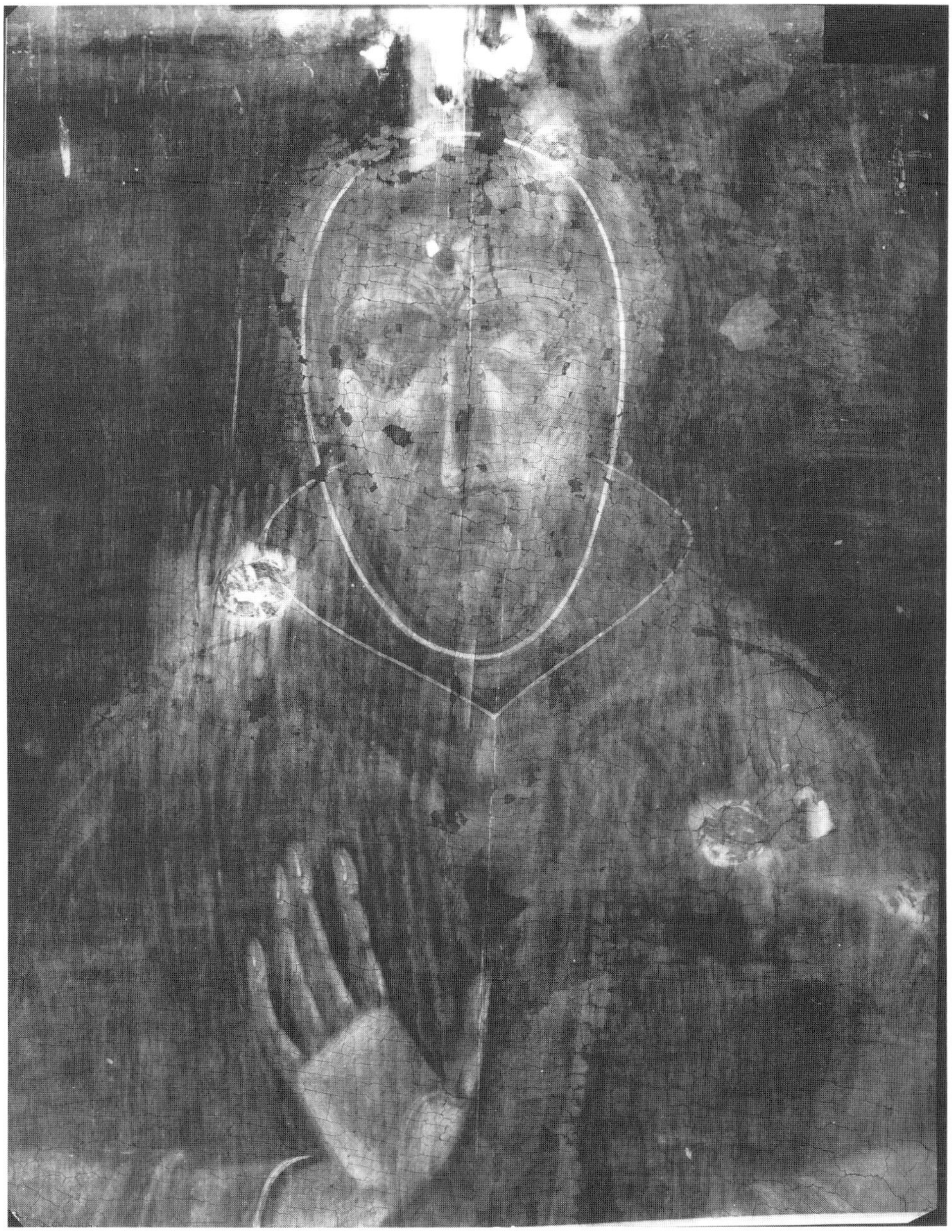

Figure 58. Margarito d'Arezzo, *St. Francis* (Arezzo), x-radiograph of face (The Harvard University Art Museums, Cambridge, Mass.)

that, generally, careful attempts had been made to preserve the outlines and modeling systems of the original, the x-radiographs revealed some significant changes to the face and hood. In the revised image, the eyes had been lowered and made smaller, the nose had been lengthened, the neckline altered from a high collar with a slight "V" at the front to a round neckline, and the hood, which originally fully covered the top of the saint's head and fell directly behind, had been pulled back to expose part of the bald crown, with the point of the hood falling over toward the right. In addition, a linear white border was added around the hood, framing the saint's face.[14] The repainting, which may not be by Margarito himself, though it adheres closely to Margarito's style, can perhaps be attributed to a close follower trained by Margarito and dated c. 1270–5, about ten to fifteen years after the original.[15]

Careful examination of the original paint surface where exposed on the panel and where evidenced in the x-radiograph gives us no reason to believe that the image was repainted to repair a damaged original.[16] Nor was it reworked for reasons of style. Instead of updating Margarito's work, the artist responsible for the new surface seems to have taken much trouble to imitate closely many of the stylistic features of the obscured image. However, some elements of the portrait were markedly transformed, and these portions may provide a clue to the reasons for repainting. As mentioned before, the facial features of St. Francis were changed in significant ways. These changes seem to have been effected to intensify the characterization by transforming the physiognomy of the saint from a general male type found in Margarito d'Arezzo's repertoire to a specific type of St. Francis, one more pleasing than the man depicted initially in Berlinghieri's 1235 dossal, but one authenticated by Thomas of Celano's verbal portrait.[17] This was to become a sanctioned likeness of St. Francis reproduced in many subsequent portraits such as the one in Castiglion Fiorentino by Margarito's workshop. All follow the basic features of the Arezzo image with minor variations, and repeat the new rounded neckline and exposed tonsure of the repainted version.[18] Indeed, as the subsequent reproductions of the painted likeness of St. Francis in the Arezzo panel suggest, the image helped to establish an iconographic model of the saint that functioned as demonstration and proof of his sanctity. Nevertheless, the reason why the Arezzo *St. Francis* was reworked in this way can only be fully explored by investigating the devotional context in which images of this kind and this image in particular functioned.

Hellmut Hager and Henk van Os have argued that the numerous images of St. Francis that proliferated after his death were a result of the vitality and intensity of the saint's personality.[19] Francis affected the minds and hearts of the Italian people to such an extent that he needed to be remembered; and this remembrance took the form of painted portraits. Images of the saint began to appear in the places he had visited and in the monasteries, convents, and churches he had founded.[20] Visual representations of the saint became a necessity in every Franciscan institution and even within lay domestic environments.[21] Painted portraits were venerated as souvenirs of his physical and spiritual presence.

Whereas the large, historiated altarpieces with St. Francis's portrait in the center and scenes from his life to either side seem to have been commissioned for side chapels in Franciscan churches, it has been suggested that the simpler, isolated images of the saint performed a different function. They were hung on pillars in Franciscan churches and became focuses of veneration independent from an altar space.[22] Although this is very plausible, a broader range of locations within a Franciscan institution, including placement in an assembly room, should also be considered. The volumetric quality of the Arezzo prototype, with the figure modeled emphatically and set in a rectangular, boxlike space defined by the recession of the floor on which the saint's bare feet are placed, also makes one wonder whether this group of portrait images arose as painted facsimiles of sculpture. Although no isolated sculpted figures of St. Francis have survived from this period, polychrome wooden figures of patron saints remain from the late thirteenth and fourteenth centuries in Umbria and in Siena, and an older local tradition for such figures may be recorded in part by the survival in Arezzo of polychrome wooden Crucifixes from the twelfth century.[23] It is an attractive possibility that painted wooden statues of St. Francis were fashioned following his death and canonization as commemorative and devotional images. Margarito's painted portraits would then have been designed as two-dimensional equivalents, capturing on panel the presence of the saint.

The provenance of the Arezzo panel can be traced back as far as the sixteenth century. Giorgio Vasari in his *vita* devoted to "Margaritone" refers to an image of St. Francis, "ritratto di naturale," at the Franciscan monastery of Sargiano near Arezzo.[24] Significantly, in 1872, our painting was transferred to the gallery in Arezzo from Sargiano.[25] Salmi suggested, on account of the importance of this image as a prototype, that it may have been designed originally for the shrine established at La Verna, the monastery near Arezzo where Francis had undergone the stigmatization.[26] Indeed, it does seem most likely that the painting was created for a Franciscan church or monastery near Arezzo (perhaps the one at Sargiano) like other portraits of the saint produced by Margarito and his workshop, for instance, the panel from San Francesco in Castiglion Fiorentino and the panel from the monastery of San Francesco at Montepulciano and now in the Museo Civico there.[27]

Positioned in a prominent location in a Franciscan monastic church or adjacent building, an image like this one would have provided Francis's followers with an emblematic portrait of their mentor and could have functioned also as a focus for spiritual thoughts and worship.[28] Francis had himself, through his own spiritual experiences, encouraged image worship

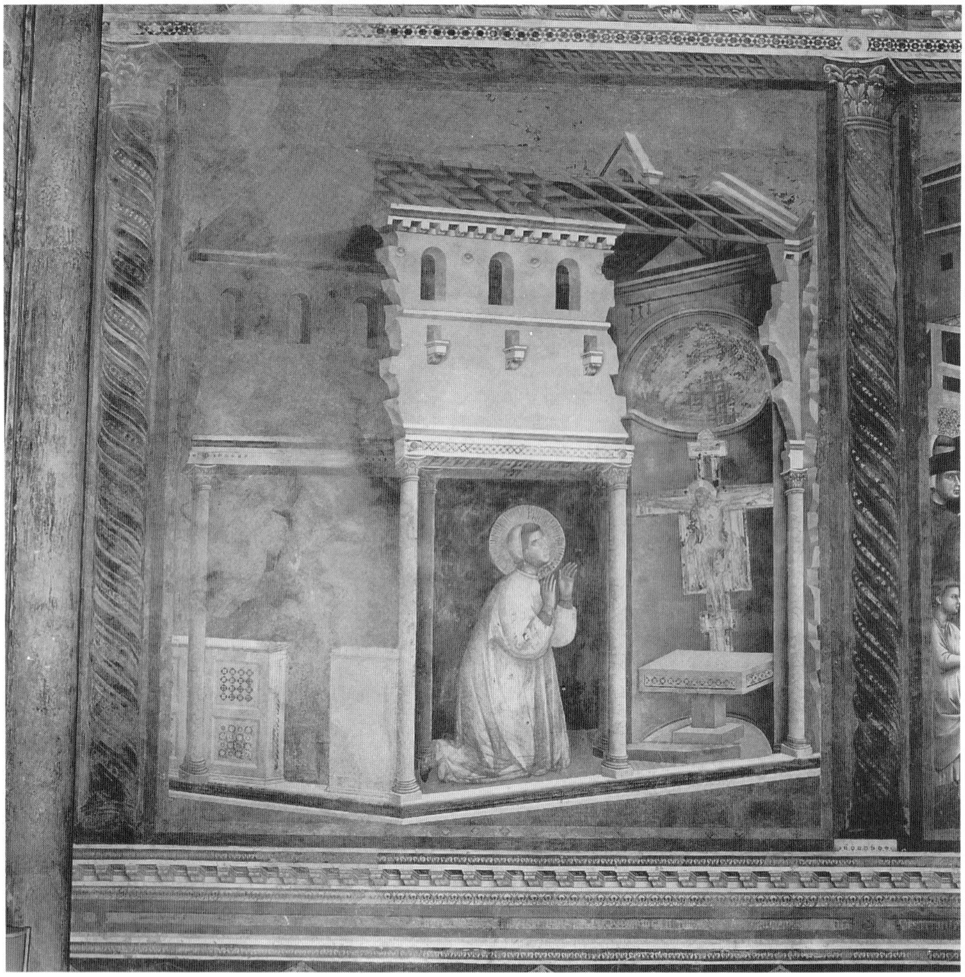

Figure 59. Master of the St. Francis Legend, *Miracle at San Damiano*, c. 1300–5, Assisi, S. Francesco, Upper Church (Roma, Istituto Centrale per il Restauro – Archivio fotografico)

among his followers. From the outset, he had expressed his devotion toward Christ and the Virgin by worshiping in front of material representations. In particular, Francis's miraculous experience with the early painted panel of Christ Crucified at the ruined church of San Damiano near Assisi, in which the image came alive and spoke to Francis directly, asking him to strive to restore the church, would have sent a message to his followers about the power inherent in images (Fig. 59).[29] In turn, Franciscans became important patrons of painted images in the Dugento and later. One late-thirteenth-century panel that evidences well this concern with material images as the focus for devotion is Duccio's *Madonna of the Franciscans* of about 1295 in the Pinacoteca of Siena (Fig. 60). In the tiny panel, three Franciscan

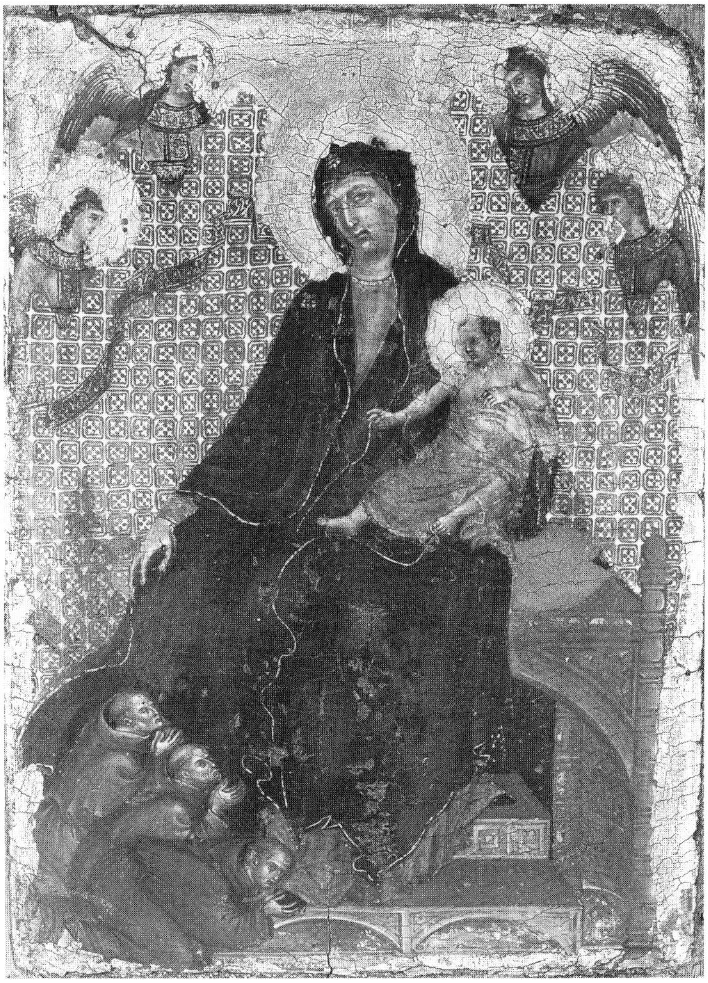

Figure 60. Duccio, *Madonna of the Franciscans,* c. 1295, Siena, Pinacoteca Nazionale (Fotografia di Fabio Lensini, Siena, Italy)

friars are shown kneeling in prayer and adoration as donors at the feet of the Virgin and Child enthroned in majesty. The painting encapsulates the involvement of images in Franciscan piety.

We can understand the repainting of the Arezzo *St. Francis* in the context of Franciscan interest in images and devotion to the person of their spiritual founder. It is plausible that Francis's followers would have desired an image of their mentor that accurately represented the standard for his appearance recorded in Celano's legend and that softened the harsh persona of Berlinghieri's altarpiece. As he was a new saint, this "friendly" image would have familiarized the friars, in a comfortable way, with his physical features as remembered by Celano. Also, a convincing likeness would enable the brothers to as it were "recognize" Francis if he appeared to them in a dream or vision, and would likewise ensure that the mentor they focused on in their meditations had a standardized appearance.[30] Such standardization functioned to strengthen the effective power of the saint.

However, I would like to suggest tentatively that the portrait face of the Arezzo *St. Francis* may also contain reference to Francis's status as *Alter Christus*. This doctrine of Francis as the second Christ was of primary importance to Franciscans and should be kept in mind when evaluating the iconographic meanings of images of the saint such as the Arezzo portrait.[31] Soon after the saint's death and canonization, the doctrine began to be disseminated in Franciscan literature and visual imagery. Already in the 1240s, in the first series of frescoes painted in the Lower Church of San Francesco at Assisi, scenes from Christ's Passion, painted on the right side of the nave, are paralleled to events from the life of St. Francis, depicted opposite, on the left wall (Figs. 61 and 62). Reading the narratives in tandem, one is presented with a full doctrinal account of Francis's *imitatio Christi*. Later in the century, evidence of Francis's special status also pen-

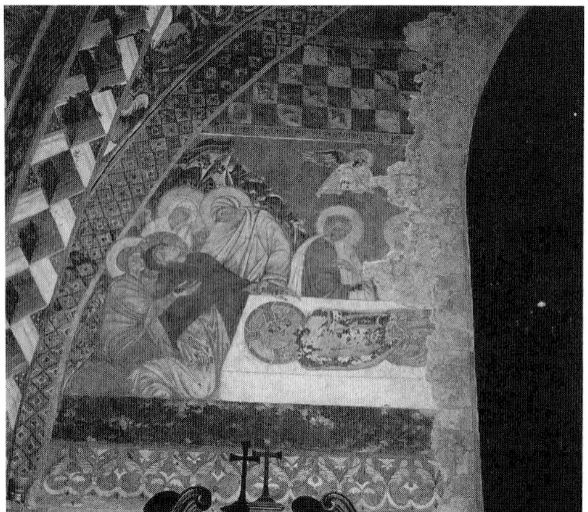

Figure 61. St. Francis Master, *Lamentation*, 1240s, Assisi, S. Francesco, Lower Church (Roma, Istituto Centrale per il Restauro – Archivio fotografico)

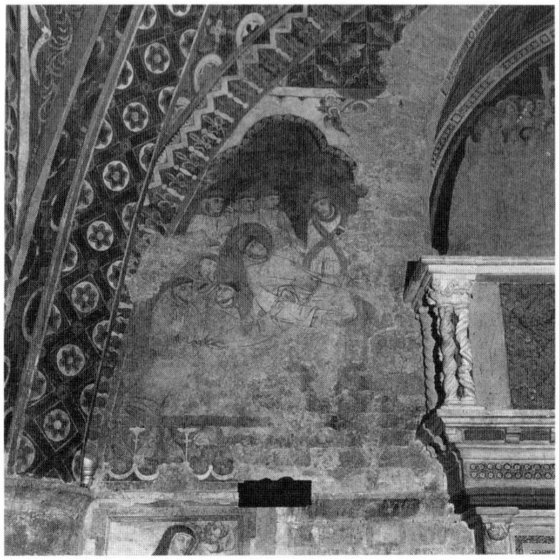

Figure 62. St. Francis Master, *Death of St. Francis*, 1240s, Assisi, S. Francesco, Lower Church (Roma, Istituto Centrale per il Restauro – Archivio fotografico)

etrated standard visual iconography such as the Crucifixion. One example is the *Crucifix* in the Pinacoteca at Perugia, attributed to the St. Francis Master and dated 1272, in which Francis is represented in a privileged position at the foot of the Cross, bending over and gesturing toward the bleeding wounds in Christ's feet (Fig. 63).[32] In Franciscan literature, the doctrine was most fully articulated in Saint Bonaventure's influential *Legenda major* of 1263. Bonaventure described how Francis's entire life had been infused with a deep consciousness of the significance of Christ's Passion and culminated ultimately in his physical experience of Christ's wounds during his vision of the seraphic Christ Crucified on Mount Verna. In the

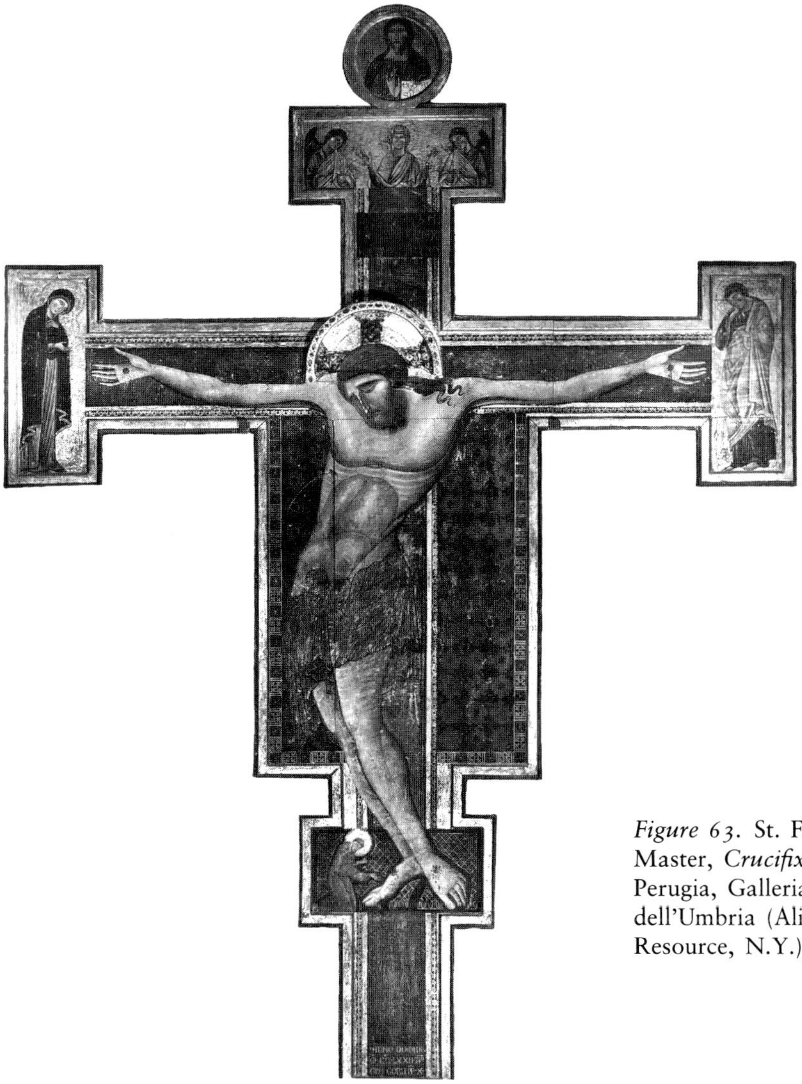

Figure 63. St. Francis Master, *Crucifix*, 1272, Perugia, Galleria Nazionale dell'Umbria (Alinari/Art Resource, N.Y.)

stigmatization, Francis's spiritual identification with and emulation of Christ were visually imprinted on his flesh.[33]

Returning to the Arezzo portrait, the repainted face of Francis, added over Margarito's original in about 1270–5, may allude to Francis's special association with Christ. With its stylized delineations of the saint's idealized and gentle features, the new face may be intended to remind the viewer of Byzantine icons of the face of Christ. The long, thin facial structure, the intensely staring eyes and thin nose, the slight moustache and beard of Francis all closely resemble the features in Byzantine cult images of the face of Christ with their softened and sympathetic renditions of the Son of God. One famous image of this kind is the Christ icon of the Sancta Sanctorum in the Lateran in Rome, dated to the seventh century. Another is the tenth-century Constantinopolitan icon of the face of Christ in the church of San Bartolomeo degli Armeni in Genoa (Fig. 64). Such Christ icons became popular devotional objects in the Medieval period in Italy as a result of Byzantine influence and would, therefore, have been well known to the followers of St. Francis.[34] The artist who repainted the Arezzo panel, subtly focused attention on the typological relation between Francis and Christ, not only by eliding their facial features, but also by framing Francis's face with a solid white line.[35] Encircled and isolated in this way, like an icon of the face of Christ, the repainted portrait of the *Alter Christus* acquired new power through its associative references to Christ's image and, as a consequence, became a stronger focus for cult worship.

THE FOGG ST. DOMINIC

Whereas Francis initiated and encouraged a personality cult among his followers, Dominic, the founder of the second important mendicant order, seems to have successfully downplayed his persona. Indeed, these differences of approach are clearly reflected in the earliest biographies of the two saints. In contrast to Thomas of Celano's *Vita Prima*, which dwells in descriptive detail on Francis's unique character, Jordan of Saxony's *Libellus* does not stress the individual attributes of Dominic as man and saint, but instead documents the foundation of the Order of Preachers and Dominic's role in this development.[36] The *Libellus*, the first and most reliable "legend" of the saint, was written by Dominic's close contemporary and successor as Master General of the order, Jordan of Saxony, between the end of 1231 and Dominic's canonization on July 3, 1234.[37] It chronicles the origins of the Dominican movement, situating Dominic within a sequence of wise and highly spiritual men who contributed to the establishment of the order.[38]

Evidence of the contrasting roles played by Francis and Dominic in the spread of their orders can also be found in early images. For whereas

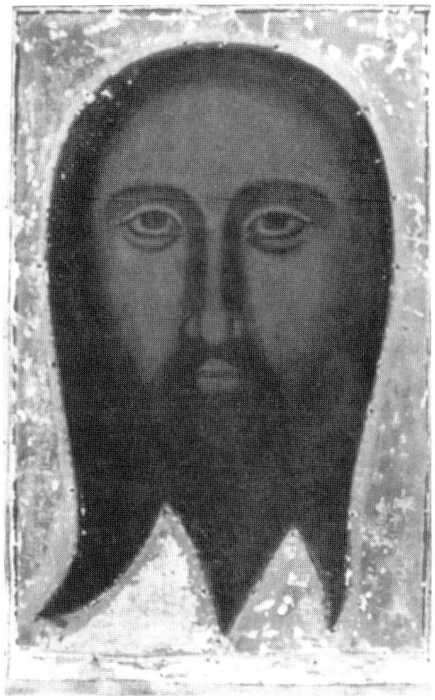

Figure 64. Byzantine, *Volto Santo*, 10th c., Genoa, S. Bartolomeo degli Armeni (Archivio Fotografico del Servizio Beni Culturali del Comune di Genova, Italy)

numerous thirteenth-century panel-paintings of St. Francis have survived as an indication of the importance of his personality, only three images on panel with St. Dominic as their focus are known from this period. The first of these, the large altarpiece of St. Dominic in the Museo di Capodimonte in Naples, is the only intact historiated dossal of this saint from the Dugento or very early Trecento (Fig. 65). Originally, in 1962, Ferdinando Bologna attributed the work to an anonymous Southern Italian master and dated it to the end of the thirteenth century.[39] In 1969, however, he sharpened the attribution by tentatively connecting the altarpiece with a Pugliese artist, Giovanni da Taranto, documented in Naples in 1304.[40] St. Dominic is represented full-length, in an attitude of blessing, with two friars kneeling at his feet and receiving his instructions in the form of a book held open to the passage from the Gospel of St. Mark: "*Euntes in mundum universum predicate*" ("Go into all the world and preach").[41] Twelve scenes from the saint's legend, depicted in a style reminiscent of contemporary miniatures, occupy vertical strips to either side of the central panel and may, possibly, have been added a little later. The altarpiece came to the Capodimonte from the church of S. Pietro Martire in Naples, but it is not clear for which Dominican church it was originally commissioned.[42] A second panel, showing St. Dominic full-length but in isolation, is also of Southern Italian origin (Fig. 66). It is attributed by Bologna to a Neapolitan master of the late thirteenth century, c. 1290, and can be found in the important church of S. Domenico Maggiore in Naples.[43] The third surviving panel-painting of

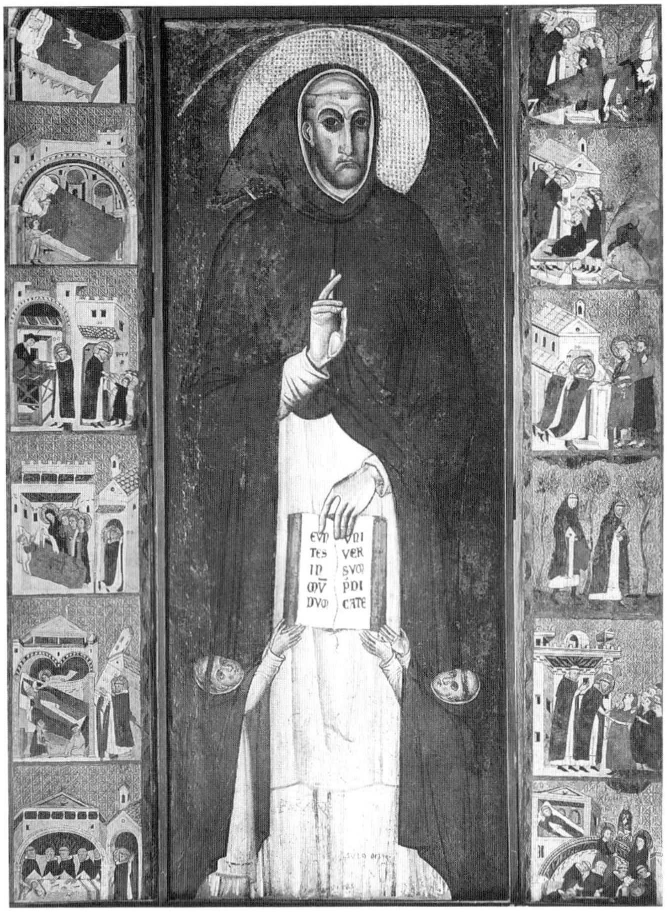

Figure 65. Giovanni da Taranto, *St. Dominic and Stories from his Life*, c. 1300–5, Naples, Museo di Capodimonte (Soprintendenza per i Beni Artistici e Storici, Naples, n. 31826)

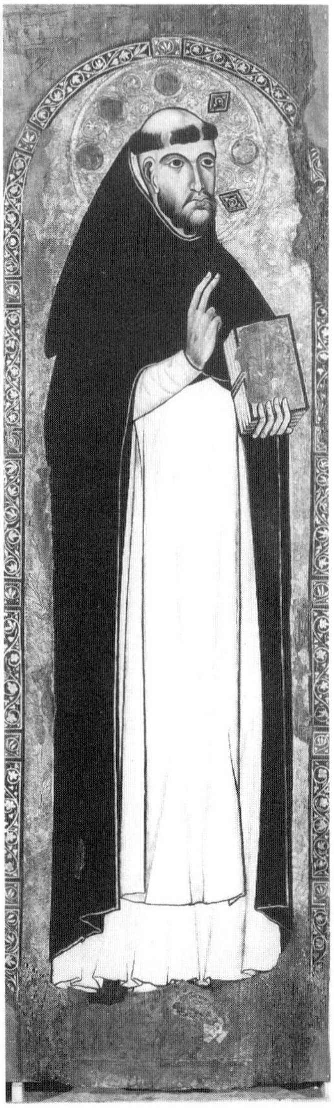

Figure 66. Neapolitan, *St. Dominic*, c. 1290, Naples, S. Domenico Maggiore (Soprintendenza per i Beni Artistici e Storici, Naples, n. 19861)

St. Dominic from the Dugento is, however, of Sienese workmanship. This is the well-known "portrait" of the saint in the Fogg Art Museum in Cambridge, Massachusetts. Because of its hybrid structure, the Fogg *St. Dominic* will be our focus.

The Fogg panel shows a fully frontal image of St. Dominic standing but cut off below the waist (Pl. 1 and Fig. 67). The figure has a simple and striking silhouette made more prominent by the gold background, now extensively abraded. He is dressed in characteristic Dominican robes, with a black hooded mantle and a white surplice beneath. The hood only partially covers the top of his head, leaving the tonsured crown in evidence. His face is austere with emphatically outlined staring eyes, but the effect is softened somewhat by the warm, reddish tone of his hair and beard. Dominic holds a book in his left hand, a standard attribute for the founder of an order, and his right hand is raised in a gesture of blessing. The star incised in the gold leaf to the left of Dominic's head alludes to the story of his godmother's vision, as recorded by Jordan of Saxony, that at Baptism, the future saint had a star on his forehead.[44]

In its present state, the Fogg portrait measures 116.3 × 61.8 cm. However, as close examination of the edges of the panel reveals, the picture has been cut down. Along the bottom, the gesso layer is fractured and the coarsely woven linen, applied between the poplar panel and the ground to cover imperfections in the wood and provide a tooth for the gesso, has been cut off unevenly. To either side of the figure and along the gabled top of the panel, there is fragmentary evidence of a blue linear border. At periodic intervals along the border area, small arc-shaped areas of red and white paint also remain. Thus, the bottom of the panel has definitely been cut and, in addition, the support seems to have extended farther to either side and perhaps above the present gable as well.[45]

With the knowledge that the Fogg panel had been cut down and with the fragmentary evidence of a blue linear border accented at regular intervals by red and white circular forms, Arthur Wheelock set about reconstructing the picture in 1967. He envisioned a historiated dossal with a full-length image of St. Dominic in the center, flanked by twelve scenes from his legend, each measuring 34 cm in height, a measurement derived from the spacing of the surviving border ornamentation (Fig. 68).[46] The inspiration for the basic form and configuration of the gabled altarpiece in Wheelock's reconstruction came from the *St. Francis Altarpiece* of about 1255, located in the Bardi Chapel of Santa Croce in Florence, and executed by an anonymous Florentine artist known on account of this work as the Bardi St. Francis Master (Fig. 69). Wheelock followed the layout of the Bardi altarpiece with the exception of the eight scenes below the figure of St. Francis, which he omitted. At the top, he imitated the gabled form of the Bardi

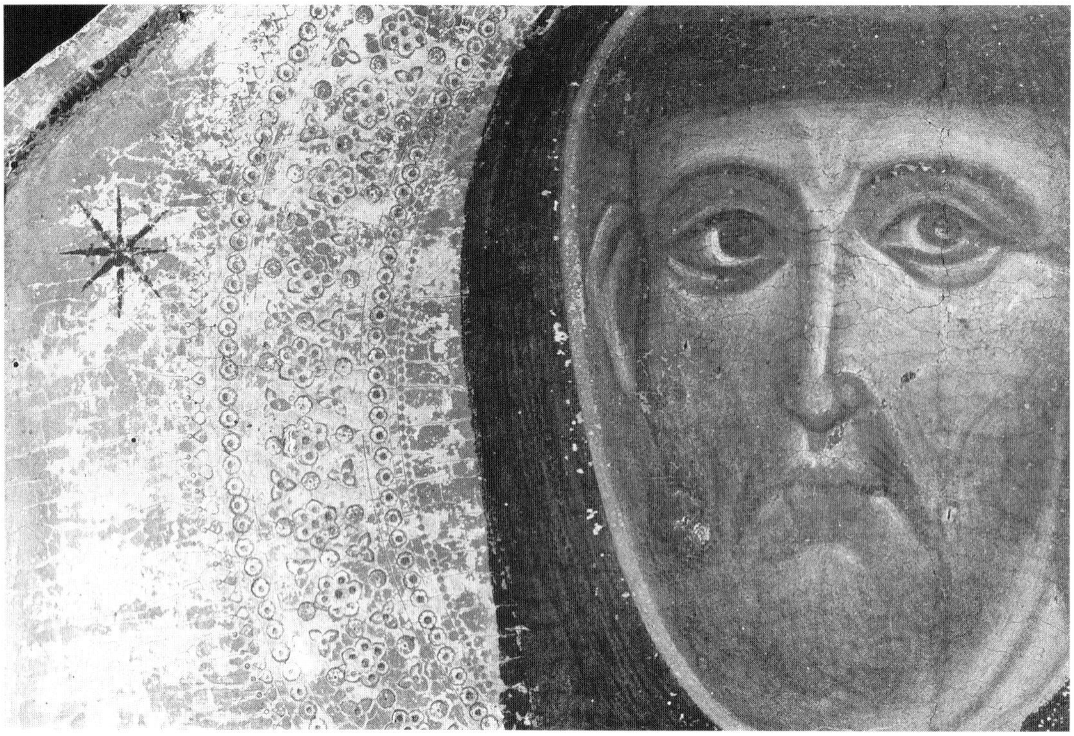

Figure 67. Sienese, *St. Dominic*, c. 1240–80, detail of face and halo, Cambridge, Mass., Fogg Art Museum (author)

altarpiece, leaving an upside-down V-shaped space analogous to the one occupied by angels there. This reconstruction is persuasive, although the arrangement at the bottom of the altarpiece must of necessity remain speculative.

According to Wheelock's model, the altarpiece would measure about 2.34 meters in height from the tip of the gable to the base and about 1.39 meters in width. This is a substantial size for a historiated altarpiece of the period and closely comparable to the Bardi *St. Francis*, which measures 2.34 × 1.37 meters.[47] Significantly, the extensive cycle of twelve scenes from the saint's legend accommodated in the reconstruction finds an echo a little later in the Naples *St. Dominic Altarpiece*, where twelve events from his life and miracles are also depicted.[48] Indeed, the Southern Italian cycle provides evidence of a tradition for the representation of St. Dominic's legend, a tradition perhaps initiated and stimulated by the Fogg altarpiece in its full, original form.[49]

Although the Fogg *St. Dominic* initially comprised part of a historiated dossal and in this way differs from the isolated image of St. Francis on the

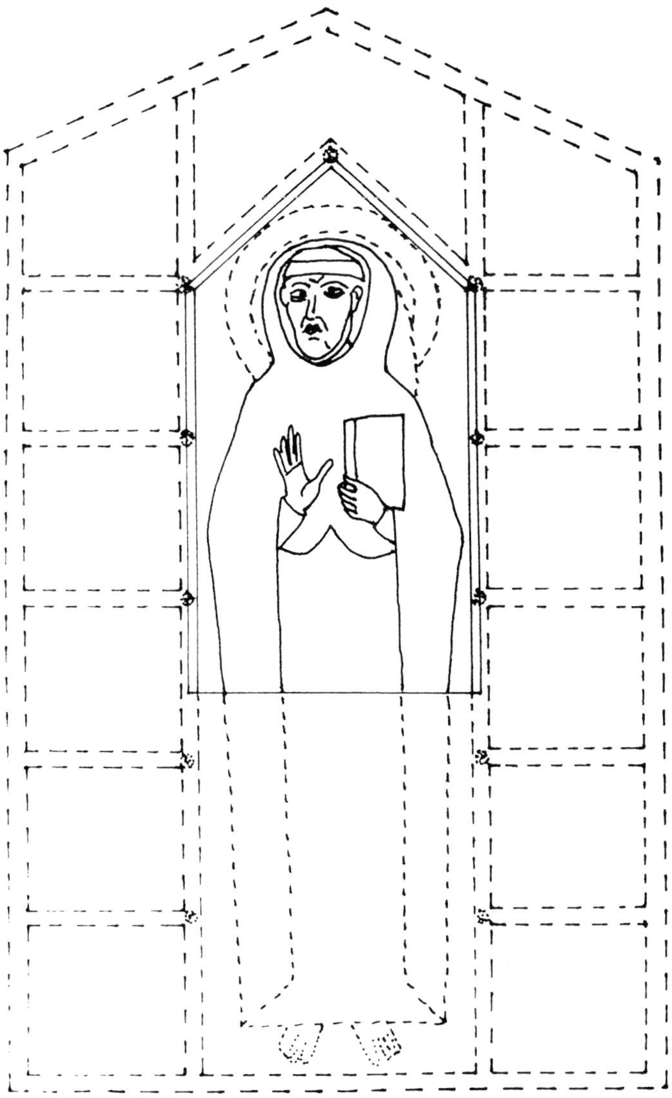

Figure 68. Reconstruction of *St. Dominic Altarpiece* after A. Wheelock (The Harvard University Art Museums, Cambridge, Mass.)

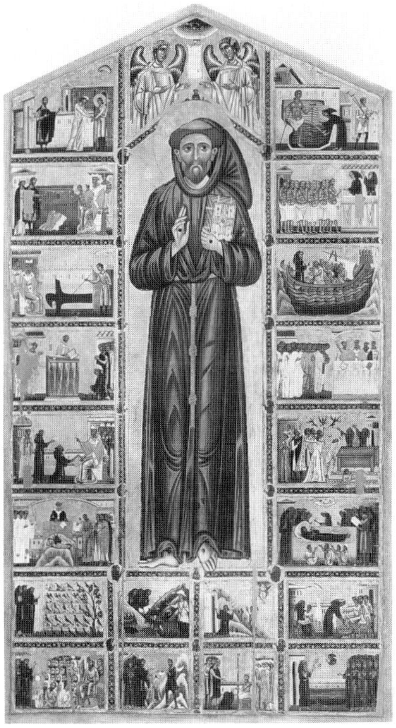

Figure 69. Bardi St. Francis Master, *St. Francis Altarpiece*, c. 1255, Florence, Sta. Croce (Alinari/ Art Resource, N.Y.)

panel in Arezzo discussed before, the two portraits of saints were both repainted at early stages in their histories. But in the case of the Fogg *St. Dominic*, the sequence of reworkings is far more complex. Areas of the panel were repainted twice in the late thirteenth century, and in the early fourteenth century, a decorative, tooled halo was also added.

The compound nature of the Fogg *St. Dominic* was first recognized by students in a Harvard University seminar in 1955 under the direction of Millard Meiss. On the basis of stylistic analysis, seminar members conjectured that portions of the image, in particular the hands and the modeling of the mantle just below, were earlier than other areas.[50] Prompted to reexamine radiographs made of the painting in the 1930s and in 1948, the technical evidence was interpreted as revealing that the head of the saint had been repainted twice (Fig. 70). On the radiograph, three separate images of the saint's right eye can be clearly distinguished, as well as two different outlines of the face, one substantially larger and to the lower right. A diagrammatic form of the three stages was eventually published in 1969, and each stage was given an approximate date on the basis of general stylistic features detectable from the radiographs, such as the shape and positioning of the eyes. The original image, thought to have been painted in Siena, was dated c. 1235–40; the second face, which was strongly modeled in lead white and showed features characteristic of the Florentine artist, Coppo di Marcovaldo, who was active in Siena in the early 1260s, was given a date of about 1260; and, finally, the third and now visible face, attributed to a follower of Guido da Siena, was dated c. 1280–5.[51]

A study of the layered structure of the painting under the microscope had helped to verify and add precision to these conclusions. Elizabeth Jones, then chief conservator at the Fogg, discovered that, whereas large areas of the panel consist of only one layer of paint, two distinct layers can be seen in the hands, the white robe, and at the edges of the black mantle. Further, as she observed, an additional third layer can be seen in the area of the head, chest, and shoulders. Her findings indicated that "the picture was refurbished locally, not entirely repainted each time."[52]

The Fogg *St. Dominic* underwent a final stage of renovation in the early fourteenth century – the punching of the halo. Already in 1929, George Stout recognized the incongruity, or as he called it, the "puzzle," of the tooled halo on the panel.[53] Whereas the final paint layer dates from the late thirteenth century, full halo-tooling using sophisticated combinations of motif punches was not initiated in Siena until about 1319.[54] More recently, Mojmìr Frinta has identified the punch motifs used to decorate the halo as characteristic of the Sienese artist, Ugolino di Nerio, in the years c. 1320–5.[55] Indeed, punch motifs found in the Fogg picture also can be identified on panels from Ugolino's dismantled Santa Croce altarpiece of c. 1325, one

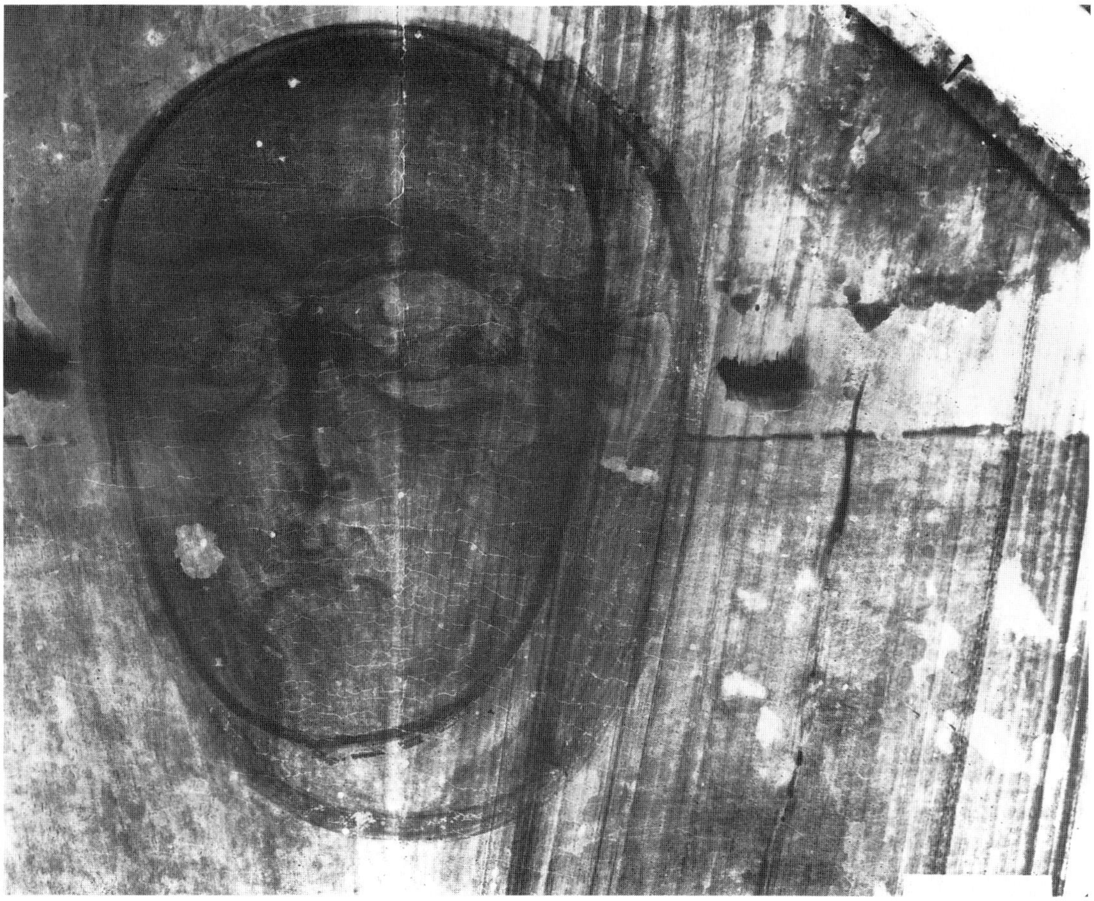

Figure 70. Sienese, *St. Dominic*, c. 1240–80, x-radiograph of face showing two earlier versions (The Harvard University Art Museums, Cambridge, Mass.)

of Ugolino's most important commissions of the period, made for the Franciscans in Florence.[56] It may be significant that in the early 1320s, Ugolino is recorded as having produced a perhaps equally spectacular altarpiece for the high altar of the Dominican church in Florence, Santa Maria Novella.[57] The embellishment of the Fogg picture would have been carried out for the Dominicans in Siena at about the same date.

The complex series of renovations experienced by the Fogg *St. Dominic* indicates that the altarpiece of which it formed the central part was the subject of strong devotional interest. In fact, the sequence of attentions that the panel underwent can be compared with the repeated repainting of wonder-working icons in the Byzantine tradition, discussed in Chapter 2. Thus, even though the historical and literary records suggest that St. Dominic's personality did not stimulate an extensive cult following analogous to the spiritual movement inspired by Francis of Assisi, individual images of the saint, such as the Fogg altarpiece, may have been the focus of intense veneration. To investigate this further, the historical context in which the altarpiece functioned must be explored.

In this instance, the provenance of the panel is of little help, as it can only be traced as far back as 1919, when the picture left the hands of the Marchese Peruzzi in Florence and through a complex route found its way into the collection of the Fogg Art Museum in 1920.[58] However, the structure and iconography suggest more about the panel's original context. Historiated altarpieces of the kind reconstructed by Wheelock were generally commissioned for side altars in churches, as has been mentioned. A large altarpiece dedicated to St. Dominic and scenes from his legend, of course, would have found its most natural place in a Dominican church. In the case of the Fogg panel, the attribution of the two last stages of reworking to Sienese workshops – the final paint layer by an artist in the circle of Guido da Siena and the tooled halo characteristic of Ugolino di Nerio's workshop – points to Siena as the place of origin. It is, therefore, tempting to connect the Fogg St. Dominic altarpiece with the Sienese church of San Domenico.[59] Even though the earliest surviving inventory of works of art in Siena, Monsignor Fabio Chigi's *Elenco* of 1625–6, does not record the altarpiece as then in San Domenico, the list is incomplete and the painting could have been removed before that date.[60] Nevertheless, it is perhaps surprising that no records of the early location of such a major altarpiece or of its subsequent dismemberment survive.[61]

As was mentioned in Chapter 2, in 1225, the Dominicans of Siena, who had been located at the hospice of Sta. Maria Maddalena outside the porta S. Maurizio since 1221, were given a piece of land outside and inside the city walls by the Malavolti family.[62] A parrochial church entitled San Gregorio may have been located on this land, and it has been widely assumed that the Dominicans were ceded the church, although this is far from certain.[63] It is clear, however, that in 1225, the Dominicans began building their own new church on the donated land, and that by 1262, the first church of San Domenico was nearing completion and presumably ready for services.[64] In Chapter 2, I related the commission of Guido da Siena's *Palazzo Pubblico Maestà* of c. 1270–80 to the establishment of the Dominicans in their new building. On the other hand, the Fogg altarpiece, the earliest stage of which dates from about 1235–40 or a little later, seems to have been ordered before San Domenico was complete and perhaps while the Dominicans were occupying San Gregorio.[65] It would be safe to assume, however, that the altarpiece was intended from the start for San Domenico, and perhaps the first repainting of the image can be linked to the transfer to this new environment. The image was refurbished in about 1260 as part of the process of spiritual renewal that accompanied the move to more grand and spacious surroundings.

The second repainting of the Fogg altarpiece may also mark an important happening in the life of the Dominicans of Siena, although this is less secure. For at about the time when an artist from the circle of Guido da Siena was hired to retouch areas of the image in c. 1280, artists from the same workshop, if not the master himself, were commissioned to paint the monumental Maestà altarpiece for San Domenico.[66] It is possible that both commissions to the same workshop were motivated by one significant event or patron associated with the new location at San Domenico.

The final reworking of the altarpiece also can be tentatively linked to a commemorative occasion in the early history of the order. In Chapter 2, I suggested that the devotional repainting of the other large altarpiece owned by the Dominicans, Guido da Siena's Maestà – involving a selective reworking of the faces and other flesh areas of the Virgin and Child as well as details of the draperies and throne – could have been carried out in preparation for the centenary of St. Dominic's death in 1321. This repainting has been attributed to Ugolino di Nerio by J. A. Crowe and G. B. Cavalcaselle and by Bernard Berenson.[67] Can it be mere coincidence that the Fogg altarpiece was rewarded with a new tooled halo at about the same time by the same workshop, or does this last stage of physical renovation likewise document a highly important moment in the religious life of the Sienese Dominicans, namely, the anniversary of their founder's death?

One qualitative feature of the renovation of the Fogg panel also merits attention. It may be very significant that the face of the *St. Dominic* was repainted more than the rest of the panel. As the microscopic examination of the surface indicated, the painting was retouched in selected areas with more layers added to the region of the face. These findings can be explained in two ways. Firstly, the repainting may represent an Italian equivalent to the Byzantine practice of refurbishing icons discussed in Chapter 2. In this case, the concentration on the saint's face could be related to the Orthodox tradition that the face and hands of a divine figure receive most attention because they are the essential, expressive portions of the image. The reworking of the Fogg *St. Dominic* would then be closely comparable to other early Italian manifestations of what was essentially a Byzantine cult practice, such as the repainting of the faces and hands in a number of Tuscan altarpieces of the Madonna and Child, most notably the renovations of Coppo di Marcovaldo's *Madonna del Bordone* and Guido da Siena's *Palazzo Pubblico Maestà*, carried out in Siena in the early decades of the fourteenth century.

A second explanation, perhaps not totally divorced from the first, is that the portrait elements of the face were an ongoing concern. Although Jordan of Saxony in his *Libellus* never refers in any detail to the physical appearance of St. Dominic, a candid, eyewitness account survives. Sister Cecilia, who took her vows under St. Dominic in Rome and subsequently, in 1223, joined the community of St. Agnes in Bologna, dictated her memories of St. Dominic some time between 1272 and 1288, and they were written down as *The Miracles of St. Dominic*.[68] The "miracles" include the following "Portrait of St. Dominic": "He was slender and of medium height. His face was handsome and somewhat ruddy. His hair and beard were reddish and his eyes beautiful. From his brow and eyes emanated a kind of radiance which drew everyone to revere and love him. . . . He was never bald, although he wore the full corona, which was sprinkled with a few grey hairs."[69] The most significant portrait features recorded in Sister Cecilia's description and present also in the ultimate stage of the Fogg panel are St. Dominic's reddish hair and beard. Further, a microscopic paint cross-section taken from the painting, from the area above the saint's right ear, revealed that the hair in the original image, painted soon after St. Dominic's death, was also red.[70]

It is impossible to arrive at firm conclusions given the sparcity of evidence concerning Dominic's actual appearance, and given the difficulty of interpreting from x-rays the images of his face recorded at three distinct moments on the Fogg panel. Nevertheless, it seems safe to suggest that the successive reworking of St. Dominic's face reflects interest in creating a legitimate "portrait" of the holy man. In contrast to the emblematic *St. Francis* by Margarito d'Arezzo, however, the Fogg portrait did not achieve the status of a sanctioned likeness, nor was it widely disseminated in the context of a broad cult. Other early Tuscan images of St. Dominic typically show the saint with dark brown or black hair and beard.[71] One example is the small figure of the saint included in the portable triptych by a Florentine master of about 1270 in the Yale University Art Gallery in New Haven. Within the central panel of the Madonna and Child, Dominic is represented in the place of honor to the right of the Virgin, and Francis is shown on her left. This small folding triptych, which includes as well as St. Dominic a second Dominican saint, probably St. Peter Martyr, on the left shutter, may have been designed to fulfill the private devotional needs of an early Dominican.[72] Another image of the saint appears in Duccio's *London Triptych* of about 1300 (Fig. 71).[73] Standing on the inner side of the right shutter, somewhat separated from the Virgin and Child, Dominic is portrayed here with exquisite naturalism. His hair and beard are a dark, walnut brown. Because of the presence in the triptych of both St. Dominic and St. Aurea of Ostia, Joanna Cannon has suggested it was made for the eminent Dominican, Niccolò da Prato (d. 1321), who was cardinal of Ostia.[74] Both triptychs provide further evidence that images of St. Dominic sometimes did play a role in the spiritual exercises of his followers, although in each

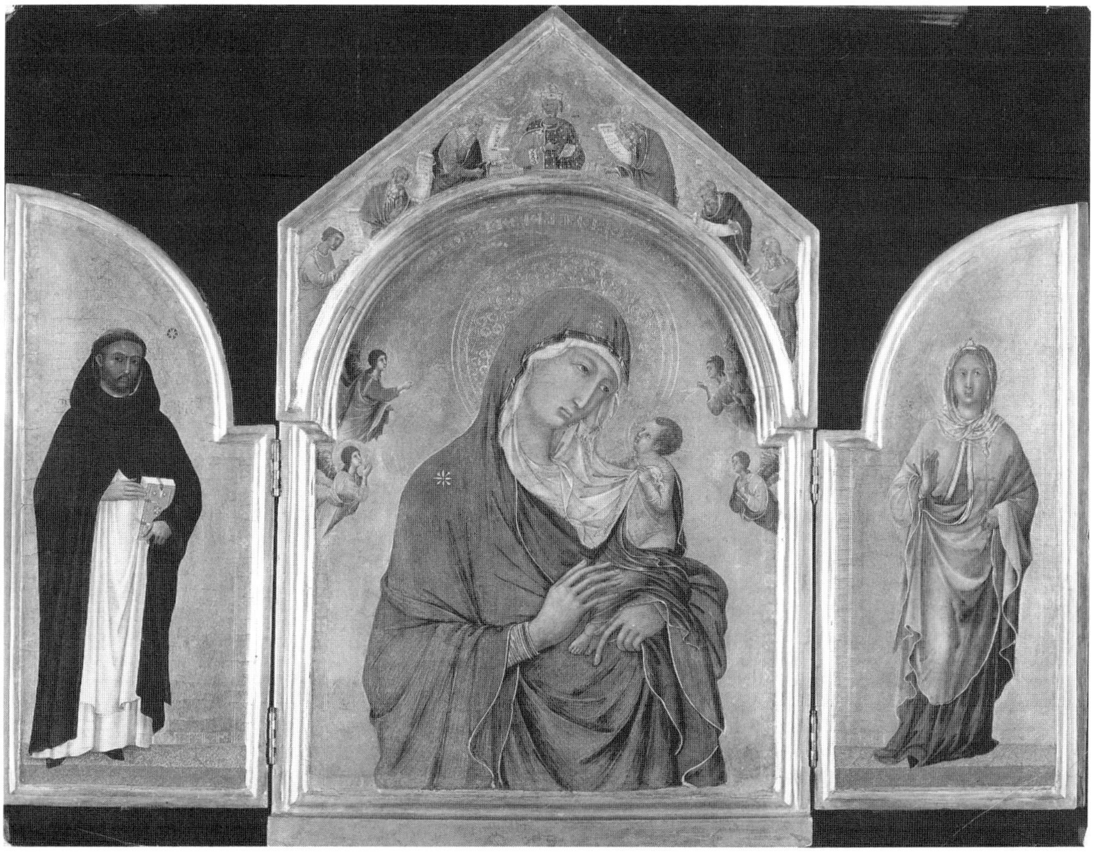

Figure 71. Duccio, *London Triptych*, c. 1300, London, The National Gallery (Reproduced by courtesy of the Trustees, The National Gallery, London)

instance, Dominic's role is secondary and circumscribed, that of intercessor with the divine.[75]

Even though the Fogg *St. Dominic* did not generate replicas comparable to Margarito d'Arezzo's sequence of images of St. Francis, it is clear that the painting did have great local significance. The repeated reworking of this once monumental altarpiece glorifying St. Dominic, with special attention paid in the renovations to his face and portrait features, reveals the importance of the persona of the saint and his image within the limited context of the Dominican community in Siena.

□ □ □

In this chapter, the physical changes embodied in two panels of St. Francis and St. Dominic have been interpreted as recording important aspects of the images' devotional functions. The Arezzo *St. Francis* was repainted, I have argued, to create a truer portrait of the holy man suitable as a focus of meditation for his followers, and the two revisions to the face of the Fogg *St. Dominic* may reflect a similar, though more local, cult interest in the persona of that saint. When examined as manifestations of specific social environments, the complex, stratified structures of these images help to document the way the paintings worked as cult objects and elicited responses over an extended period of time.

CHAPTER 5

The Reframing of Gothic Altarpieces During the Renaissance

In the fifteenth and early sixteenth centuries in Tuscany, a substantial number of Gothic altarpieces were subjected to renovations. Although the nature of the changes varies from case to case, generally the Gothic painting was transformed into a Renaissance work by altering the frame. One colorful example is Taddeo Gaddi's polyptych representing the *Madonna and Child with Four Saints* in the Metropolitan Museum of Art in New York (Pl. 7). The Gothic altarpiece, painted originally in about 1340–5, was radically remodeled in the late Quattrocento.[1] At that time, the five joined panels were removed from their pointed-arched frame and set inside a classically inspired architectural construction typical of the day. In order to effect this maneuver, the central panel of the Madonna and Child had to be cut along the top. New pieces of wood were inserted to fill the open spaces in the spandrel areas at the top. Decorative, classical-style pilasters were then painted between the saints in the areas originally occupied by the colonettes, and illusionistic images of the four Evangelists were added in the spandrels in a style attributable to the workshop of Domenico Ghirlandaio, a workshop often engaged in renovation activities.[2]

Compound altarpieces of this type have generally elicited a negative response when viewed from an aesthetic standpoint. Indeed, one art historian describes the hybrid form of Taddeo Gaddi's altarpiece as an "unhappy solution" that "imposed a unified space that was clearly contrary to Taddeo's intentions, and . . . introduced a frame all out of proportion to the figures it encloses."[3] Although reframed altarpieces of this kind clearly accorded with Renaissance tastes, modern viewers are disturbed by the mixture of Gothic and Renaissance. As a consequence, relatively few renovated Gothic altarpieces survive intact. Whenever possible, their Renaissance "accretions" have been removed and they have been returned to their original states. For instance, between 1957 and 1958, Giotto's *Badia Polyptych* was, as one art historian explains, "liberated" from its Quattrocento additions (Figs. 5 and 6).[4] Pieces had been added to the original Gothic frame to remodel the altarpiece into a rectangular form more pleasing to the Renaissance eye. Documents indicate that the cherubs between the cusps were painted by the Florentine artist Jacopo d'Antonio sometime in the years 1451–3.[5] But with the historical dimension of the object in mind, one might pause to consider: Now that all these additions are gone, have we gained or have we lost? The question is not a simple one. Although the original form of the altarpiece has been recovered, it could be argued that we have deprived the object of one layer of its meaning. Those pejoratively labeled "accretions" can be interpreted more positively as carriers of history, as providing clues to the value and meaning of the Trecento object during one later period of its history. The purpose of this chapter is to elucidate some of these historical meanings.

TYPES OF REFRAMING

The oldest instance of this type of reframing known to us is the *Maestà* in the oratory of Sta. Maria Maddalena in Pian di Mugnone near Fiesole attributed to the Master of the Horne Triptych (Fig. 72). In the late 1420s, the pointed-arched panel representing the Madonna enthroned and surrounded by angels was reframed in the form of a rectangle, with three spiral colonettes to either side. An image of the Annunciation, traditionally given to the prolific Florentine artist Bicci di Lorenzo, was painted on the two new spandrels.[6] Later reframings of single-panel Maestà images follow the same formula. One instance is the *Maestà* by the Master of the Fogg Pietà in the Collegiata of Figline Valdarno just south of Florence, which was transformed from a cusped shape into a rectangular structure through the addition of two triangular panels with images of angels to form the top corners (Fig. 73). The recently restored angels, now separated from the *Maestà*, have been identified by Alessandro Conti as early works of Domenico Ghirlandaio, associating the painting component of this reframing with his shop (Fig. 74).[7]

By the mid- to late Quattrocento, the period in which the majority of these renovations seem to have been done, two other basic types of reframing performed on more complex altarpieces of triptych or polyptych format can be distinguished. They are exemplified, respectively, by Giotto's *Badia Polyptych* and Taddeo Gaddi's *Metropolitan Polyptych*, both mentioned earlier (Fig. 6 and Pl. 7). The manner of reframing chosen seems to have

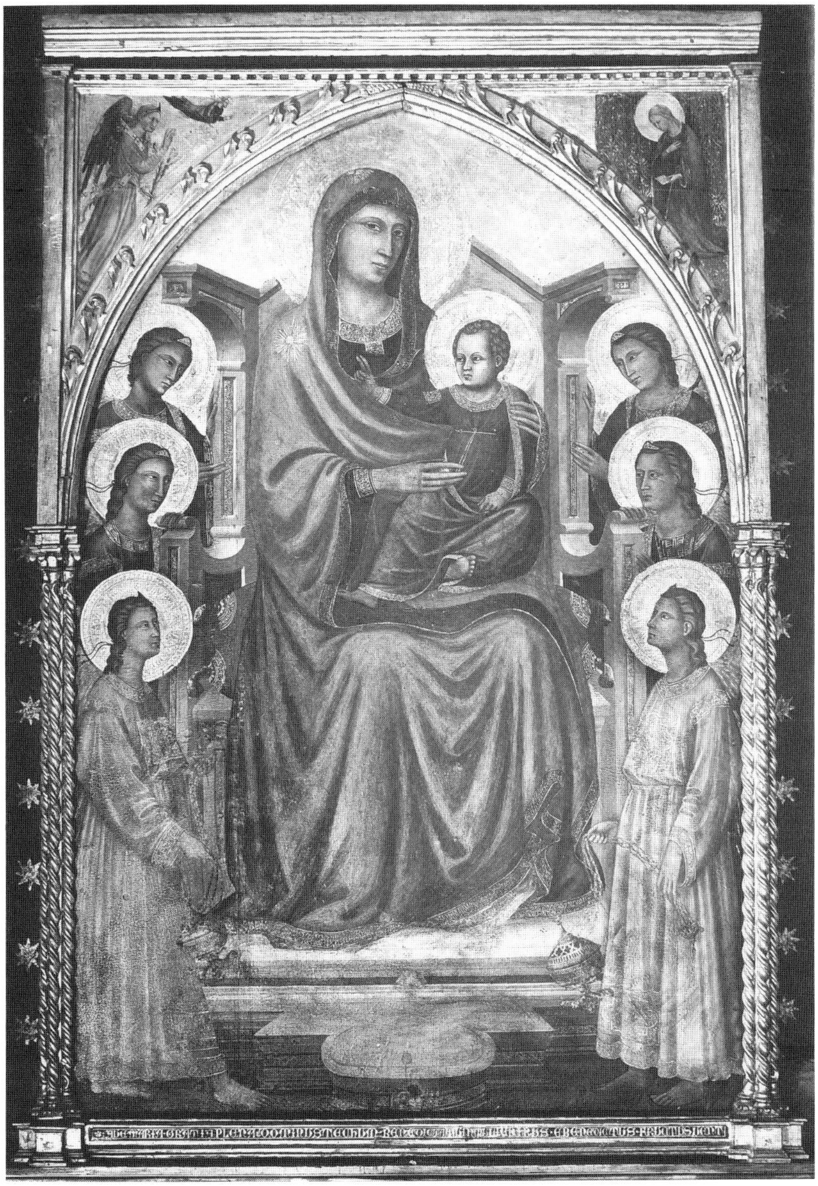

Figure 72. Master of the Horne Triptych, *Maestà*, early 14th c., Pian di Mugnone nr. Fiesole, Sta. Maria Maddalena (Alinari/Art Resource, N.Y.)

depended on the original design of the altarpiece involved. If the altarpiece took the form of a polyptych with half-length figures on the main register and small pinnacle figures in gables above and was framed in a simple manner with moldings, the pointed-arched painting was remodeled without removal of the frame by adding wood pieces to create a rectangular form. Such was the case with Giotto's *Badia Polyptych*, and many other examples

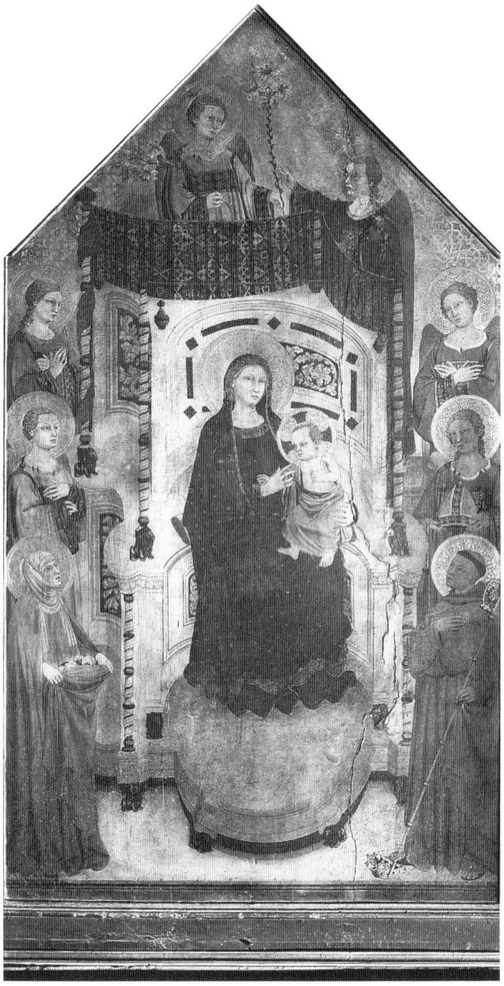

Figure 73. Master of the Fogg Pietà, *Maestà*, early 14th c., Figline Valdarno, Collegiata di S. Maria (Alinari/Art Resource, N.Y.)

could be cited.[8] On the other hand, polyptychs with full-length figures and lavish architectural frames were often more radically restored, as with Taddeo Gaddi's *Metropolitan Polyptych*. The Gothic frame was completely discarded and the old panels inserted into an up-to-date frame modeled on early Renaissance, classically inspired architecture.[9]

There are, of course, exceptions to the previous categorization of types. One unusual reframing was performed on Jacopo del Casentino's *Madonna and Child with Sts. Michael and Margaret* from the Church of Sta. Maria at Ughi in Rignano sull'Arno and at present under restoration in Florence (Fig. 75). The triptych with half-length figures was transformed by adding cherubim heads in the new spandrel areas in the typical fashion. However, the wood addition in this case extended far above, doubling the total height

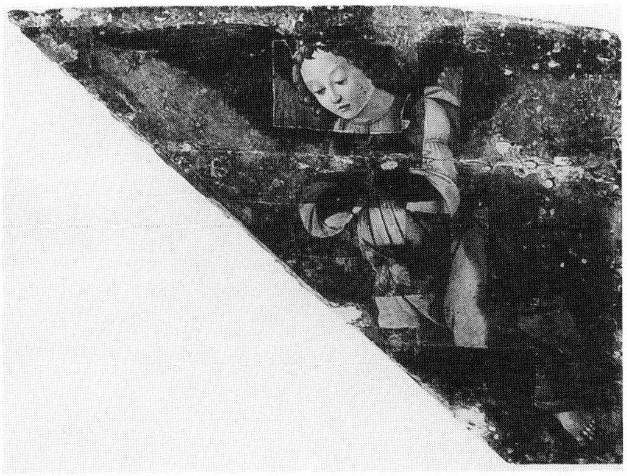

Figure 74. Domenico Ghirlandaio (?), *Angel*, c. 1480, from the Master of the Fogg Pietà's *Maestà*, during restoration of early 1980s, Figline Valdarno, Collegiata di S. Maria (Opificio delle Pietre Dure di Firenze, Italy)

of the altarpiece, with images of the Trinity in a mandorla and four saints. These late-Quattrocento additions can be attributed to a minor Florentine working under the influence of Cosimo Rosselli and Jacopo del Sellaio.[10]

MOTIVATIONS

It is important at the outset to remember the widely held thesis concerning the significance of the added frames and repaintings on Gothic altarpieces. Traditionally, hybrid altarpieces of this kind have been viewed as Renaissance attempts to disguise distasteful Gothic works. The choice of reframing was selected only as an economically feasible alternative to commissioning a completely new painting, and reflects a dismissive attitude toward the Medieval, or so the argument runs.[11] In support, one could cite Jacob Burckhardt's classic contention that in Italian Renaissance art, "a fixed prejudice showed itself against all that those centuries [the Middle Ages] had created."[12] However, a fuller investigation of the social and cultural contexts surrounding these practices may lead to somewhat different conclusions. Gothic altarpieces sometimes looked precious and meaningful when seen through Renaissance eyes.

In search of the rationale underlying renovations of this kind, one source of information to which we have recourse are the records of painting contracts describing such work. Our most informative documentary source is the work diary of the Florentine painter Neri di Bicci, kept in the years 1453 to 1475. Neri di Bicci, an idiosyncratic though interesting artist, who catered primarily to the needs and purses of the less well-to-do, kept a journal account of several work projects in which he was called upon to renovate paintings. One project deserves particular attention. Neri di Bicci records that on Thursday, October 31, 1471, he undertook the restoration of an altarpiece for Tommaso Soderini. He explains that the painting is destined for an altar in the church of San Frediano in Florence, an altar that

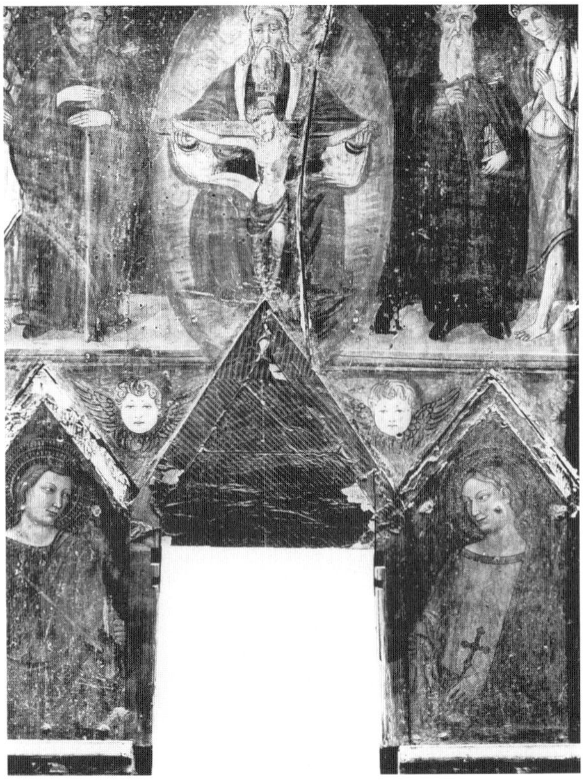

Figure 75. Jacopo del Casentino and Florentine late 15th c., *Madonna and Child with Saints and the Trinity,* Rignano sull'Arno, Sta. Maria a Ughi (Opificio delle Pietre Dure di Firenze, Italy)

has been recently renovated and thus updated. The altarpiece, which Neri describes as "made in the old manner with finials and foliate designs according to the usage of that older time," is to be "restored and brought back to the taste of today, that is, with pilasters on either side, and above an architrave with a frieze and a cornice."[13] In other words, an old altarpiece, framed in the Gothic style with the typical decorations of foliage carved into the crowning portions of the polyptych, is to be renovated by replacing the frame with a modern one in the classical style of Neri's day. Although the commission is given to Neri, he will carry out only the painting and gilding and will subcontract the wood carving of the frame to Domenico da San Tommaso and his son Zanobi, regular collaborators with Neri.

Neri's matter-of-fact account reveals clearly his awareness of the stylistic features distinguishing the Gothic altarpiece, which he describes as "made in the old manner," from the products of early Renaissance taste. It is the framing of the altarpiece that he identifies as making the work aesthetically out of date, the aspect of the work most obviously distinguishable as of an earlier style. But, it is also significant that the altarpiece was not singled out for renovation on its own. Indeed, the modernization seems to have been undertaken as a consequence of the renovation of the altar where it was to be rehoused. Neri's work diary leads one to believe that the Soderini altarpiece was updated at the request of the patron so that it might fit, aesthetically, within its Renaissance chapel space. In search of corroborative evidence, the historical context surrounding particular examples of reframed altarpieces will be examined.

THE BARONCELLI ALTARPIECE

To begin with the most famous of the surviving reframed Trecento polyptychs, the *Baroncelli Altarpiece* painted by Giotto and his workshop in about 1330, this altarpiece was designed for the chapel of the Baroncelli family in the Florentine church of Santa Croce, and stood there in its Gothic frame until about 1480 when it was quite radically renovated (Fig. 1).[14] During this procedure, the altarpiece was removed from its original frame and the top portion of the central panel with an image of God the Father was discarded.[15] The painting was then carefully set inside a new, ornate frame in the *all'antica* style and images of cherubim, painted in vermilion against a steel-blue background, were added in the spandrel areas.

Interventions of this kind are often difficult to attribute on the basis of style alone because of the sparseness of the evidence, and because late-Quattrocento frames in the *all'antica* style often look more similar than unique. The frame of the *Baroncelli Altarpiece* is, however, an exception. It is a luxurious frame, unique and remarkable for its high quality and for its distinct classical detailing. The cornice and the side pilasters are decorated with raised gilt ornamentation, including swirling acanthus leaves, cherub heads, and palmettes, all set off against a rich blue background. Indeed, the exceptionally lavish form of framing used in this instance can be tentatively associated with a particular workshop, that of the architect and wood sculptor Giuliano da Maiano, on the basis of stylistic comparisons. The Baroncelli frame closely resembles sculpted frames on contemporary works by Giuliano's brother and affiliate, Benedetto da Maiano, most notably the frame of his *San Bartolo Altar* in the church of San Agostino in San Gimignano, usually dated 1492–4, which shows a similar use of *all'antica* relief ornament (Fig. 76).[16] Giuliano da Maiano ran one of the most active framing businesses in Florence in the second half of the Quattrocento, working together with various painters including Neri di Bicci, Alesso Baldovinetti, and Domenico Ghirlandaio.[17] In the case of the *Baroncelli Altarpiece*, the commission for the frame may have come through his brother, who had been busy on other projects in the church of Santa Croce during the period of the renovation. The magnificent marble pulpit in Santa Croce that Benedetto da Maiano designed for the Mellini family

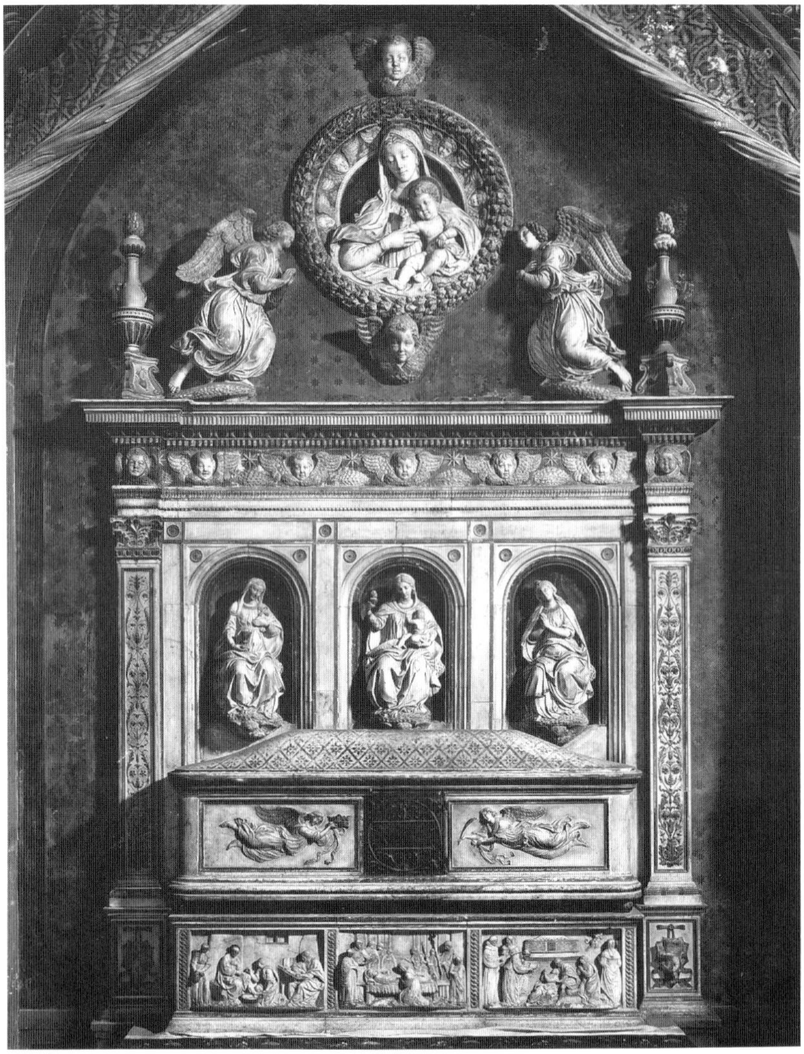

Figure 76. Benedetto da Maiano, *San Bartolo Altar*, c. 1492–4, San Gimignano, S. Agostino (Alinari/Art Resource, N.Y.)

is datable on the basis of style to the early 1480s.[18] The Baroncelli, perhaps impressed by the result of his labors, turned to the same family business when in need of a frame design.

On the other hand, it might seem foolish to attempt to attribute the painted portions of the *Baroncelli Altarpiece* – the cherubim in the spandrel areas – to a particular hand as the images are aguably more formulaic than they are stylistically unique. Nevertheless, circumstantial evidence can assist us in narrowing down the possibilities. In the early 1480s, the period when the altarpiece was reframed, other painted renovations were carried out in the Baroncelli chapel. The entire west wall was covered with a fresco representing the *Assumption of the Virgin with St. Thomas* probably designed by Ghirlandaio but executed by his assistant Sebastiano Mainardi (Fig. 77).[19] The pastel-colored earth pigments of the mural, as well as the grey tones of Mary's tomb and the mural's illusionistic carved marble frame, were carefully selected to blend in with the earlier decorations in the chapel: Taddeo Gaddi's frescoes, the Baroncelli sepulchral monument, and the pietra serena floor. In addition, to either side of the fresco at the bottom, Mainardi was instructed to add the Baroncelli arms – Argent, three bends dexter gules – as an indication of the family's continuing patronage over the chapel space. It seems likely that the painter's workshop called upon for the redecoration of the west wall was also commissioned to perform the repainting necessary on the family altarpiece.[20]

Thus, the renovation of the *Baroncelli Altarpiece* would represent a collaborative project between the two prominent Florentine workshops of Domenico Ghirlandaio and Giuliano da Maiano. Perhaps, as in the case of the Neri di Bicci commission mentioned before, it was the painter Ghirlandaio who received the initial contract for the chapel redecorations with the condition that the altarpiece project be subcontracted out to Giuliano da Maiano for the carpentry portions of the work. Other collaborations between the Ghirlandaio and da Maiano workshops attest to their regular association.[21]

Mainardi's fresco of the *Assumption of the Virgin*, added to the west wall of the Baroncelli chapel, was probably part of a larger redecoration program for the chapel ordered by the Baroncelli during the early 1480s. This spacious image of the Virgin being received bodily into heaven and dropping her girdle to St. Thomas enriched the iconographic program of the chapel, which was dedicated to the Life of the Virgin and culminated with her Coronation in the *Baroncelli Altarpiece.* Representations of the Assumption and the Giving of the Girdle had played a strong devotional role in Florence since the mid-Trecento as a result of the proximity, at Sto. Stefano in Prato, of the celebrated relic of the Virgin's *cintola*, with an active cult following in Florence.[22] In conjunction with the important addition of this devotional fresco, improvements were ordered for other aspects of the chapel progam as well. These may have included refreshing Taddeo Gaddi's frescoes of the *Life of the Virgin* on the walls of the first bay. And it is within this larger project of renovation that the reframing and repainting of the *Baroncelli Altarpiece* should be seen.

Redecorations and modernizations of this kind were carried out in the competitive environment of Florentine family chapel patronage for a variety of complex and interwoven motives. The family was the primary unit of status and power in Quattrocento Florence, and it was in the context of the assertion and consolidation of the family name that private chapels in churches were not only built and endowed but also maintained and kept up to date.[23] In redecorating a family chapel, the family publicly asserted its financial ability to keep abreast with changing fashions and tastes, and through its ability to pay, the family also affirmed its power. However, chapel redecoration has a less secular significance as well. These renovations also need to be examined in relation to contemporary religious practices. As Samuel Cohn has recently demonstrated for Siena, by the end of the Quattrocento, a substantial amount of the money left in wills as pious gifts was left to erect new family chapels or to renovate old ones.[24] It could be argued more generally for Tuscany that it was through the foundation and redecoration of private family chapels that many testators sought not only to assert their familial status publicly, but also, in a more private way, to express their piety and, thus, to ensure their salvation.[25]

The same combination of motives, on a smaller scale, lies behind the modernization of a family altarpiece. Giotto's *Baroncelli Altarpiece*, enshrined in its magnificent new frame, stood in part as an expression of the Baroncelli's financial power and taste. The Baroncelli coat of arms, painted on the sides at either end of the predella box, was a badge of ownership, proudly linking the altarpiece in its original and then in its new form to the family. But also, the modernized altarpiece, whose transformation would have been paid for as part of an account reserved for church spending, can be understood as a pious gesture, a devotional statement.

And yet why did the Baroncelli decide, when redecorating their chapel, to reframe an old polyptych instead of ordering a totally new altarpiece. Economic concerns do not seem to have been an issue. After all, the Baroncelli had gone to considerable expense to decorate other parts of the chapel, and at the same time selected a particularly lavish frame to enshrine their family altarpiece. It is, however, possible that the Baroncelli altarpiece was rewarded with a new frame at least in part out of regard for the master who had painted it.

Despite his Gothic style, Giotto's works were highly valued during the Quattrocento. Evidence of this regard can be found in numerous historical and humanist writings, including the *Commentaries*, Lorenzo Ghiberti's writings on art composed in about 1450. Ghiberti incorporated into this treatise a brief history of art up until his own day described as two separate developments, that of antiquity and that of modern times. The two periods are divided by the gulf of the Dark Ages when art, according to Ghiberti, was virtually dead. But with Giotto, the revival known subsequently as the Renaissance, a revival based on the study both of nature and of models from classical antiquity, was initiated. Giotto, "leaving behind the faintness of the *maniera greca* [the Byzantine style] caused the new art to begin."[26]

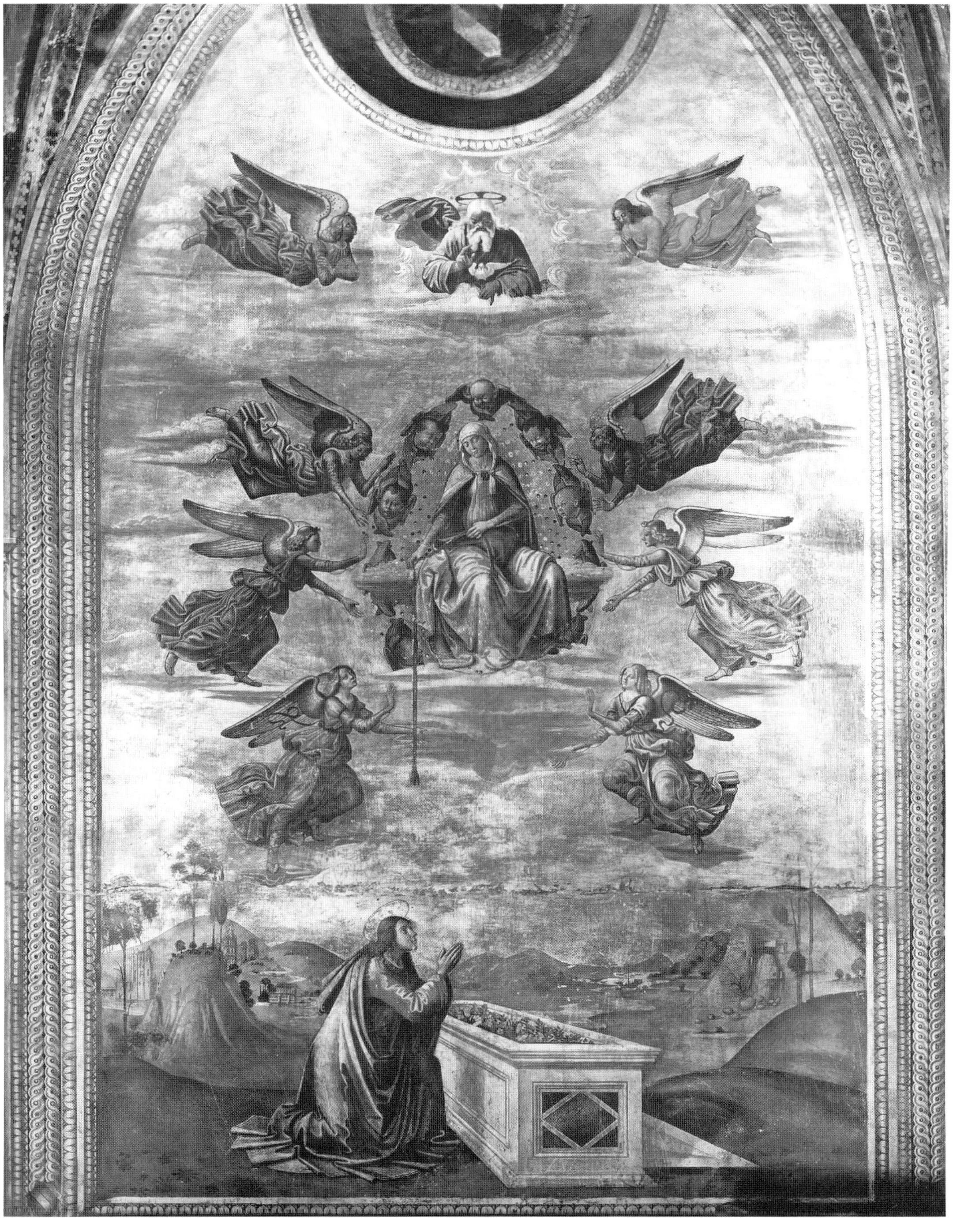

Figure 77. Sebastiano Mainardi, *Assumption of the Virgin*, early 1480s, Florence, Sta. Croce (Alinari/Art Resource, N.Y.)

Thus, Ghiberti saw Giotto not as negatively Medieval but as the essential forerunner of the new style. And as such, he came to be revered during the Quattrocento by humanist critics and art patrons alike.[27] The *Baroncelli Altarpiece* is only one expression of this phenomenon of Giotto veneration.[28] The Baroncelli, in a gesture of pride as owners of the revered example of Giotto's craftsmanship, singled out the altarpiece for renovation as part of their enterprise of chapel redecoration. The original Gothic frame was abandoned as aesthetically out of date, but the value-laden painted portions of the work were retained and rehoused in an ornate, classical frame more in line with late-Quattrocento tastes.

LIPPO MEMMI'S "MADONNA DEL POPOLO"

On the other hand, many of the altarpieces selected during the Quattrocento and early Cinquecento for reframing were by artists less highly revered than Giotto himself, and consequently different sets of motivations seem to have been at play. One example is the *Servite Madonna* by the Sienese Gothic artist Lippo Memmi, later called the "Madonna del Popolo" because of intense veneration (Figs. 78 and 79). The style and tooling of the panel indicate that it belongs to the second phase of Lippo's activity, which began in about 1324 when he became closely affiliated with Simone Martini perhaps as a junior partner in the latter's shop.[29] Although the image was probably ordered by the Servites, the traditional association of the painting with a document dated October 16, 1319, recording a petition by the monks of Sta. Maria dei Servi to the commune of Siena for one hundred lire to help pay for a panel of the Madonna and Child they had commissioned, is untenable.[30] The original location of this prized panel within the church is unknown, but by the late fifteenth century, it had been acquired by Ambrogio Luti for his family chapel located at the end of the left transept.[31] The Luti were a Sienese patrician family who contributed greatly to the growth and development of the Servite church. The family established their tomb in the church and funded the construction of both chapels at the ends of the arms of the transepts.

Among the Luti family members active at Sta. Maria dei Servi during the second half of the Quattrocento, the knight, Francesco Luti, stands out in greatest prominence. He was the head of the *operai*, the deputation of notable citizens in charge of church works, during the important period of reconstruction beginning in the mid-1460s.[32] At this time of renovations, Francesco Luti acted as a model for other patrician families involved in the church by leaving money in his will to ensure that his family chapel would be beautifully decorated. He provided funds for an altar, a family tomb, and a tabernacle for the church's relic of the Corpus Christi. In order to be absolutely certain that the funding would be sufficient to cover these expenses, he abstemiously restricted the cost of his funeral to the absolute minimum, in this way saving a further fifty florins.[33]

Francesco Luti's family chapel was located at the end of the right arm of the transept, directly across from that of his relation Ambrogio Luti. Perhaps it was Francesco's generous testament gift, or a competitive spirit, that encouraged Ambrogio to likewise carry out renovations in his own family chapel, and as part of this project to fund the reframing of the Lippo Memmi *Madonna*. The iconic image of the Virgin and Child was set into a highly elaborate and ornate late Quattrocento or early Cinquecento frame, decorated with music-making angels and with architectural elements taken from the classical repertory. The addition of the stemma of the *popolo* (a white rampant lion against a red background) and of the Servite church (a white "S" inserted in gold ornamentation against a blue background) to the base of the new frame records the continuing significance of the altarpiece for the larger community of worshipers of which the Luti were only a part.[34]

In this case, the painting was retained despite its outmoded style and singled out for attention not because of reverence due to its painter, Lippo Memmi, but because of the intrinsic powers of the image itself. The reframing probably should be evaluated in the context of the chronic Sienese devotion toward the Virgin – Siena was the City of the Virgin – and also in the context of Servite reverence for the Virgin as their special patron saint. Perhaps because of a miracle worked through this image of the Virgin on the behalf of some member of Ambrogio Luti's family, or more likely simply with the aim of gaining her goodwill for the wider church congregation as a whole, Luti provided for the reframing. In a gilt inscription on the frame below the image, we can still make out the congregation's invocation to the Virgin to intercede: "Blessed Mary Mother of God, pray for your people, intervene on behalf of the clergy."[35]

TWO ALTARPIECES AT S. MARTINO A MENSOLA

Two reframed altarpieces survive intact in another Tuscan church, the church of San Martino a Mensola, just outside Florence. In each instance, a Gothic polyptych was taken out of its original frame and set inside a new frame of classically inspired design. These reframings, once again, must be seen in the context of more extensive renovations carried out in the church and in family chapels during the late Quattrocento.

The small parish church of San Martino a Mensola, founded as early as the ninth century, had become by the eleventh century a convent church for Benedictine nuns.[36] By the early fifteenth century, documents record

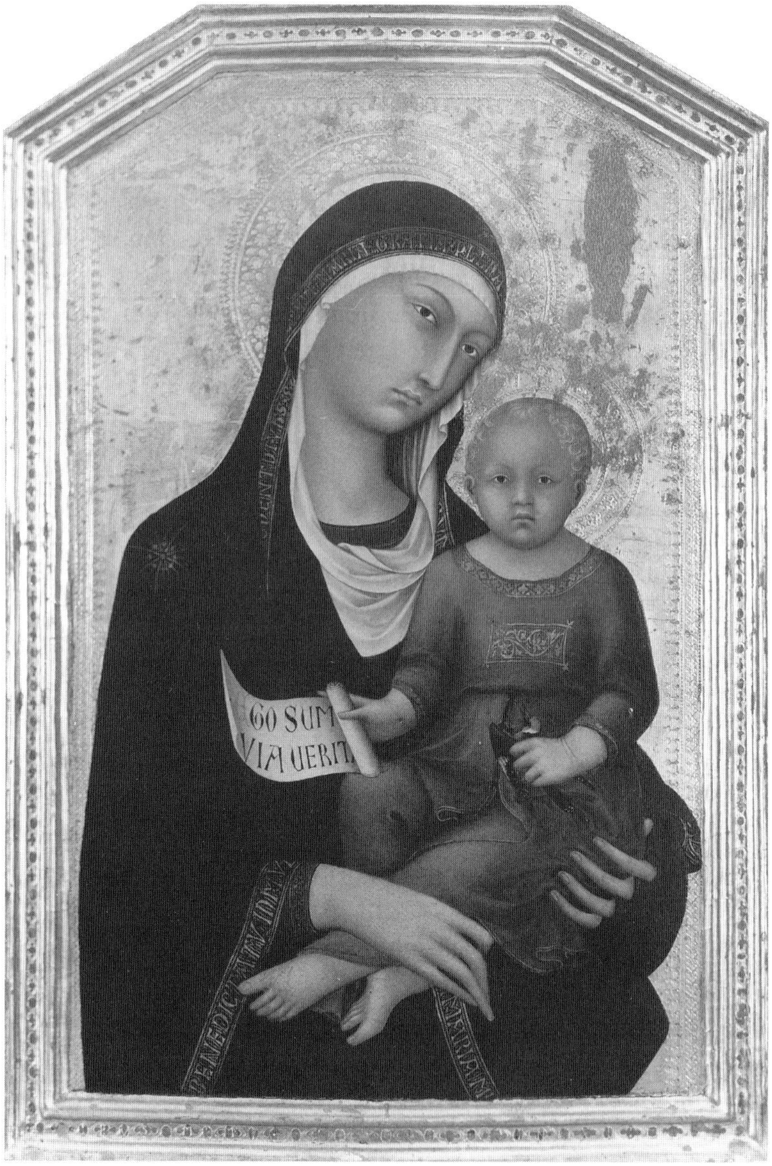

Figure 78. Lippo Memmi, *Servite Madonna*, c. 1324, Siena, Pinacoteca Nazionale, on loan from Sta. Maria dei Servi (Foto Soprintendenza per i Beni Artistici e Storici di Siena, Italy)

the convent as being in a state of great decline and almost deserted, but in 1450, efforts were already underway to effect restoration.[37] The church was reunited with the Badia in Florence, and in 1451, Jacopo di Santi di Giovanni, a man renowned for his piety, was invested as priest. The document of his investiture makes the condition that he restore the church both physically through architectural renovations and spiritually to new life.[38] It must have

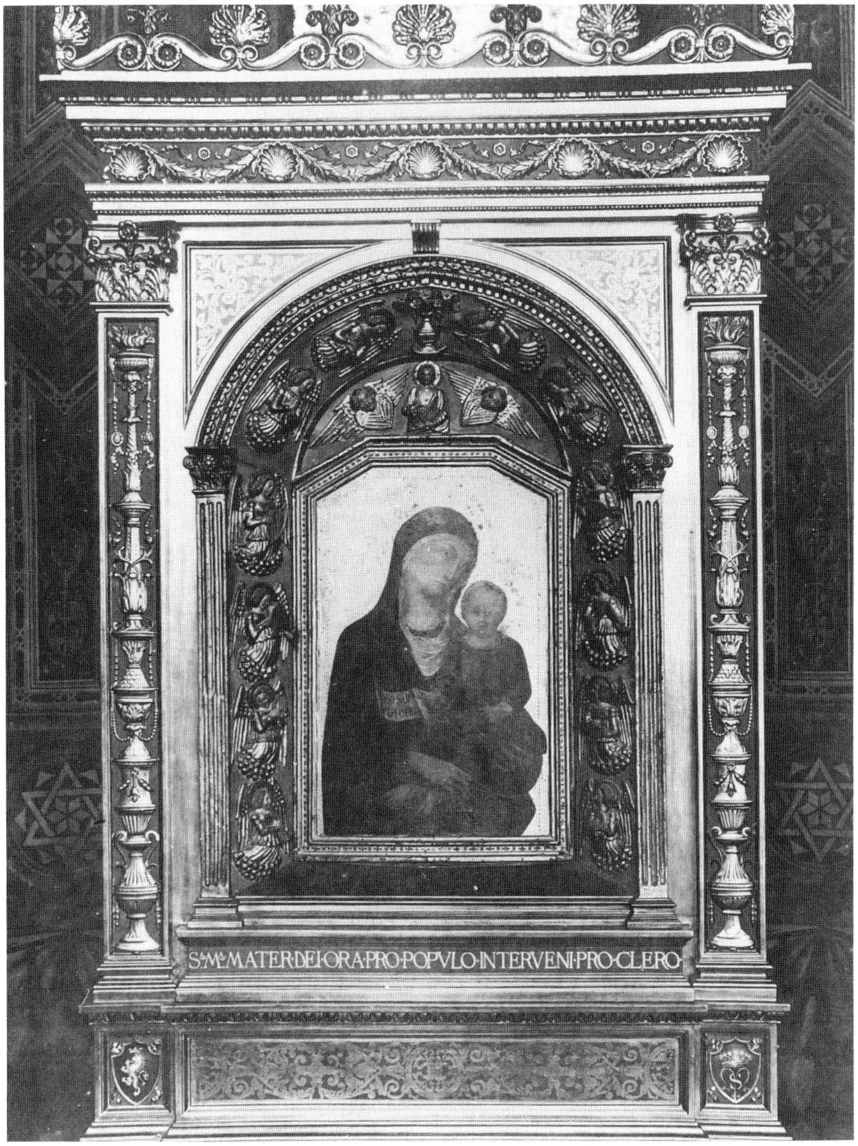

Figure 79. Lippo Memmi, *Servite Madonna*, with late 15th- or early 16th-c. frame (Foto Soprintendenza per i Beni Artistici e Storici di Siena, Italy)

been during Jacopo di Santi's term that the restoration of the Gothic church in an early Renaissance style recalling Brunelleschi was begun (Fig. 80).[39]

A component of the restoration was the redesign and redecoration of the chapel spaces to which local families were encouraged to contribute. The Zati family, who held patronage over the main altar chapel, recorded their financial help and their ownership by adding the family crest to the new

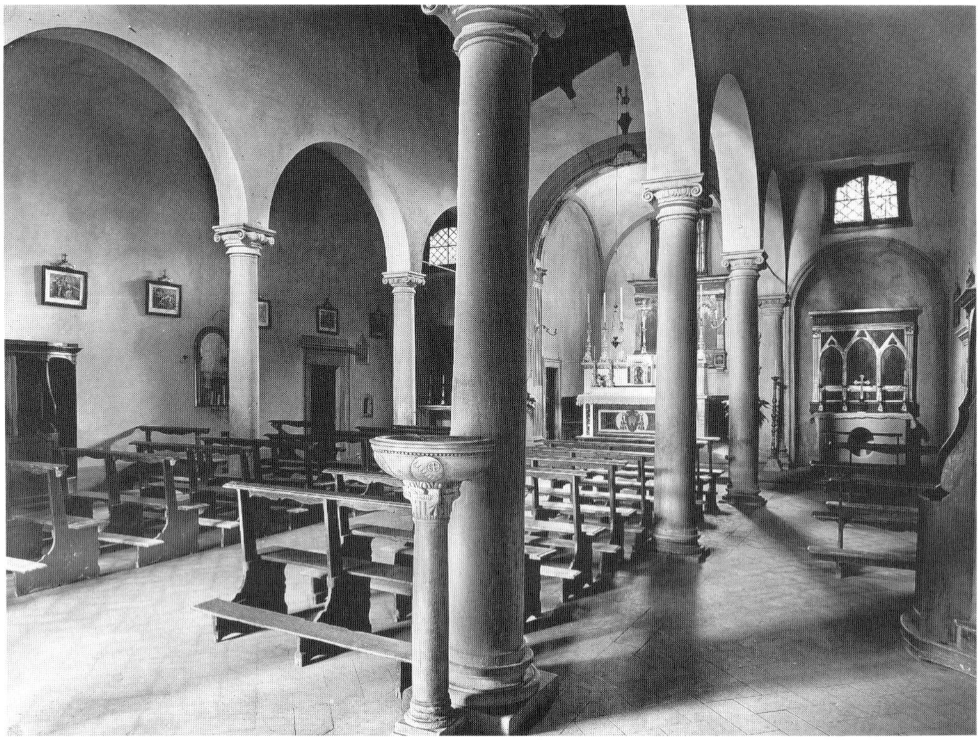

Figure 80. S. Martino a Mensola, Ponte a Mensola nr. Florence, interior (Alinari/Art Resource, N.Y.)

classically inspired decoration of the semicircular entrance arch. Their contribution also included the renovation of the main altarpiece, probably in the 1480s, in a frame whose classical details – fluted pilasters surmounted by composite capitals – echo those of the surrounding architecture (Fig. 81). Cosimo Rosselli, a second-rank Florentine painter, seems to have been commissioned to carry out the painted additions: four prophet figures in the new spandrel areas.[40] Significantly, the painted wooden door of the stone tabernacle housing the Eucharist in the main chapel is also attributed to Rosselli.[41] Rosselli subsequently became an important artist in the life of the church, contributing to several projects during the late Quattrocento and early Cinquecento.[42] He may have been attracted to S. Martino a Mensola by the Zati family after making contact earlier in the 1480s when Rosselli was active at San Ambrogio in Florence, the Zati family's neighborhood church in the city.[43]

The polyptych was a personalized work that had belonged to the Zati family for generations. It was originally painted in 1391 by a Florentine artist known as the Master of S. Martino a Mensola. An Orcagnesque artist who developed under the influence of Agnolo Gaddi, this master was also

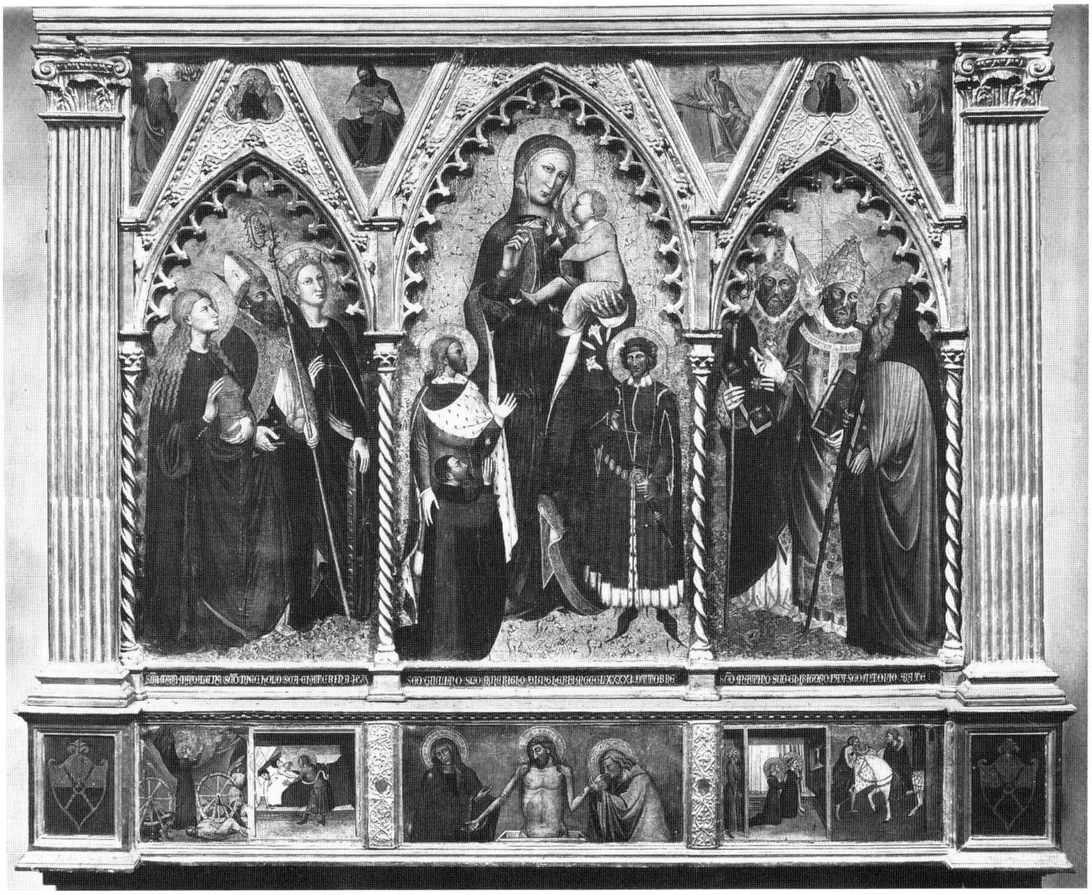

Figure 81. Master of S. Martino a Mensola, *Madonna and Child with Saints*, 1391, Ponte a Mensola nr. Florence, S. Martino a Mensola (Alinari/Art Resource, N.Y.)

affected by the earliest currents of the International Gothic in Italy as his rhythmic drapery folds and the naturalism of his portraiture reveal.[44] The central panel shows the Zati ancestor, Amerigo Bartoli Zati, as a kneeling donor being presented by his patron saints, Amerigus of Hungary and Julian, to the standing Virgin and Child. In the side panels stand Sts. Mary Magdalen, Nicholas, and Catherine of Alexandria, to the left, and Sts. Martin, Gregory, and Anthony Abbot, to the right. The central predella panel bears a devotional image of the Man of Sorrows between the mourning Virgin and St. John, and to the left and right are scenes from the lives of Sts. Catherine, Julian, Amerigus, and Martin. But perhaps most striking are the detailed representations of the patron saints and the donor figure in the central panel on the main register. The donor's name saint, Amerigus of Hungary, is dressed in aristocratic red robes with slit sleeves, ermine borders, and a metallic belt at the waist. St. Julian, who stands presenting the donor, wears a grey tunic and over it a mantle lined with white flecked fur. Although the donor is simply dressed, his portrait is the most meticulous of all. Amerigo Zati's middle-aged physiognomy is rendered with convincing naturalism and great attention to detail. Here we have an example of an important family altarpiece, representing the founding father of the family dynasty, which was reframed by the heirs about eighty years after its initial completion.

In this instance, the renovation can be associated with the Renaissance phenomenon of ancestor worship. The altarpiece, with its portrait of Amerigo Zati, played an important part in the family cult by preserving a record of the ancestor for his descendants. Painted portraits could awaken and activate interest in ancestors. Furthermore, it was within the realm of family chapels that ancestors such as Amerigo Zati were commemorated and the family line celebrated. Endowments in family wills often included clauses requesting that commemorative masses be said for the testator and for other previously deceased relations, and devotional exercises of this kind would have been performed in private chapels such as the one at S. Martino a Mensola. The renovation of the altarpiece documenting Amerigo was a related reverential act: a demonstration of continuing devotion on the part of heirs to their ancestor's memory and to the outward religious manifestations of the family as seen in the altarpiece and chapel space. Running in tandem with this was the ubiquitous desire to remain in good taste.

The second renovated altarpiece surviving in San Martino a Mensola, Taddeo Gaddi's *Madonna and Child Enthroned with Sts. Lucy and Margaret* of about 1340, was reframed and repainted in the manner generally typical for triptychs of this kind (Fig. 82).[45] In this instance, the carpentry is particularly rough and inexpert, indicating a workshop assistant of poor quality. On the other hand, the painted portions – the frieze of cherubs and the prophets in the spandrel areas – can be attributed on the basis of style to Sebastiano Mainardi, whose work we encountered earlier in relation to the renovations of the Baroncelli chapel and altarpiece.[46]

A testament of 1482 records that the chapel in which the Taddeo Gaddi triptych now stands was established at that date through a pious bequest left by one Giusto d'Antonio di Michele Betti di Corbignano, a member of the Betti di Corbignano family prominent in the area and in the life of the parish church.[47] Presumably, once again, the renovation of the altarpiece can be associated with a financial donation to the church and seen in the context of the contemporary expression of piety.[48]

Yet, in contrast to the Zati altarpiece, the original iconography of this painting betrays no tie of particular meaning to the Betti di Corbignano family. Rather, the predominance of female saints – Sts. Lucy and Margaret

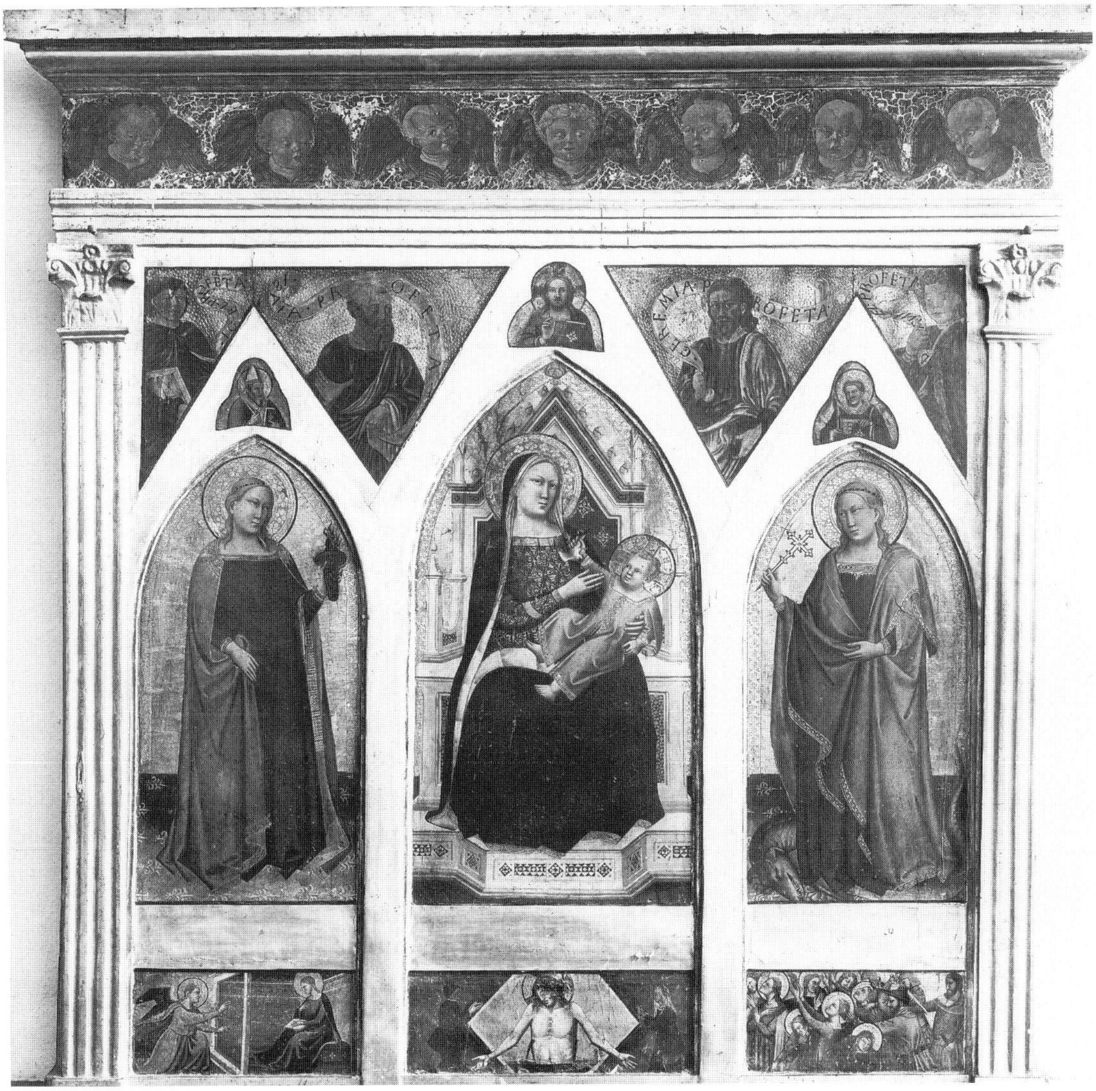

Figure 82. Taddeo Gaddi, *Madonna and Child Enthroned with Sts. Lucy and Margaret*, c. 1340, Ponte a Mensola nr. Florence, S. Martino a Mensola (Alinari/Art Resource, N.Y.)

on the main register, and the Martyrdom of St. Ursula and her companions in one predella compartment – suggests that it originally belonged to the Benedictine nuns of San Martino.[49] As such, it may well have been revered for its religious associations. After the Betti di Corbignano family appropriated the image for their new chapel, their family renovated the altarpiece to bring it up to date and into line with the surrounding architecture, but most significantly, to make an appropriated, second-hand object the family's own. Consequently, as part of the renovation, they had Sebastiano Mainardi add a donor couple – presumably representing Betti di Corbignano and his wife[50] – in the central predella panel to either side of the Man of Sorrows, replacing what must have been earlier images of the mourning Virgin and St. John. These donor portraits are the literal manifestation of the Betti di Corbignano's new ownership and as such represent an assertion of family status. On an equally public level, the minutely rendered portraits – both kneeling in prayer, the wife veiled and holding a rosary – are the literal expression of the Betti di Corbignano's devotion, a devotion made manifest through their financial support of the renovation, a devotion that they would have wanted recognized. They had the Trecento painting redone and their persons incorporated into it in order to get closer to Christ and, hence, to Salvation.

From the examples investigated so far, a number of general conclusions can be drawn. First of all, in each case, the reframing seems to have been carried out in the context of more extensive architectural and painted renovations to the chapel space in which the altarpiece was housed and, on occasion, to the church as a whole. Second, just as these chapel renovations represent both the public expression of family status and taste, and also the more private display of religious piety, so the altarpiece renovations also must be seen in light of this combination of interwoven secular and sacred concerns. And, finally, it cannot be said that these reframings or modernizations reflect a wholly negative attitude of the Renaissance toward the Medieval. For although the frames were identified as out of date and discarded, the paintings themselves were preserved. Indeed, it could be argued that the process of reframing represents an early Renaissance attempt to preserve and honor valued relics of the Medieval past. In the last three cases discussed, the Medieval nature of the enclosed, painted objects may even be virtually irrelevant. It is their familial and devotional associations that count.

FRA ANGELICO'S SAN DOMENICO ALTARPIECE

One final and slightly later example of a transformation through reframing, the well-known renovation of Fra Angelico's *San Domenico Altarpiece*, demonstrates the continuation of the values and motivations outlined so far into the early years of the Cinquecento (Fig. 83). The chronicle history of the monastery and church of San Domenico near Fiesole records that the "high altarpiece was renovated, both remodeled into a square format and repainted . . . by the painter Lorenzo di Credi" in about 1501.[51] But how exactly did the original altarpiece look, and what changes were made?

Following a close technical examination of the renovated structure, involving study of the paint surface, incisions in the gesso ground, and x-radiographs, Umberto Baldini has concluded that Fra Angelico's original altarpiece took the form of a late Gothic polyptych similar to his *Cortona Altarpiece* (Figs. 84 and 85). According to Baldini's reconstruction, the *San Domenico Altarpiece* was a residual polyptych composed of five dividing arches that resolved into a three-part format with two saints housed to either side of the Virgin and Child in the space of the side panels. Each pair of side saints was separated from the Virgin by a pilaster or colonette, but a continuous floor space unified the composition. The altarpiece had a gold leaf background and housed its figures in a relatively confined space typical of the Tuscan late Gothic style.[52] It could be categorized as transitional in format between the earlier polyptychs of the "Madonna and Saints" type with their rigid divisions, and the eventual spatial and psychological unification of the *sacra conversazione*.

As far as the exact date of Fra Angelico's original altarpiece is concerned, it can be placed in the late 1420s, about 1428, on the basis of its style. Because the tile pattern on the floor of the *San Domenico Altarpiece* continues along the width of the composition in front of the marble throne of the Virgin, the spatial formula of the painting represents a development on Fra Angelico's *St. Peter Martyr Altarpiece* (Florence, Museo di San Marco) of about 1425–9. However, it must be considered slightly earlier than the *Virgin and Child Enthroned with Twelve Angels* in the Staedel Institute in Frankfurt and datable c. 1430–5, which provides a more developed portrayal of the *maestà* configuration.

More than seventy years after Fra Angelico originally designed the high altarpiece, it was radically renovated by Lorenzo di Credi. In order to effect this transformation, Credi must have completely dismantled the wooden structure of the altarpiece and, in the process of reassembly, added new panels along the top to increase the height greatly. As a consequence, the tripartite dimensions of the original predella, now in the National Gallery in London, do not correspond perfectly with the divisions of the main register.[53] Substantial portions of the original frame were retained – specifically, the lateral pilaster components and the predella box – but new corinthian capitals were added to complete the pilaster shafts and the architectural construct was crowned with a heavy entablature.[54] The newly expanded background of the altarpiece, still partially covered with the original gold leaf, was overpainted with a deeper, illusionistic space. Credi designed a classically harmonious architectural backdrop consisting of a loggia with the side arches open to reveal a panoramic landscape. In the center, a closed arch acts to frame and secure the image of the Virgin in space. A rich blue cloth-of-honor extends behind her and is surmounted by a matching blue *baldacchino*, a furnishing derived from imperial iconography that serves to emphasize the Madonna's role as Queen of Heaven.

In short, Lorenzo di Credi transformed the late-Gothic polyptych into a

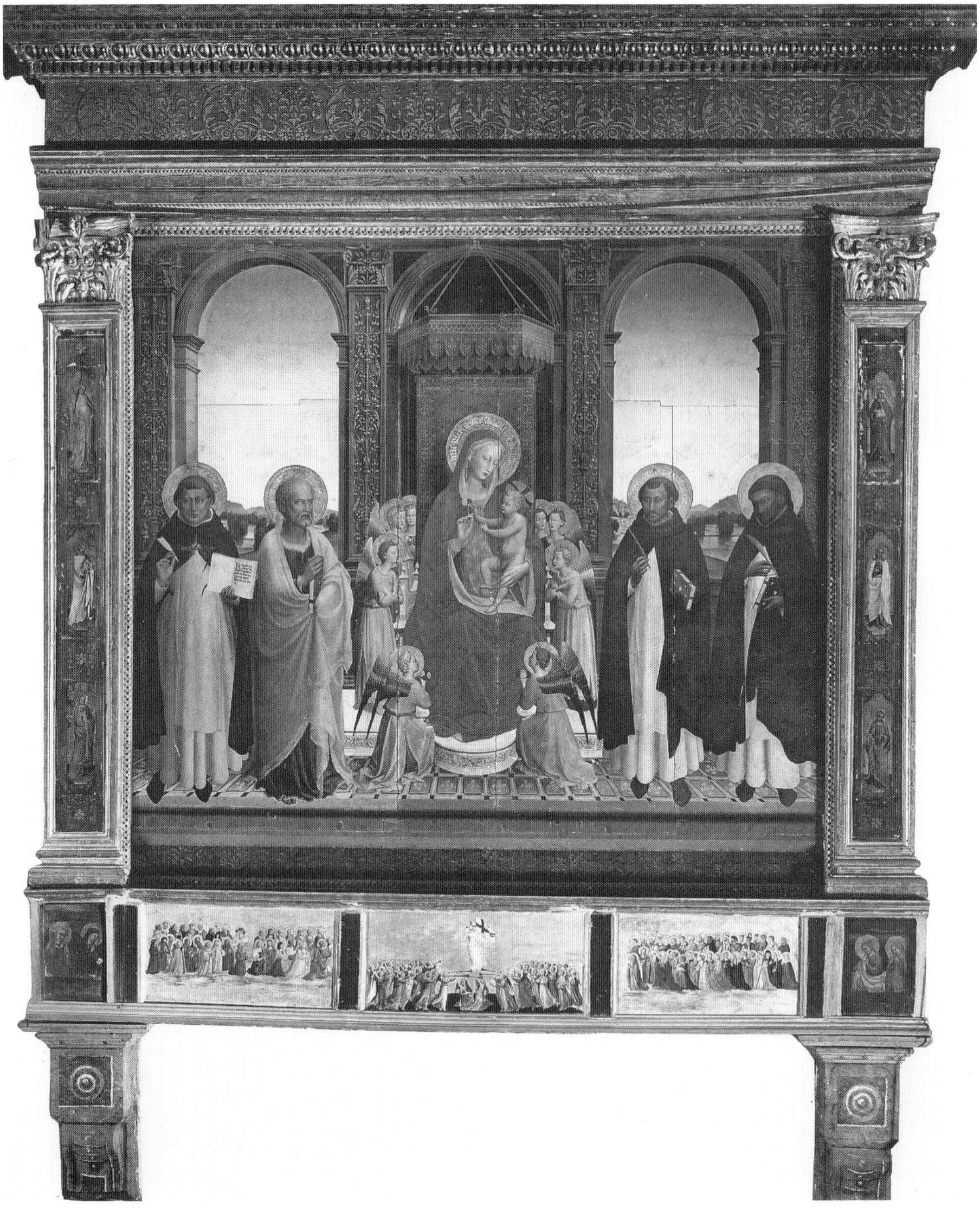

Figure 83. Fra Angelico, *San Domenico Altarpiece*, c. 1428, nr. Fiesole, S. Domenico (Alinari/Art Resource, N.Y.)

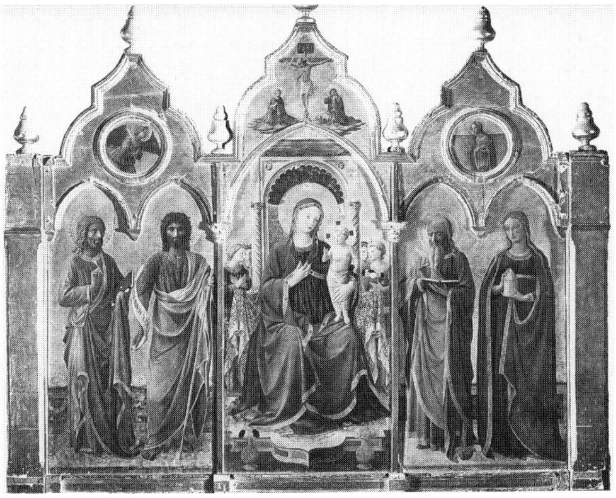

Figure 84. Fra Angelico, *Cortona Altarpiece*, c. 1430–5, Cortona, Museo Diocesano (Alinari/Art Resource, N.Y.)

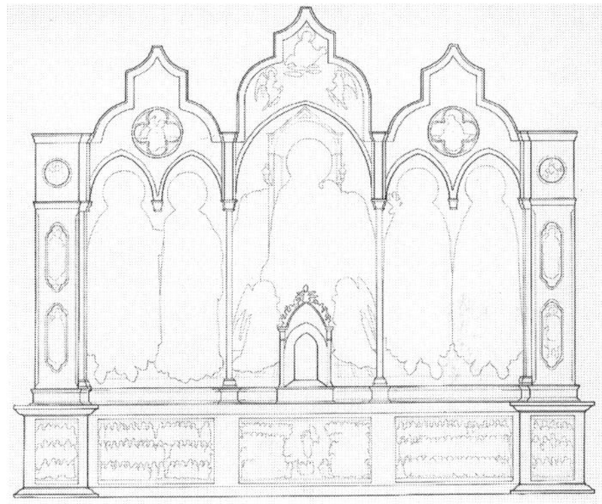

Figure 85. Reconstruction of Fra Angelico's *San Domenico Altarpiece* by U. Baldini (Opificio delle Pietre Dure di Firenze, Italy)

Renaissance pala taking the form of the more developed and unified *sacra conversazione*. In the new arrangement, the frame becomes a window frame in the true Albertian sense, through which one looks into the world of the painted vision beyond. The potential for communication between the viewer and the religious event is established through the use of linear perspective, and neither the frame nor a reflecting gold background inhibits this dialogue. In a subtle way, the hierarchic relationship of the Madonna and Saints, formerly established by the triptych format of the original frame, was retained in the painted loggia of the Renaissance solution.

According to Vasari, the San Domenico altarpiece was changed in this way "for the worse" to make up for damages to the original.[55] However, a more informed interpretation, and one that accords better with the motivations typically underlying renovations of this kind, can be found in the chronicle of the monastery. As the chronicle explains, in about 1501, during the priorate of Fra Dominici de Mugello, the tribune of the main chapel of San Domenico was renovated, and as part of these renovations, the high altar was removed and placed against the wall.[56] The details of this architectural transformation deserve further investigation.

The renovation of the tribune and high altar space at San Domenico was part of a sequence of modernizations carried out in the church beginning

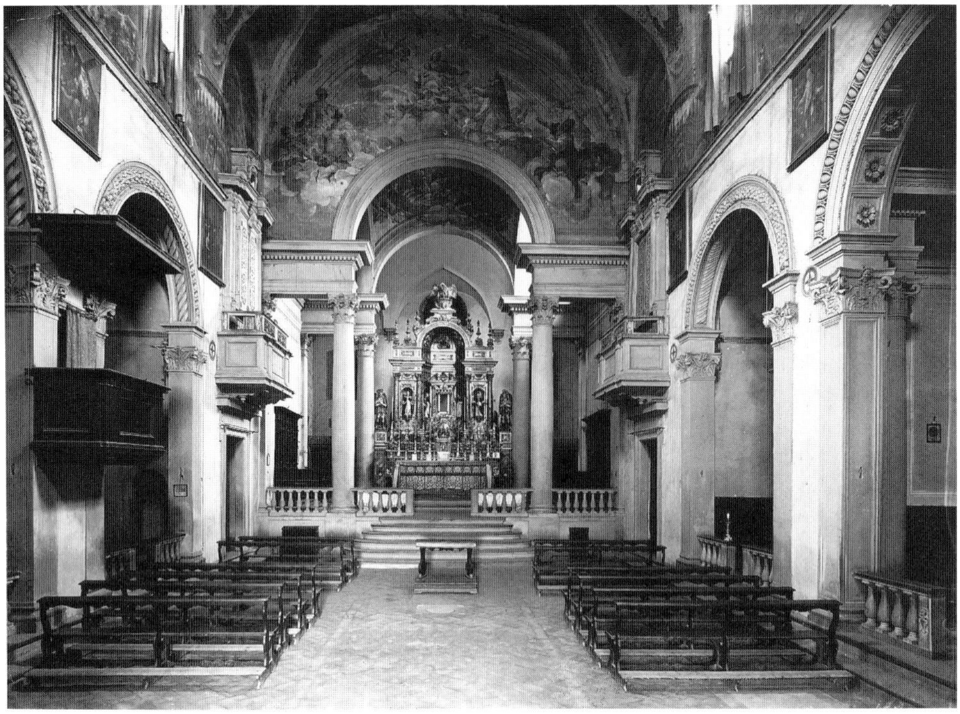

Figure 86. S. Domenico, nr. Fiesole, interior (Alinari/Art Resource, N.Y.)

in the late Quattrocento. Although few vestiges remain of the original church completed by the Dominicans in the years following 1418, examination of the present structure indicates that the earlier church was a much smaller building with a simple apse housing the main altar on which Fra Angelico's altarpiece stood.[57] Expansion and modernization of the convent and church began in 1486 under prior Fra Bonifazio da Salodio, funded by several Florentine citizens. The church interior was transformed starting in 1488 with the erection of four new family chapels, three off the left side of the nave and one off the right side, in a period of about ten years (Fig. 86).[58] Then, in 1501, as part of this process of rebuilding paid for by donations from various Florentine families, the original apse was torn down and an innovative tribune with a double-arched opening was constructed to house the main altar. The altar was reconsecrated on February 24, 1503, when the rebuilding of the apse space must have been complete.[59]

Although the tribune at San Domenico was subsequently rebuilt in the Baroque period, in layout the high altar space is thought to have resembled the format found at the Dominican oratory of Sta. Maria Maddalena in Pian di Mugnone near Fiesole, built in the years following 1460, where the altar table is set back against the wall behind the double-arched opening of the tribune and the tribune is separated from the rest of the church by a

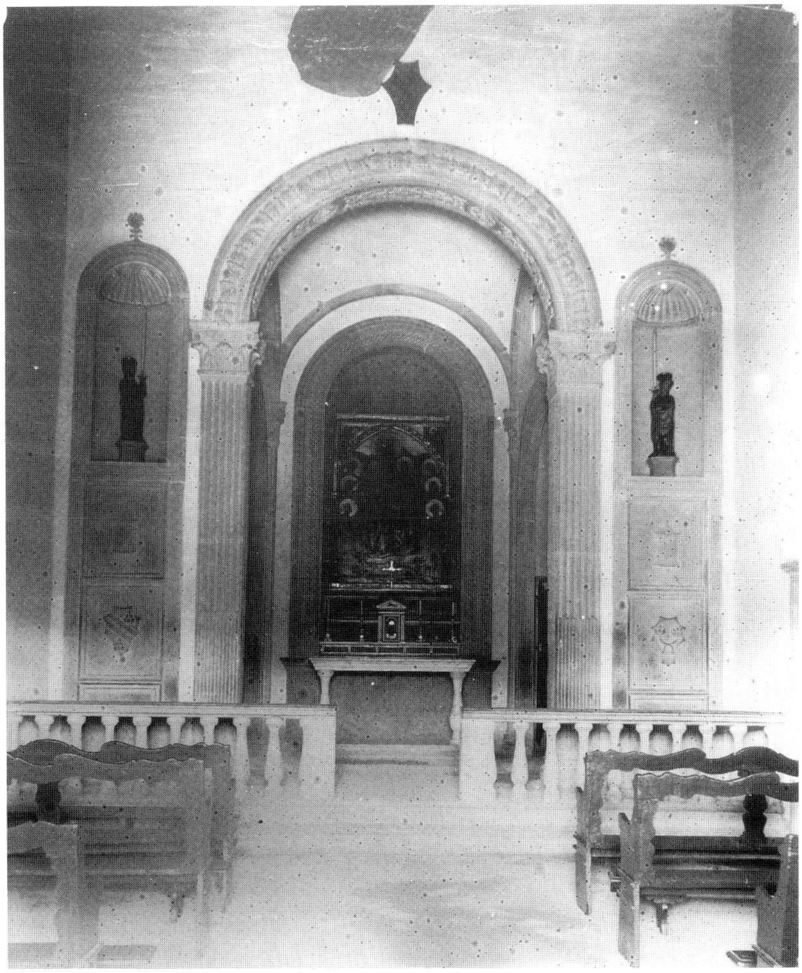

Figure 87. Oratory of Sta. Maria Maddalena, Pian di Mugnone, high altar (Archivio Fotografico Soprintendenza per i Beni Artistici e Storici di Firenze)

stone ballustrade (Fig. 87).[60] Framing the main chapel space at Sta. Maria Maddalena is a decorative architectural border in pietra serena applied to the semicircular entrance arch. Designed in a classicizing style reminiscent of the work of Michelozzo, the decoration also closely resembles that found in the late-Quattrocento family chapels at San Domenico. This style was presumably employed at the church in 1501–3 for the embellishment of the tribune space as well.

When Lorenzo di Credi renovated Fra Angelico's high altarpiece, he took into consideration this new architectural ambient. In the painted architecture of the setting, he designed a loggia that must have echoed in its *all'antica* vocabulary and its dark grey pietra serena material the decorated rounded arches of the church tribune. Credi also created the illusion that the back wall of the tribune, against which the altarpiece rested, had been magically pierced by a window leading into the paradisal world of the Madonna.

As in the case of several of the earlier reframings, Lorenzo di Credi's transformation of the *San Domenico Altarpiece* was partly occasioned by a need to harmonize the painting aesthetically with its remodeled altar space. However, Credi's "improvements" should not be interpreted as an implicit critique of Fra Angelico's style. Rather, the changes reflect a desire to perpetuate the devotional efficacy of a highly valued image by turning it into the kind of fully painted and illusionistic altarpiece best able to communicate with early sixteenth-century worshipers. Although the older painting was still appreciated, modernization took place.

□ □ □

Additions such as the Renaissance elements in this sequence of Gothic altarpieces can carry rich historical meanings. Although sometimes considered "accretions" by art critics and restorers determined on their removal, when examined in a more favorable light, it becomes clear that they illustrate important dimensions of the social and cult history of the objects, and provide insight into the way the Renaissance viewed art of the Gothic past. Although during the Quattrocento and early Cinquecento a stylistic awareness existed distinguishing "old" Gothic works from those of the new Renaissance period, the transformation of Trecento altarpieces was not motivated simply by a negative conception of these earlier paintings. It was, in large part, the need to save and rejuvenate revered Gothic objects, and rejuvenation was effected through renovation in the contemporary style.[61] In specific circumstances, Gothic altarpieces looked valuable to Renaissance eyes.

CHAPTER 6

Restoring Wall-Paintings

Wall-paintings often deteriorate quickly as a result of a complex combination of factors, including the technique in which they were executed, moisture percolating through the walls, and other chemically induced disturbances. As a consequence, they demand frequent repairs and retouchings. When this was the case in the late Medieval and Renaissance period in Italy, the walls were often simply whitewashed and new frescoes painted on top; the subjects or styles of the old ones were no longer deemed to be of note. One important example is the fresco decoration of the main altar chapel in Sta. Maria Novella, Florence, originally carried out by Orcagna in the midfourteenth century with scenes from the lives of the Virgin and St. John the Baptist. Martin Wackernagel relates how initially in 1469 Francesco Sassetti proposed to replace the damaged and "unsightly" Trecento frescoes with a new cycle devoted to his patron saint, Francis, and how the Dominicans rejected Sassetti's proposal because of the change in iconography. Eventually, in 1486, a plan presented by the Tornabuoni was approved and, rather than restoring Orcagna's originals, the two cycles were recast and painted afresh by Domenico Ghirlandaio.[1] In a number of cases, however, concerted efforts were made to repair and even to update existing wall-paintings, and the way in which these renovations were carried out can be of considerable interest.[2] In this chapter, the restoration of two of these early mural decorations will be investigated, the Trecento *Maestà* frescoes of Siena and San Gimignano by Simone Martini and Lippo Memmi, respectively. Both were central public images decorating the council rooms in town halls, and this civic context must be considered when evaluating the reasons for repainting.

SIMONE MARTINI'S *MAESTÀ*

About four years after Duccio's double-sided altarpiece of the *Maestà* had been carried through the streets of Siena in 1311 in an extravagant religious and civic procession to its destiny on the high altar of the cathedral, Simone Martini was commissioned by the commune to paint an image of the same subject on the wall of the council room in the town hall (Fig. 88). Although the commission is not specifically documented, a record of October 20, 1315, in which Simone is debited against a credit account with the commune, has been traditionally associated with the painting of the fresco.[3] In addition, a fragmentary inscription below the lower frame of the fresco has been decoded to yield the artist and date of completion: MILLE TRECENTO QUINDICI VOL . . . / [E] DELIA AVIA OGNI BEL FIORE SPINTO / [E] IUNO GIA GRIDAVA IMI RIVOL . . . , and lower down, somewhat separately: S . . . A MAN DI SYMONE. These poetic lines can be interpreted as signifying that with the passing of spring and the arrival of the month of June, the year 1315 is gone and the new year of 1316 (which according to the Sienese calendar began on Annunciation Day, March 25) is in progress.[4] It is, therefore, now generally assumed that the *Maestà* was completed by Simone in 1316, although it may have been started as early as 1311.[5] In fact, the presence of a strong horizontal seam in the *intonaco* of the mural roughly at the level of the hips of the front row of saints suggests the painting may have been carried out in two separate stages.[6]

The painting of this *Maestà* fresco amounts to the translation of an image created initially for a religious and civic context – Duccio's Siena cathedral altarpiece – into a more fully political sphere. Following Duccio's archetype quite closely, the composition shows the Virgin as Queen of Heaven, elevated and enthroned with the Christ Child on her lap, surrounded by her court of saints and angels. Secular imperial associations are evoked through the iconography. For example, according to Medieval political theory, the king was in a state of power while on a raised throne, and so, in this state, the painted Queen of Heaven carries out her divine duties.[7] Simone enriched upon the court iconography of Duccio through the inclusion of a large canopy or *baldacchino* that unifies and enshrines the members of the company. Such a furnishing would have brought to mind the honorary presentation of a contemporary ruler or church official in a throne room or public procession.

At the foot of the Virgin's throne kneel two angels who present the Virgin with flowers, and the four patron saints of Siena: Ansano, Savino, Crescenzio, and Victor. These patron saints are effectively turning over the civic community under their protection to the Queen of Heaven, thereby making Siena the "City of the Virgin."[8] Further, as poetic verses inscribed

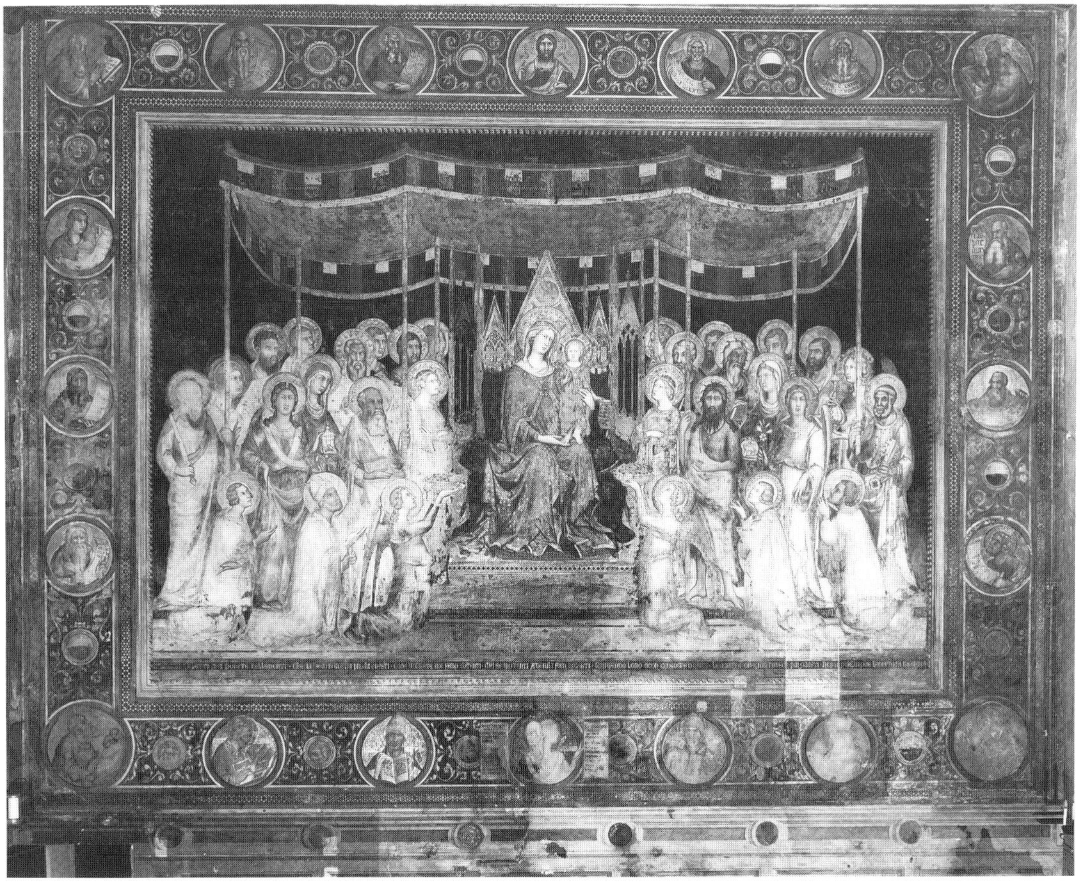

Figure 88. Simone Martini, *Maestà*, 1315–16, Siena, Palazzo Pubblico (Fotografia di Fabio Lensini, Siena, Italy)

on the base of the Virgin's throne indicate, they are engaged in a dialogue with the Virgin. In two lyric stanzas, she responds to the angels and saints in a tone of warning that any attempts on the part of the people of Siena to seek intercession with her through gifts of flowers and through prayer will be tried in vain by those who betray her or who exert oppression. It is a political message directed at the councillors of Siena who would have been seated just below the fresco.[9] The conditional nature of the Virgin's patronage is evoked as a threat, in order to ensure the just proceeding of government in Siena. She appears in the council room of the town hall as the standard of good and just rule.

The theme of justice, which underlies the Virgin's lyric responses, reverberates throughout the mural. On the Virgin's knee stands the Christ Child holding a scroll bearing the message: "Love justice, you who judge the earth." In this erect position, the Christ figure takes on the adult role of the teacher of wisdom, in contrast to the benevolent seated Child in Duccio's *Maestà*. An iconographic echo is found directly above in the framing band of medallions where the central tondo carries a bust-length image of Christ as Judge, presaging the Last Judgment.[10] Far below, in the central medallion of the lower border, a female figure with two faces, one old and one young, represents the Old and New Law, reinforcing the message of justice still further. Around the double head are inscribed the names of the cardinal and theological virtues with Temperance significantly occupying the position of greatest importance at the top.

The standards of justice that the Virgin through her official presence in the fresco encouraged, formed the code of civic conduct of the day in Siena. Good government involved the fair treatment of citizens, and also the enhancement of the success of the city as a whole, rather than private individual or family ends. Siena's system of rule was designed specifically to foster justice by controlling corruption and violence, especially that occasioned by the powerful noble factions. During this period, Siena was led by an oligarchic government of nine men known as the *Nove*. This system of shared rule by nonnobles had been developed to circumvent the problems of the signorial approach – where power was held by a dictator or by one family – by bringing together a governing council of individually less powerful men to strive for communal well-being.[11]

Although the fresco would have been commissioned by an appointee of the Nine – the master of works of the cathedral who was hired to supervise the government's artistic and architectural projects – and, therefore, would have mirrored the political directives of the oligarchy, it was the members of the General Council who met in the Sala del Consiglio and who were intended to learn from the mural. According to William Bowsky, Siena's General Council played a crucial role in the administration of civic justice as "the commune's chief deliberative and legislative body."[12] The council was made up of 300 men elected by the Nine, with 100 drawn from each of the three areas of the city; but members of a group of about 200 other officials often joined in their meetings. During their six-month term, the councillors considered both important legislation and more routine issues. For instance, they were responsible for maintaining the city's supplies of food and water as well as for defense. They also heard numerous petitions from individuals. Archival records suggest, however, that meetings may often have been rather mundane and boring, as the strict rules of conduct were frequently broken and fines levied for not attending, for making an irrelevent speech, and for not paying attention.[13] With an average attendance of about 250 members, the room would have been fairly full; nevertheless, the frequent and tedious sessions would have allowed time to contemplate Simone's magnificent image and to review its pertinent didactic message.[14]

In order to bring to life in High Gothic form this civically important image of the Queen of Heaven as Justice, Simone adopted an extremely decorative technique. He worked on the wall in a method indebted to contemporary panel-painting, a method that incorporated texture, relief, and light-reflecting metallic surfaces, qualities unusual in mural works of the period (Pl. 8). For instance, the haloes were decorated with flower, leaf, and star motifs by pressing gouged-out matrices into a built-up area of plaster. When dry, these patterned haloes were gilded. Semitransparent colored oil-glazes were used on the painting, applied over metal leaf to decorate select areas such as the cusps of the throne, the clothing of the Virgin, and her crown. In addition, diamond-shaped pieces of painted glass were set into the halo of the Christ Child and the pinnacles of the throne. To create these luxurious effects, Simone had to work primarily on dry plaster, *a secco*, applying rich-toned pigments based on minerals and dyestuffs with tempera binders and affixing metal leaf. Originally, the painting must have rivaled its prototype, Duccio's *Maestà*, in brilliance of color and shimmer of gold.[15]

THE RENOVATIONS OF 1321

Yet despite his great effort and technical ingenuity, already in 1321 Simone was paid for fixing up the mural that he had completed only five years earlier. The communal account books record that on December 30, 1321, Simone and his assistants were paid twenty-seven lire for the gold and colors required to mend the *Maestà*.[16] It is very likely that as part of this mending process, Simone touched up the colors of the mural and the gold work in places. This general repair work seems to have been necessitated by Simone's original use of experimental *secco* techniques as opposed to the more time-tested true fresco methods.

But much more surprising is the discovery that as part of this campaign, Simone totally replaced the heads and hands of eight principal figures and repainted them in a markedly different technique on new whiter plaster. The following areas were replaced: the face and entire headdress of the Virgin and her hands; the face and hands of the Christ Child and a small area of his tunic just below the Virgin's left hand; the faces and hands of the two kneeling angels and of Sts. Ursula, Catherine, and Crescenzio; the face of San Ansano and the right hand of St. Paul.[17] In these areas, Simone scraped away the old *intonaco*, applied new patches of a lighter-colored plaster, and painted the flesh and drapery tones afresh while the plaster was still wet. We may never know whether Simone made significant changes to

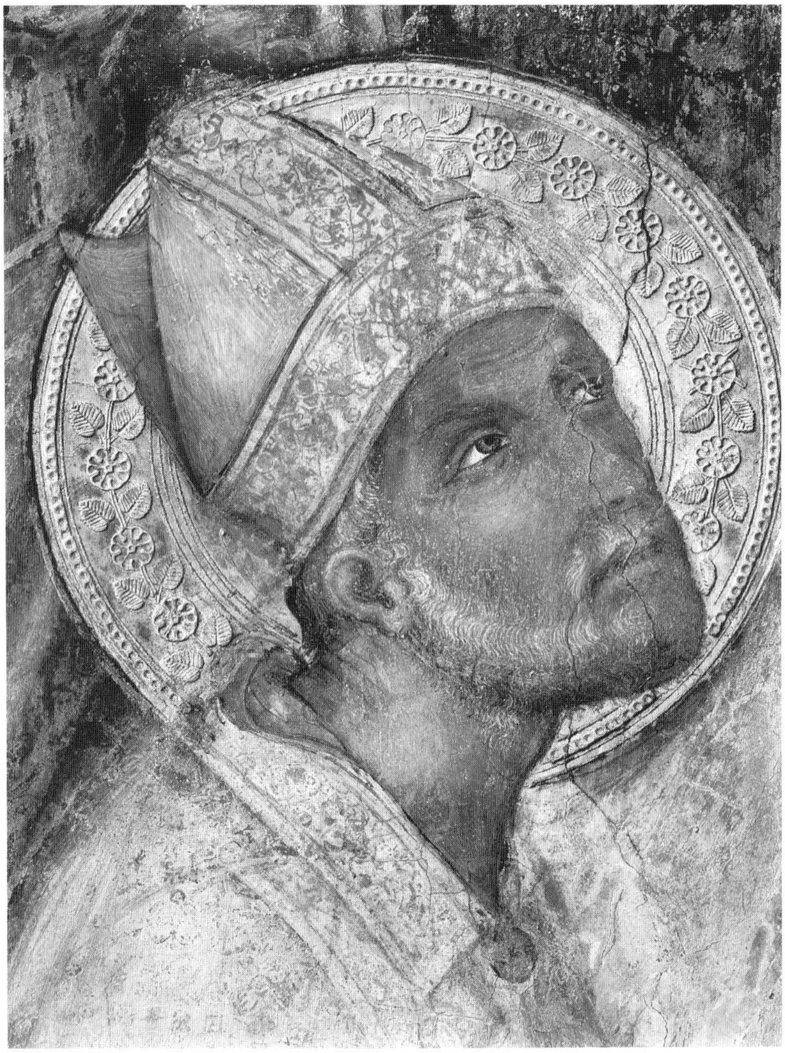

Figure 89. Simone Martini, *Maestà*, detail, St. Savinus (Kunsthistorisches Institut, Florence, n. 637)

the style of the faces; whether, for instance, the original face of the Virgin was frontal, resembling the iconic face of St. Louis in the Naples altarpiece and providing the model for the Virgin in Lippo Memmi's subsequent San Gimignano *Maestà* of 1317.[18] What one can tell from the present surface is that a major change was made in technique. For the faces, the difference in appearance between the new and the original ones seems to be largely due to the use of clear silica sand instead of the darker tufo as a major component of the plaster. In terms of the paint itself, the flesh areas of the new faces appear lighter and more luminous because of the use of green earth (*terre verte*) and red earth as replacements for the darker natural- and

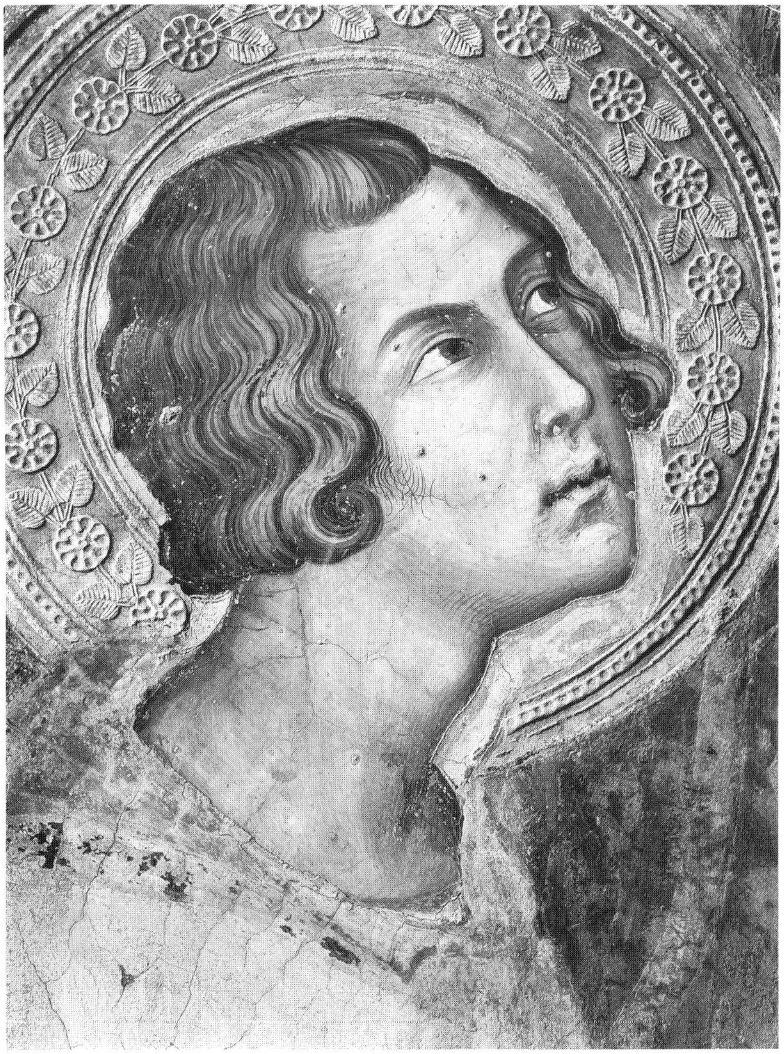

Figure 90. Simone Martini, *Maestà*, detail, St. Ansanus (Kunsthistorisches Institut, Florence, n. 521)

burnt-umber tones (Figs. 89 and 90).[19] As Eve Borsook remarked: the new "heads are lighter and brighter than the others and harder, more calligraphic, in style. . . . It is an entirely different kind of painting. . . ."[20]

MOTIVATIONS

The reasons that propelled Simone to redo eight of the heads in the *Maestà* in a completely different technique have not been fully discussed. The generally agreed upon explanation is that Simone was redoing badly damaged faces in a more durable technique.[21] However, this explanation leaves one wondering how the most extensive damage to the fresco could have been so specifically and apportionately located in eight of the principal faces. It is more likely that Simone chose to remedy a general and widespread problem in the fresco, namely, that the flesh tones were too dark, with a partial solution. Perhaps it had been recognized that when viewed from a distance, the essential attributes of the communicating figures in the fresco, their facial expressions and hand gestures, did not stand out emphatically enough because of the technique in which they had been painted.[22] Repainting all the flesh areas would have been an immense task, but Simone hit on an effective compromise. He carefully selected eight of the most prominent heads and hands for total renewal. From a distance, these essential protagonists would emerge from the background of more darkly painted figures and effectively tell the story. Thus, the primary motivation behind the selective renovation of the *Maestà* probably lay in the need to create a more visually effective image. The new faces, lighter and more emphatically modeled, stood out and were more expressive and successful from a distance. As these restored faces were strategically placed within the image, the effect of the selective restoration was cumulative.

It has also been traditionally assumed that the initiative to renovate the *Maestà* came from Simone himself. Motivated by an aesthetic impulse and with the desire to try out a new and improved wall-painting technique, Simone occasioned the renovations, or so the theory runs. Yet this scenario seems doubtful. We should not forget that the fresco was not merely a private artistic accomplishment; rather, it stood as a didactic emblem of standards of good government and just rule in the city of Siena. Others have associated Simone's repainting with the early Trecento updating of Coppo di Marcovaldo's and Guido da Siena's *Maestà* altarpieces, but clearly Simone's mural served a quite distinct function and, hence, the renovation should be evaluated differently.[23] In Simone's case, it was the commune who paid for the restoration of a civic symbol. Probably, therefore, governmental concern to enhance the expository message of the fresco as well as the desire to maintain the impressive appearance of civic decorations were the primary motivating factors behind the renovation.

Contemporary documents provide insight into the reasons why the Sienese government might have been anxious to preserve and improve the appearance of an important civic fresco like Simone's *Maestà*. One document highlights communal pride as the rationale for civic renovations. It is a petition of 1316 in which some citizens of Siena complain to the governing body about damage to a "very beautiful picture" in the residential quarters of the city governor or podestà and call for its restoration:

> It is delightful to the eye, joyful to the heart, and pleasing to each human sense, and also of great honor to individual communes when their rulers and officials

dwell in fair and splendid residences, both for their own sake, and, also, for those foreigners who for many and various reasons come to visit them. This, considering its greatness, is of importance to the commune of Siena. . . .[24]

The general thrust is that Siena, with its buildings, monuments, and images, should be kept in fine condition to maintain an environment that the citizens can be proud of and that will incite foreign admiration and envy. Other contemporary documents lay equal stress on pleasing the Virgin by maintaining the beautiful appearance of her city and its buildings. Siena was fashioned into a city that the Virgin would be proud of and willing to favor.[25]

Both reasons may well have stood behind the renovation of Simone's *Maestà*, the desire to honor the Virgin and to provide an occasion for pride in Siena's citizenry. But as well as such general impulses, more specific concerns involving the iconography of the fresco must have been of primary importance. Communal expenditure for the physical maintenance and selective improvement of the mural indicates how valuable the communicative force of this politically expressive image was deemed to be. It was important that Sienese councillors, other citizens, and distinguished visitors as well, be able to read clearly this visual statement about the Virgin's patronage of Siena and the commune's adoption of divine standards of justice and good government.

LIPPO MEMMI'S *MAESTÀ*

The restoration history of a related *Maestà* fresco located in another important Tuscan public building provides an equally interesting subject for investigation. In 1317, Lippo Memmi's *Maestà* was added to the political and civic imagery that already covered the walls of the council room in San Gimignano's town hall (Pl. 2). A document of 1317 records payment to Memmo di Filippuccio and through him to his son Lippo Memmi for the painted figures in the council room.[26] However, Lippo alone signed the mural at the bottom center and it was probably carried out by an extended workshop under Lippo's direction.[27]

Since the late thirteenth century, the large, rectangular council room had been decorated with three bands of fresco paintings that circled the room and covered the entire wall space from the top edge right down to the basemento. Although these images are now only very faint shadows of their former selves, they have been deciphered as follows: in the narrower upper band, the coats-of-arms of San Gimignanese families and other communes, as well as the fleur-de-lis of the Angevins; in the wide middle band, a courtly homage scene on the short end wall and a number of horsemen and soldiers on other portions of the band; in the lowest strip, representations of nobles and hunting activities.[28] The decoration is generally attributed to the communal painter "Azzo" who was paid for work in this room in July and August 1291.[29] However, with the addition of Lippo Memmi's *Maestà* the earlier scheme was disturbed. A large part of the long wall was covered over by the new image and the focus of the room shifted from the homage scene on the short end wall to the large and brightly colored new work.

Lippo's *Maestà* is an adaptation of Simone's earlier fresco, made specifically relevant to San Gimignano by the inclusion of local saints and the present podestà and captain of the people, the Sienese citizen Nello di Mino Tolomei. Pictured as a kneeling donor, Nello holds a scroll with an inscription in which he is recommended to the Virgin by his patron saint, Nicholas of Bari. The podestà may have been responsible for stimulating the commission of the fresco so reminiscent of the one in his own home town. Yet although particularized in time and place by the inclusion of this contemporary portrait, the San Gimignano *Maestà* also carries some of the same wider reverberations as Simone Martini's *Maestà* fresco, which it so strongly echoes. As in Siena, so here, too, the primary meaning of the fresco is as a political emblem of the participation of the Virgin in the maintenance of standards and just government in San Gimignano.

THE TWO RESTORATIONS

It has long been recognized that Lippo Memmi's *Maestà*, as it survives today, constitutes an expanded and extensively repainted version of the original. As early as Vasari, the painting was believed to have been restored by the Florentine artist Benozzo Gozzoli.[30] Closer to our own day, in 1908, Crowe and Cavalcaselle developed this line of argument by assigning the reworking as a totality to Benozzo, on the basis of the Latin inscription bearing the artist's name in the lower right corner of the mural, as well as a document of 1466 commissioning him to "refresh and repaint all the figures."[31] However, a recent technical examination, carried out by the conservator Leonetto Tintori in 1980, has revealed that the transformation was actually the result of two separate reworkings. The fresco was repainted at least twice during the fourteenth and fifteenth centuries.

The first of these projects, carried out in the late fourteenth century, was primarily an expansion. The composition was extended at each end so that four extra saints could be included (Fig. 91). Violating the original boundaries of the mural, two figures were added at either side, representing, on the left, Sts. Anthony Abbot and Fina, and on the right, Blessed Bartolo of San Gimignano and St. Louis IX of France (Figs. 92 and 93). This additional painting was executed in a style and technique relatively close to the original

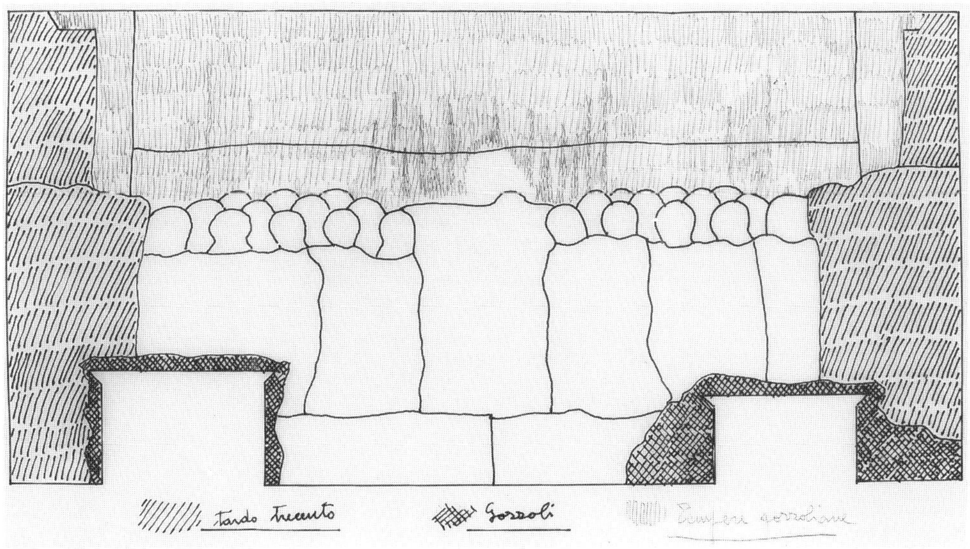

Figure 91. Diagram of Renovations to San Gimignano *Maestà*, by L. Tintori, showing: original central section by Lippo Memmi, 1317; lateral extensions by Bartolo di Fredi, c. 1370–80; repairs and retouches by Benozzo Gozzoli, 1466–7 (Foto Soprintendenza per i Beni Artistici e Storici di Siena, Italy)

and can be attributed to the Sienese painter, Bartolo di Fredi. The portrayal of the penitent St. Anthony Abbot in the fresco, for example, has been compared with Bartolo di Fredi's similarly grim and haggard representation of the saint in the side panel of his *Nativity Triptych* in Torrita di Siena (Fig. 94).[32] Furthermore, the use of floral motifs to pattern the gilded haloes of the four new saints, at a time when decorated haloes of this kind were no longer the fashion in wall-painting, points likewise to the participation of Bartolo. For in Bartolo's most important mural project in San Gimignano, the Old Testament scenes in the Collegiata, motifs were also used to decorate some of the haloes.[33] In the *Maestà*, Bartolo's continuation of this ornamental technique for the haloes of the four added saints can be interpreted as a sensitive attempt to harmonize his contributions with the earlier style and technique of the fresco. Sensibly, however, he did not imitate the technique of the earlier painting as a whole; Bartolo chose to execute the new areas in pure fresco rather than following the fragile technique of the original.

Lippo Memmi's *Maestà*, like Simone Martini's before it, had been executed primarily in the *a secco* wall-painting technique, on a dry plaster layer applying pigments with tempera binders. *Buon fresco* work on wet plaster was limited to the faces of the saints and angels (excluding the faces of the Virgin and Child and the face of the podestà).[34] Such a method enabled Lippo to work slowly, with luminous mineral pigments and a

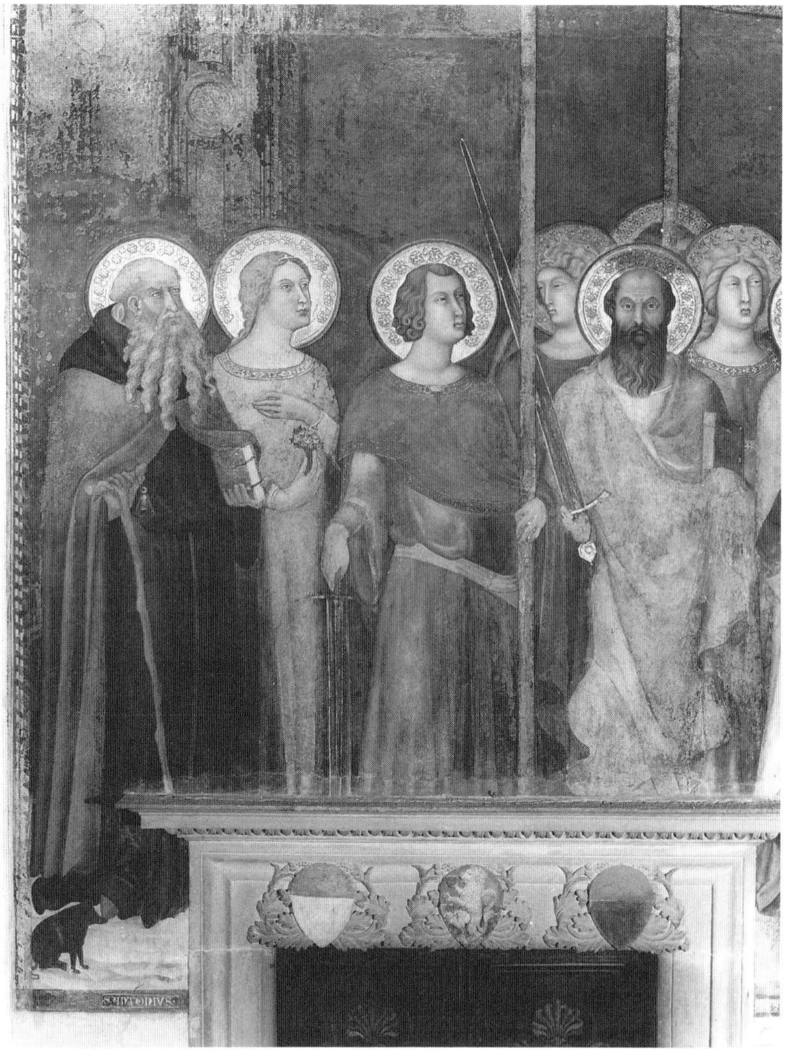

Figure 92. Lippo Memmi and Bartolo di Fredi, *Maestà*, left side, San Gimignano, Palazzo Comunale (Foto Soprintendenza per i Beni Artistici e Storici di Siena, Italy)

variety of kinds of metal leaf, in order to achieve the extraordinary effects of light and color usually associated with works on panel rather than paintings on the wall. According to Leonetto Tintori, the pigments used include verdigris, azurite, vermilion, red lake, and other mineral pigments that required adhesive binders. In addition, the painting was extensively gilded and at points the metal layers were glazed to simulate gem stones or enamels (Fig. 95).[35] The result was a visually stunning work, but one lacking in durability. It must have been in an effort to preserve the already deteriorating work that Bartolo di Fredi, as part of his late fourteenth-

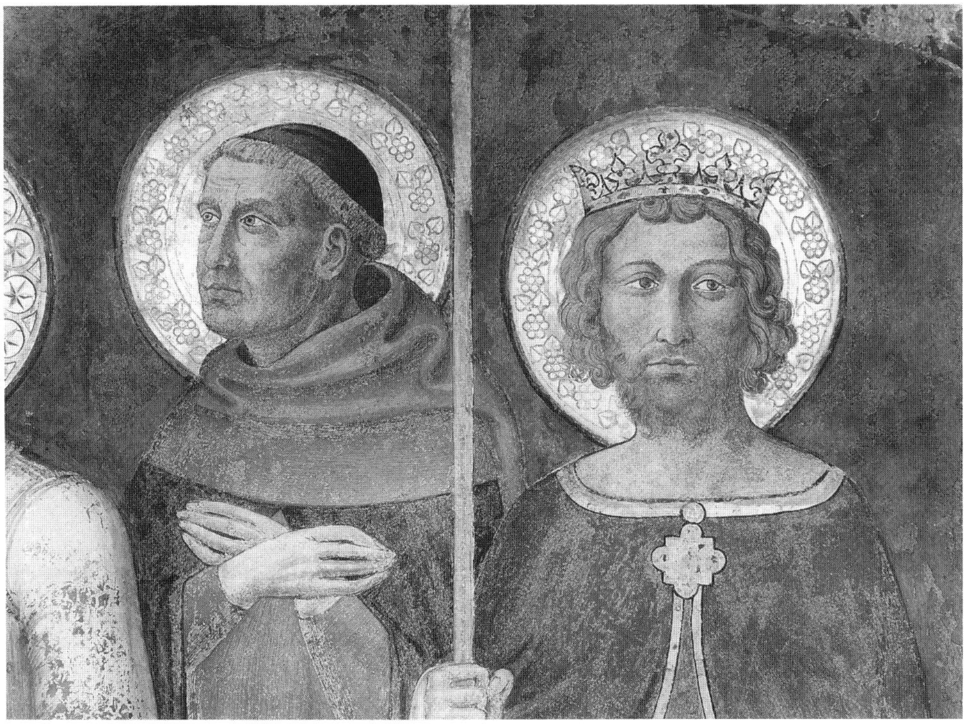

Figure 93. Lippo Memmi, Bartolo di Fredi and Benozzo Gozzoli, *Maestà*, detail of right side (Foto Soprintendenza per i Beni Artistici e Storici di Siena, Italy)

century renovations, added a layer of an organic fixative – most likely white of egg – to the surface of the entire painting. It would have been intended to act as a protective adhesive coating or varnish, securing the pigment layer and at the same time enhancing the colors. Ironically, however, the fixative initiated a chemical-physical transformation that undermined the fragile tempera layers even further and provided at least part of the occasion for the later restoration of the work by Benozzo Gozzoli in 1467.[36]

In the commission document of 1466, Benozzo was hired to *rinfrescare e riattare*, to refresh and repair the entire fresco. Interpreted at its most literal and technical level such refreshing involved repainting the damaged areas of the mural where the color, applied *a secco*, had largely fallen away. Accordingly, Benozzo seems to have retouched the blue sky and several of the draperies. His skills were also required for two much more obvious areas of repair. In December 1461, the town council had voted to construct two rooms, the audience room and the chancellery, leading into the Sala del Consiglio, and when built, the two new doors pierced the wall that contained Lippo's *Maestà*, their large, classically inspired cornices extending

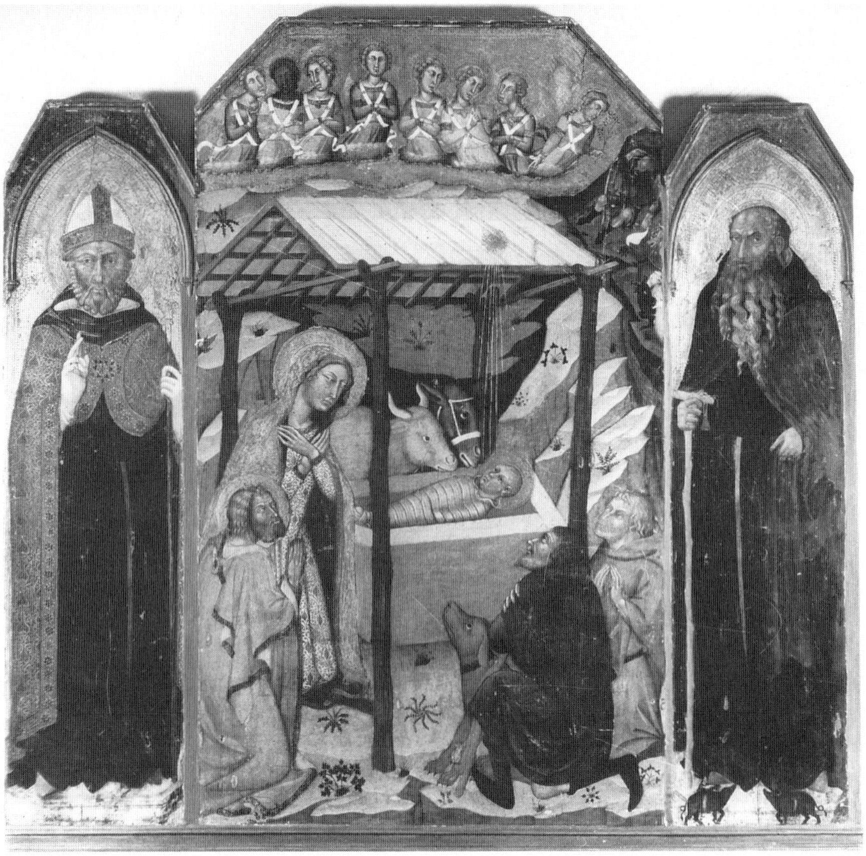

Figure 94. Bartolo di Fredi, *Nativity Triptych*, Torrita di Siena (Fotografia di Fabio Lensini, Siena, Italy)

right up into the field of the painting (Pl. 2).[37] Benozzo's task was to repair the mural around these openings. His workmanship is particularly visible in the proper left foot of John the Baptist and right around the upper frame of the right door where he replastered and painted afresh (Fig. 91). But in addition, Benozzo's alterations, done in a highly calligraphic and thoroughly Quattrocento style, are evident in areas that did not immediately cry out for repair on account of their poor condition. Benozzo took the liberty of reworking the faces of two of the saints recently added in *buon fresco* in the late fourteenth century, the faces of Blessed Bartolo of San Gimignano and St. Louis IX of France (Fig. 93). This is particularly evident for Blessed Bartolo, whose new, subtly modeled visage has the depth of characterization of a contemporary portrait. Perhaps working from descriptions of the physical appearance of this local saint, Benozzo brought his presence more effectively to life. Indeed, the frescoed portrait of Blessed Bartolo resembles a contemporary terracotta bust of the *beato* attributed to Pietro Torrigiano

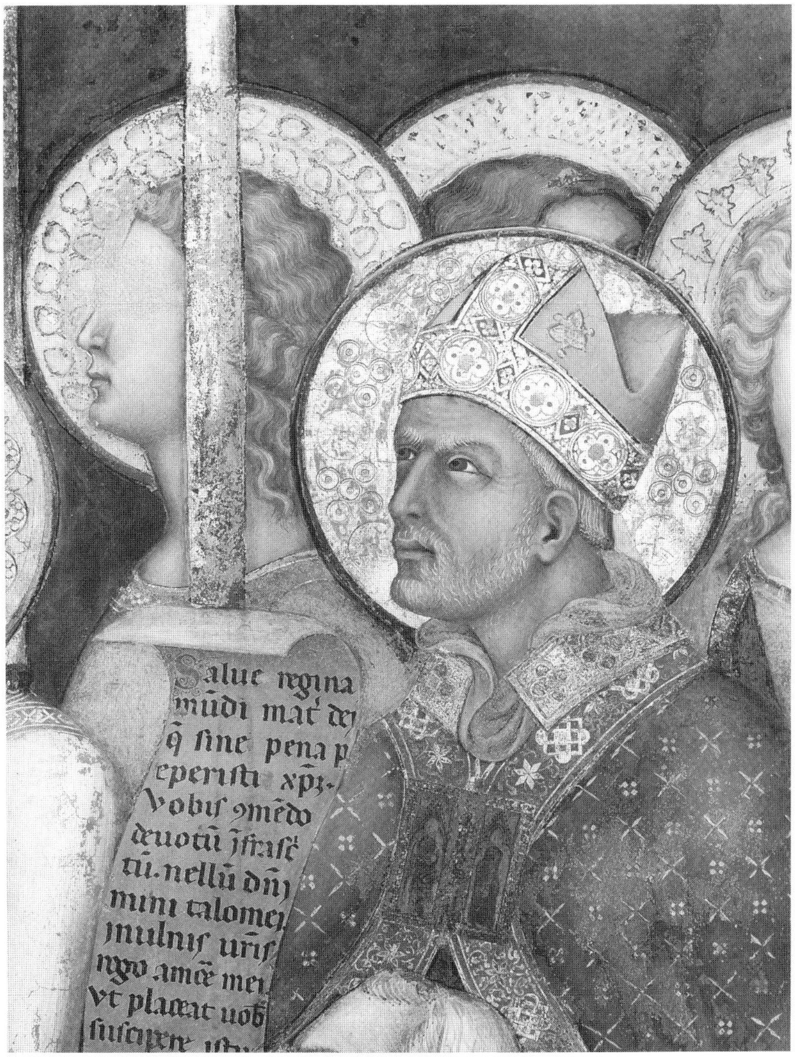

Figure 95. Lippo Memmi, *Maestà*, detail showing morse worn by St. Nicholas, made to simulate enamel work (Foto Soprintendenza per i Beni Artistici e Storici di Siena, Italy)

and now housed in the Museo of the Palazzo Comunale, suggesting that records of Bartolo's appearance survived in Benozzo's day (Fig. 96).

These two separate stages of renovation – by Bartolo di Fredi and Benozzo Gozzoli – can be explained partly as simple repairs to a damaged mural, undermined by the technique in which it was originally executed. However, for a deeper understanding of why the painting was also effectively transformed, first by extending it and then by substantially updating it in a Renaissance hand, the broader social context of the mural's contemporary political and civic function must also be considered.

CONTEXTUAL EXPLANATIONS

As suggested before, Lippo Memmi's *Maestà*, like Simone Martini's mural in the council room of Siena's town hall, had an emblematic significance for the commune of San Gimignano. The painted presence of the Virgin as Queen of Heaven established her authority to set the standards for just government in the city. She presided. Hence, the mural was a highly important civic image recording the participation of the Virgin and Child, together with an impressive gathering of saints, not only in the rule, but also in the protection of San Gimignano. Local saints, most notably the traditional guardian of the city, San Gimignano, were present in their role as civic patrons and communal advocates before the Virgin.

Thus, to begin with the late fourteenth-century expansion of the *Maestà* by Bartolo di Fredi, this initial transformation can be understood best in relation to the mural's civic function. For the sake of keeping the painting up to date and of continuing relevance for the commune, four new saints were included as part of the protective umbrella serving San Gimignano. It was a way of recording the patronage of these saintly personages in a highly public and visual manner. But, perhaps more significantly, it was also a way of securing their continued help. Once publicly honored in paint, their participation was ensured.[38]

When considered initially within the broad socioreligious context of the contemporary civic cult of saints, the dual function of the expanded *Maestà* fresco as recording patronage and securing continued assistance from saints becomes clear. In the late Medieval period, a large number of Italian communal governments became heavily involved in the promotion of devotional cults surrounding local, minor, and often uncanonized, saintly persons. These cults, in their most obviously detectable form, involved the official communal celebration of the saint's feast day with offerings of candles brought in procession to the church or chapel where his/her grave and relics were housed. In addition, celebrations could be extended to include recreational activities (for example, the Palio in Siena), a market, or a fair. The celebration of the feast of one new local advocate of San Gimignano, Blessed Bartolo (d. 1300), is first mentioned in the documents for 1314. The festivities included a fair that lasted five days.[39]

The interest of communes such as San Gimignano in the cult worship of local *beati*, in addition to more traditional and fully sanctioned saints, stemmed from the belief that a city had the best chance of security when protected by the largest number of saintly patrons. Local saints were especially coveted because of the civic patriotism they were thought to possess. As the guardian of the Franciscans in Siena in 1329 contended in a petition in favor of the local *beato* Pietro Pettinaio:

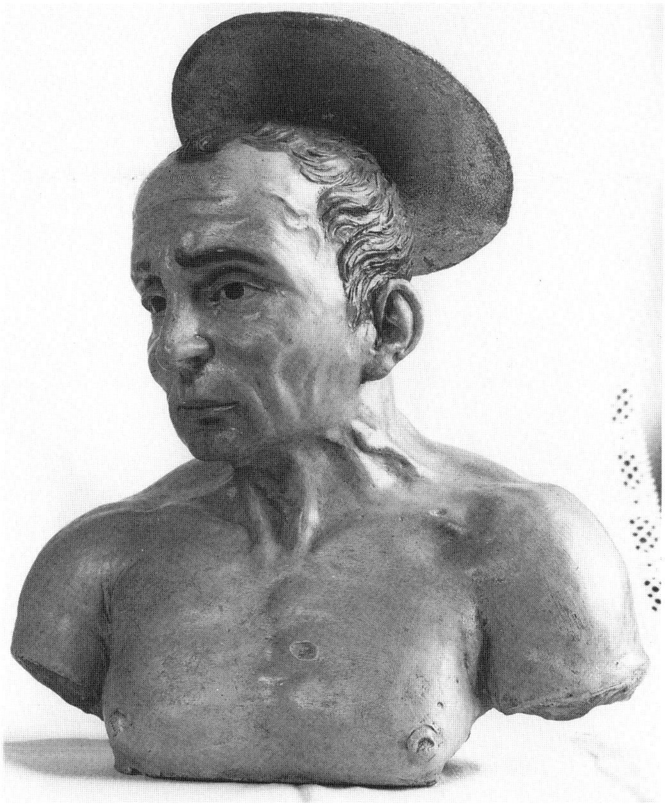

Figure 96. Attributed to Pietro Torrigiano, *Bartolo of San Gimignano*, mid- to late 15th c., San Gimignano, Museo Civico (Foto Soprintendenza per i Beni Artistici e Storici di Siena, Italy)

it is firmly believed and hoped that the veneration of the saints that formerly was undertaken in the city of Siena by the said commune and its officials conferred many advantages upon the aforesaid commune, and brought to an end and protected the city from any evils and perils.[40]

Furthermore, to explain the specific importance of Pietro Pettinaio, the guardian continued: "he was born in this city and because of this natural love, he has a particular benevolence for the city and for its citizens."[41] The citizens of San Gimignano felt the same way about their local favorites, Santa Fina and Beato Bartolo. Therefore, the inclusion of these new favorites, along with St. Anthony Abbot and St. Louis IX of France, in an expanded *Maestà* fresco reflects the commune's concern to firmly establish its enlarged security force of divine advocates.

It is possible, in addition, to pinpoint more specific reasons underlying the expansion of the *Maestà* fresco. Why was there a particular need in the late fourteenth century to garner and record the assistance of four new saints, and why were these four – Anthony Abbot, Fina, Blessed Bartolo of San Gimignano, and Louis IX of France – chosen? The answer seems to lie in the devastated state in which the commune found itself during the second half of the fourteenth century as the result of periodic visitations of the plague.

The plague struck Tuscany several times during the fourteenth century, leaving in its wake greatly decimated populations in the cities and a deserted countryside. The Black Death reached San Gimignano in 1348. Contemporary novels and chronicles record the huge loss of life only in general terms as a "*grande mortalità.*" However, a census of households taken in 1332 and again in 1350 suggests that, as elsewhere in Tuscany, in San Gimignano about three-fifths of the population perished.[42] This would mean that of a preplague population of about 15,000, only about 6,000 survived. We do know that of the nine signori of the commune, only four survived, and that the podestà, M. Umberto Visdomini, was among those who perished. Further, when in 1349, Florence requested the military assistance of San Gimignano in the form of thirty foot soldiers, the commune could only send twenty-four and one captain.[43] Another wave of the plague in 1363 that affected most of Tuscany reached San Gimignano by July. Although it is again difficult to arrive at an exact estimate of the destruction, that the commune sought the assistance of Florence in alleviating the dangers is recorded.[44] There were two more epidemics in 1390.

These successive waves of the plague must have created an atmosphere of desperation in the city. People turned to every available means of support for help, including patron saints. Significantly, three of the saintly figures selected for inclusion in the *Maestà* in the late fourteenth century were noted for their curative powers.

Of these, the most generally appreciated was St. Anthony Abbot, widely invoked in times of pestilence.[45] One of the patriarchs of monasticism, Anthony Abbot was an early Christian hermit saint celebrated for his power against demons, for directing the spirit, and for curing infirmities. The popular veneration of the saint among the common folk can be traced back to early Medieval times. He was sought after particularly for his aid against illnesses, including contageous diseases, the so-called "St. Anthony's fire," and the plague. The saint's attribute, a small pig – which figures prominently in the left foreground of the *Maestà* in San Gimignano (Fig. 92) – may allude to these curative powers, for lard from the pigs kept by the Order of St. Anthony was used as a balm against plague sores.[46]

Santa Fina was a local saint who early on became one of San Gimignano's special patrons. Born Fina de'Ciardi, from an early age, she turned her heart toward Christ and led a brief life of penitence and charitable deeds. Her choice of a bare plank for her bed was characteristic. After she died

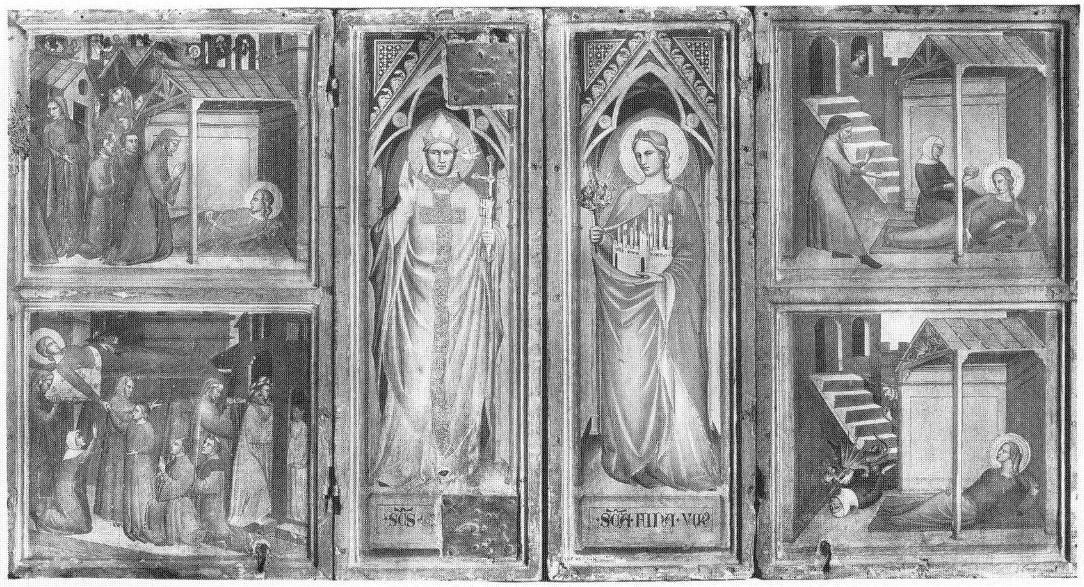

Figure 97. Lorenzo di Niccolò Gerini, *Sta. Fina Altarpiece*, 1402, San Gimignano, Museo Civico (Alinari/Art Resource, N.Y.)

in 1253 at the age of twelve, a tradition of miracles worked through her intercession sprung up. One story, recorded by Lorenzo di Niccolò Gerini in his *Sta. Fina Altarpiece* of 1402 (San Gimignano, Museo Civico), is that just after her death, when Fina's body was being carried to church, her hand suddenly gripped the crippled arm of her devoted nurse, Beldia, miraculously curing the handicap (Fig. 97).[47] Hearing of such wondrous acts, large numbers of infirm and possessed citizens worshiped at her grave. Fina's reputation for curing was such that by 1255, statutes record the erection of a charity hospital for the sick poor in her name.[48] The institution, which survived on donations from the faithful and testament gifts, must have been flooded with victims during the plague years. The evocation of her continued assistance through the inclusion of her portrait in the civic *Maestà* fresco is readily understandable in this context.

Blessed Bartolo of San Gimignano was a second local religious hero of extreme importance. Born in 1227, it is said that he exhibited divine qualities from birth, and in order to be able to attend to the care of the sick, the poor, and pilgrims, he entered the ministry and became a Franciscan tertiary. A model of charity, obediance, and abnegation, he lived a long life of austerity and penitence. At the age of fifty-two, Bartolo contracted leprosy, which he suffered from with heroic patience for the last twenty years of his life. As a result of this harsh trial, he became known popularly as the "Job of Tuscany."[49] After Bartolo died in 1300 and was buried in Sant'Agostino, his body began to work miracles, particularly in curing those possessed.[50] This has a simple logic, as leprosy, from which he suffered physically, was then believed to be caused by demonic possession. Nevertheless, his grave attracted the sick of all varieties and in such great numbers that in 1359, the decision was taken to erect a grating around the tomb, located in the center of the church, to protect from the ever-increasing flood of worshipers.[51] In the plague years of 1348, 1363, and 1390, many of these faithful would have been plague victims and their families. Thus, as with Sts. Anthony Abbot and Fina, the decision to include Bartolo in the *Maestà* in the later years of the fourteenth century can be seen to result from his special reputation for curative power.

The only figure not accounted for in this explanation is St. Louis IX of France, the final saint on the right of the San Gimignano *Maestà*. As Louis of France was not associated with the plague or with more general curative abilities, alternate reasons must be put forward to explain his inclusion. Firstly, it should be noted that the qualities generally associated with Louis of France accord well with the broader themes expressed by the *Maestà* fresco. For Louis, who inherited the throne of France in 1235 after his mother, Blanche of Castille, was famed during his lifetime and subsequently as the ideal sovereign. As a sincerely religious man and an impartial and merciful administrator, he personified the highest ideals of the Medieval Christian ruler.[52] Thus, it may have been as a representative of the standards of just government that he was chosen in the late fourteenth century for incorporation as part of the newly expanded *Maestà*.

On the other hand, more specific political motivations may lie behind the inclusion of Louis. As former king of France, and as uncle of Louis of Toulouse and Robert of Naples, Louis IX may stand here as a representative of the Angevin dynasty. During the period of c. 1260 to 1343, there had been a strong Angevin presence in San Gimignano and Tuscany more generally. Beginning in the midthirteenth century, when they fought on the side of the Papal States to expel the Hohenstaufen and Ghibellinism from Tuscany, the Angevins held sway alongside the Guelphs for a period of about eighty years until the death of Robert the Wise in Naples.[53] The Angevin coat-of-arms, included in Azzo's late-thirteenth-century decoration of the council room and on the *baldacchino* in Lippo's *Maestà*, attests to this allegiance. Although the frescoed image of Louis of France was only added to the *Maestà* much later, some forty years after the destruction of the alliance in 1343, there may have been good reasons for recalling these ties. Perhaps the present podestà or another prominent councillor had strong French connections.

Whatever the specific reason for his inclusion, Louis of France in his royal regalia stands somewhat apart from the other saints at the far edges of the fresco (Pl. 2). Whereas the others turn in toward the Madonna and Child at the center, preserving the cohesiveness of the group, Louis is shown frontally at the far right, looking out toward the viewer. One is left with the impression that he was selected last, after the three curative saints whose inclusion was considered essential, to maintain the balance of the composition.

Thus, the transformation of the *Maestà* fresco in the late fourteenth century through the addition of three newly important civic saints and Louis of France stands in the most general sense as a document of the commune's involvement in the widespread cult of civic saints, but more specifically as the response to a period of great suffering and hardship, the plague years. Portraits of important curative saints were included both to record their input into the life of the commune and to invoke their further assistance as a way of meeting the continuing needs of the city.

The second major renovation of the *Maestà*, by Benozzo Gozzoli in 1466–7, needs also to be considered with the political and civic functions of the fresco in mind. When Benozzo was called in to refresh and repair the fresco, it was as part of a larger project of transforming the council room in order better to monumentalize the still relevant image of San Gimignano's Virgin and Saints. In the same contract, Benozzo was commissioned to whitewash the rest of the mural decorations on that wall in the room.[54]

A contemporary story may help to make what might seem to be an obvious point: namely, that in this period, images were preserved and singled out for restoration on the grounds of their continuing power or relevance for the community, but neglected or whitewashed if in every sense their time had passed. The passage comes from a collection of anecdotal stories about one Arlotto, a historical figure who was from 1423 to 1484 cleric of a parish church near Florence in the Mugello region close to Pratolino:

> When the parish priest Arlotto decided to redo the wall of his church, he wanted to whitewash it. And first of all it was necessary, in order to get it all white, to remove all the ugly frescoes that were there, while leaving some others. Thus he went to examine which figures were to be retained and which scraped away, and together with the master he went about it. He found a San Antonio and said: "Save this one." He found a figure of Santo Sano and said: "I want this one to be destroyed. Since I've been priest here I have never seen a candle lit here. Nor have I ever realized a cent from it. Consequently, master, go ahead and destroy it." But the moment the master wanted to lay a hammer to it, a pious woman knocked on the door and said: "Priest, I have to fulfill a vow from a very beautiful favor I received at the time of the pest from a Santo Sano that you have here in the church. I've brought forty soldi here for you to say thirty masses in his honor, and a lamp which you should light for these masses. . . . Don't destroy him at all."[55]

A similar process of selection was at work with Lippo Memmi's *Maestà* and Benozzo Gozzoli's commission of 1466. When redoing the council room, the commune chose to preserve and renew the more generic and enduring image of the *Maestà* because of its contemporary value, whereas the other images – political and civic allegories with specific references – had lost their significance and were, therefore, apparently obliterated. In the renovated room, greater attention must have been drawn to the important *Maestà*, grandly isolated and framed by newly blank walls.

The 1466 renovation, however, has implications of a more political nature as well. Although the *Maestà* image was fundamentally Sienese in origin having been adopted by San Gimignano during a period of strong Sienese domination, ironically, a Florentine was chosen for the extensive restoration of 1466. Already in 1353, San Gimignano had fallen under the jurisdiction of the Florentine territorial state, yet in artistic matters, the commune maintained its ties with Siena until well into the fifteenth century. Significantly, Benozzo's bold and highly evident repainting of the fresco can be interpreted as a reflection of the commune's eventual and total subjection to Florentine power and Medici standards of taste. By the 1460s and for about twenty-five years, led by the director of the cathedral works, Onofrio di Pietro, the most fashionable Florentine artists were chosen to embellish the architectural monuments of San Gimignano. Benozzo Gozzoli effectively initiated this overtly Florentine trend that climaxed with the renovations to the Collegiata later in the century, most notably the creation of the Santa Fina chapel, designed by Giuliano da Maiano in about 1468, housing a tomb sculpted by his brother, Benedetto da Maiano, in about 1475, and including fresco decorations by Ghirlandaio and members of his workshop.[56]

As one of the chosen exponents of Florentine Quattrocento taste, Benozzo Gozzoli repainted the *Maestà* in the town hall with some flourish. He made his additions in a boldly calligraphic fashion and proudly signed the fresco just below the lower right corner in large Renaissance letters: "Benozzo, Painter of Florence, restored this. 1467." Thus, when Benozzo renovated the fresco, he did so blatantly in his own style, making little effort to conform to the methods of the rest of the painting. One wonders whether this was his own choice or that of the commune and whether stylistic and technical consistency was ever even considered. As a self-conscious Renaissance artist – and a practitioner of the fashion patronized by the Medici – did he feel it beneath himself to adopt the techniques of the previous century? Or did the commune expect him to make his mark in this way? All the evidence suggests that additions of this kind in different artistic styles, rather than detracting from the overall value of the painting, actually seem to have been desired. They contributed to ensuring the painting's continuing vitality and force. Considered in this light, the instructions in Benozzo's contract, to refresh – *rinfrescare* – the *Maestà*, become more allusive. They constitute an invitation to rejuvenate the fresco, at the most fundamental level, by enhancing the color, but also through the addition of up-to-date stylistic flourishes.

□ □ □

In this chapter, the early restorations carried out on two important public murals – Simone Martini's *Maestà* in Siena and Lippo Memmi's *Maestà* in San Gimignano – have been investigated in relation to the civic contexts in which the paintings functioned. Great efforts were taken to repair and update both *Maestà* frescoes even at a time when other mural-paintings around them, having lost their relevance, were covered over by whitewash. Indeed, the layers of repaint on the murals – the improvements, extensions, and transformations – can be interpreted as records of individual and communal attempts to maintain and even increase the effectiveness of images valued by the city. They are additions that were evidently appreciated as they contributed to the continuing power of important public emblems.

CHAPTER 7

Conclusion: Living Images

In this book, I have attempted to demonstrate, through a sequence of case studies, the historical significance of early additions to certain late Medieval Tuscan paintings. Five sets of primarily religious images that were transformed to ensure their continuing efficacy have been considered in detail to reveal how the physical renovations were intimately tied to specific social contexts. For instance, I link the selective repainting of Coppo di Marcovaldo's *Madonna del Bordone* in the early fourteenth century in Siena to two primary factors: the contemporary impact of Byzantine artistic practices, specifically, the tradition of revitalizing devotional icons through retouching; and the replacement of Siena cathedral's old Madonna with Duccio's new *Maestà*. In combination, these contextual factors help to explain why the Servites chose to rework their Madonna along the lines of Duccio's new prized image in order to effect a renewal of devotional power. To understand the selective repainting of Margarito d'Arezzo's *St. Francis*, on the other hand, a quite different network of contextual factors was assembled. I argued that images of this type functioned as emblematic portraits imbued with the saint's attributes and values. Viewed in this light, the repainting reveals the Franciscans' need to create a more convincing and lovable mentor by adding definition to Margarito's uncharacterized earlier version. Revisions and renewals of this kind acquire new meaning once their historical circumstances are understood. Seen in context, the physical changes tell of important sacred and secular concerns.

All of the images discussed in this study were designed at the outset to fulfill devotional or civic functions. Because the paintings acquired their physical additions as a consequence of their roles, the added layers or parts are intimately bound up with these functions and take their historical meaning from them. The renovations, carried out for the sake of revitalizing or adapting the images, provide an indication of the continuing meaning and function of these works generations after their creation. The physical changes are a key to tracking the sacred or civic lives of the images over a period of time.

Yet works of this kind pose a problem for the art community as I suggested already in the introduction to this book. Because of their hybrid structures, which incorporate paint layers, painted supports, or frames of different dates and styles, the aesthetic concerns of the connoisseur come into conflict with the interests of the historian. More often than not, in traditional galleries, the paintings are displayed as aesthetic objects and restored accordingly; usually, no effort is made to evoke the original context. With the removal of later components, because they obscure the original master's artistic statement or because they are by an inferior hand, comes the loss of the historical dimension of the object as part of a process involving an existence and change through time. On the other hand, the most strict historical approach – advocating only minimal conservation treatments for the sake of stabilizing condition, and striving to recreate the original context if not returning the object there – would fail to meet aesthetic requirements. Moreover, it is only as a result of exploratory excavations and examinations by restorers from the aesthetic camp that the historical dimension of paintings like the formerly layered *St. Luke* in the Uffizi have been discovered – an irony that should not be forgotten.

Given such conflicting concerns, is it possible to arrive at a compromise solution, preserving some of the historical sense of the work without ignoring the aesthetic importance our society accords to the earliest layer and original format? Although decisions of this kind are best arrived at on a case-by-case basis after careful discussions involving curators, conservators, and art historians, it seems worthwhile to consider a few general guidelines however tentatively.

Cesare Brandi's principle of absolute compromise, enunciated in the context of the restoration of Coppo's *Madonna del Bordone*, may initiate discussion: "a work of art has two aspects, historical and aesthetic, and one cannot be sacrificed for the sake of the other."[1] It follows that an aesthetically disfiguring addition should only be removed if it is not of historical importance for the image. Gauging historical importance, however, can be difficult. In general, renovations contributed soon after the original have been considered more valuable than substantially later additions, because of their temporal and emotional closeness to the original. In the 1952 restoration of the Bandini Crucifix, for example, the eighteenth-century repainting of the thirteenth-century image was not deemed worthy of preservation.[2]

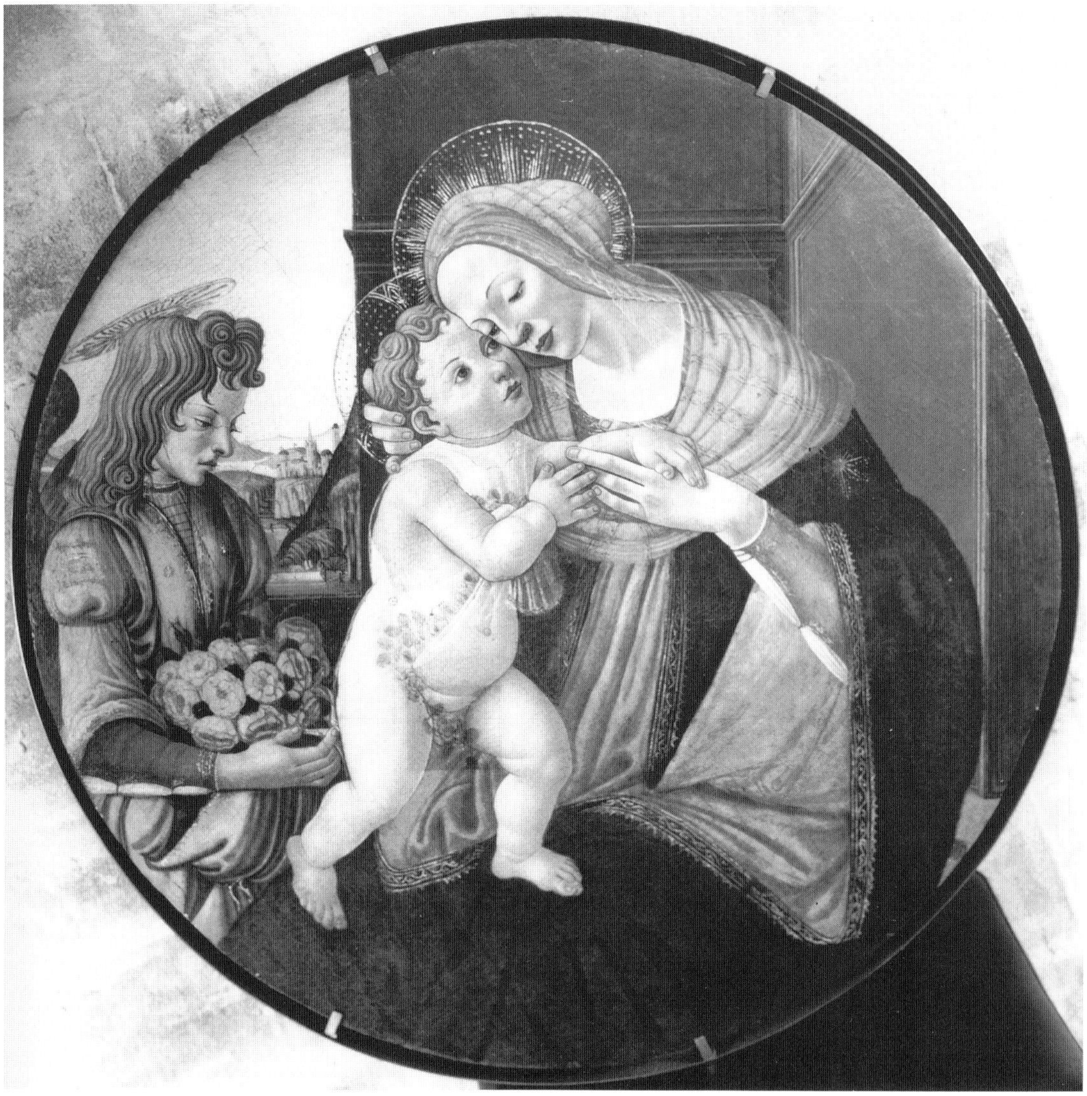

Figure 98. School of Botticelli, *Madonna and Child with an Angel*, c. 1490, Avignon, Musée du Petit Palais, after restoration of 1979 (Musée du Petit Palais, Avignon)

It had, of course, totally obscured the aesthetic appreciation of the underlying thirteenth-century figure. A contrasting decision in favor of the historical value of a late revision was made in the less complex case of a tondo of the *Madonna and Child with an Angel* (Avignon, Musée du Petit Palais) of c. 1490 attributed to the school of Botticelli and conserved by Nicole Delsaux in 1979 (Fig. 98). Perhaps as late as the nineteenth century, the last bloom on the spray of roses covering the Christ Child was rendered more opaque in order to obscure His genitals. Because the repainting was minor and did not inhibit the beauty and quality of the work, it was preserved as evidence of later taste.[3] Some late additions to works of art can indeed have importance as social or cultural documents. Then if they do not interfere with the aesthetic of the painting, it would seem wise not to remove them unless the process is reversible or the removed portions can be salvaged intact.

The case is strongest for early additions. As the changes are close to the original in time and spirit, they are more likely to be integrally related to the historical context for which the image was created and in which it functioned. Only when the renovations hamper in a major way the aesthetic appreciation of the painting in its original form should a compromise solution be attempted.

And yet in practice, it can be virtually impossible to reach the state of compromise suggested by Brandi's principle. In many instances, the goal of aesthetic harmony as it has been traditionally defined entails a destruction of historical dimensions whereas, conversely, historical aims interfere with aesthetic contemplation of the object in its original form. The difficulties involved can be illustrated by two recent restorations of layered works of art in which attempts were made to reach compromise.

The first example concerns a Florentine dossal of the *Last Supper* attributed to the workshop of the Magdalen Master and dated about 1280 (Fig. 99). It was restored in 1976 in preparation for an exhibition at the Musée du Petit Palais in Avignon. As well as extensive nineteenth-century repainting, conservators discovered that the panel had been selectively retouched at a considerably earlier date, perhaps during the early sixteenth century. At this time, the hair, hands, and clothing of the figures were reworked, the

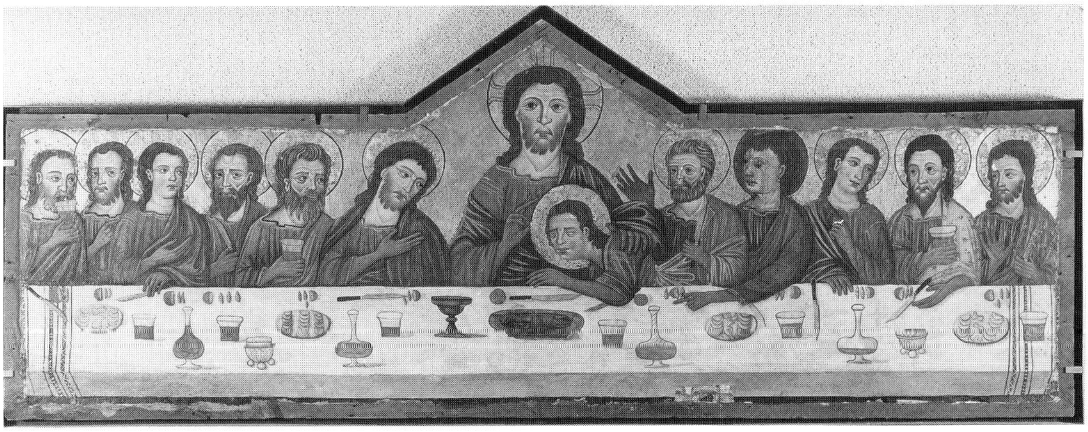

Figure 99. Workshop of the Magdalen Master, *Last Supper*, c. 1280, Avignon, Musée du Petit Palais, after restoration of 1976 (A. Guerrand, Avignon)

tablecloth was repainted, and new dishes were added to the table. The conservators decided to remove the nineteenth-century repaint but to retain the sixteenth-century additions with the exception of one small area that was cleaned to reveal the original, late Dugento tablecloth. They also decided not to inpaint several scratches to Judas's face, retaining them as evidence of early religious responses to the image.[4]

Those involved in the Avignon project argued for the preservation of the sixteenth-century retouching on historical grounds, conceding that these additions – by a "provincial and mediocre" artist – were of little artistic importance.[5] At the same time, by removing a patch of the sixteenth-century tablecloth and, thereby, providing a glimpse of the original, they made a gesture in the direction of compromise. That their solution is not fully satisfying to either side of the debate is an indication of the dilemna involved. Aesthetically, the work remains impure because the original has only been partially revealed. For the historical purist, on the other hand, compromise has led to the creation of a disturbing artefact. The result of partial and uneven removal of later layers is a newly hybrid structure, no longer corresponding to a past historical moment, but characteristic, one fears, of the late twentieth century – an ironic situation mentioned in relation to the cleaning of Guido da Siena's *Palazzo Pubblico Maestà* in the late 1940s.

In the treatment of Andrea del Sarto's *Holy Family* (Paris, Louvre) of c. 1516 by Nicole Delsaux in Paris in 1979–80, the aim was also to balance the aesthetic and historical dimensions of the object (Fig. 100). Although the painting was originally executed on a circular panel, it was transferred before 1784 to canvas and enlarged to form an oval under the influence of Baroque taste. During restoration, the oval extensions were retained because it was felt that they did not hinder contemplation of the original and because the painting's wide sculpted frame would eventually cover the additions. At the same time, Delsaux subtly drew attention to the initial form of the painting by removing the darkened varnish layers from this circular area alone and by retaining a thin white mastic line circumscribing the original.[6] With the help of a little imagination, the painting – when removed from its frame – can now be admired in its High Renaissance or Baroque form even though neither historical moment has been retrieved in its totality.

Evidently, when dealing with hybrid works of art, compromise is not easily achieved. For satisfactory solutions, both sides in the debate will be compelled to become more flexible and to adjust their standards of aesthetic harmony and historical veracity. Connoisseurs will have to develop a taste for or at least a tolerance of hybrid works like Taddeo Gaddi's reframed polyptych in the Metropolitan Museum of Art in New York.

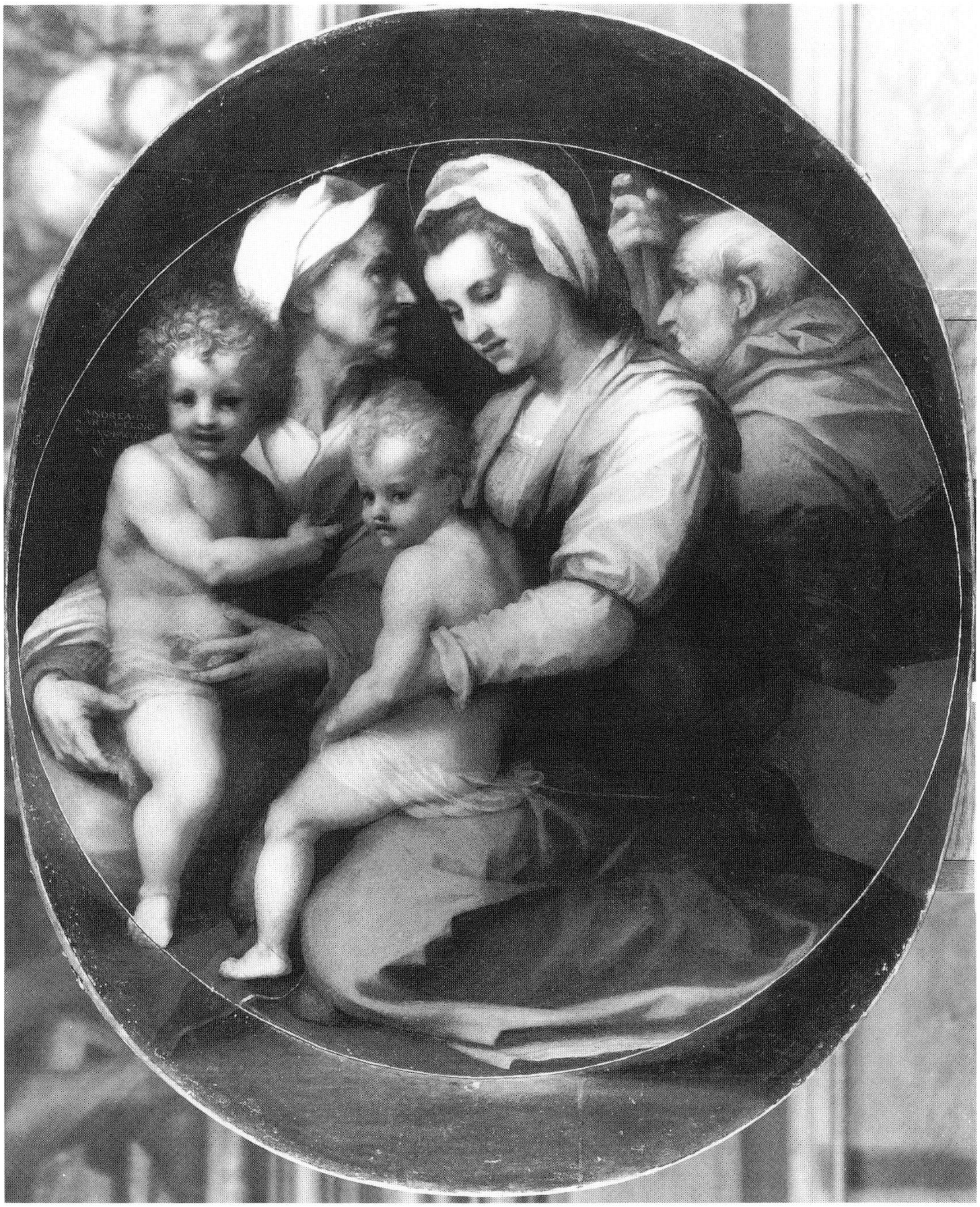

Figure 100. Andrea del Sarto, *Holy Family*, c. 1516, Paris, Louvre, after restoration of 1979–80 (© Photo Réunion des Musées Nationaux, Paris)

Similarly, historical purists will have to make some concessions to the connoisseurs, and to allow certain hybrid works to be removed from their contexts and treated, with caution, by conservators. Although it may be possible in future decades to obtain a high-quality image of the underlying layers of a repainted work with minimum destruction through sophisticated radiation techniques and computer enhancement, for the moment, the original can be revealed only by physically removing overlying layers. At present, limited exploratory treatments will have to be allowed, provided valuable historical dimensions of the images are not irretrievably lost. It is also important for the historian to recognize that no past moment in an image's existence can ever be recaptured absolutely. Every intervention, however historically motivated, brings the object into a new state tied to the values of the present.

Yet if seen in a positive light, balanced late-twentieth-century restorations of hybrid works become evidence of our modern desire to perpetuate the lives of these images through revitalization. In a careful restoration of a layered image, the conservator, in consultation, reinterprets the painting for the contemporary viewer and brings it to new life by drawing attention to both its interesting historic and its beautiful aesthetic features. Museum curators involved in the presentation of such extraordinary works can mediate in an equally enlightening way.

It could be argued that within the context of the Western art gallery with its connoisseurship-based value system, the display of religious paintings as purely aesthetic objects is fully appropriate. Nevertheless, more flexible curators may allow the new interest in contexts to play a role in reshaping museum exhibits. It would certainly be artificial, let alone virtually impossible, to attempt to recreate the original historical circumstances absolutely; however, relatively simple gestures can be made in the direction of compromise.

In the case of Taddeo Gaddi's *Metropolitan Polyptych*, for instance, the late-Quattrocento frame and painted additions have been retained, but the museum label describes them as unfortunate accretions. Instead of the negative perspective, a caption could be designed that briefly explains why Florentine Gothic altarpieces frequently were renovated in this way. A small sketch reconstructing how the altarpiece and frame may originally have looked would assist the aesthetic imagination.

Similar minor adjustments to the display of the once hybrid *Crucifix* in the Museo Bandini in Fiesole would help to evoke contextual circumstances. Although the present exhibit includes brief labels describing the process of discovery of the layers during restoration, the display could be enhanced by a series of photographs charting how the object looked at each stage of its transformation. A short explanation of the cult reasons underlying the changes would also further appreciation of the image's historical dimensions.

Designing a display for the Fogg *St. Dominic*, now preserved in storage, presents a particular challenge, as the panel has survived in its complexly layered state. An exhibit sensitive to contextual issues might include a label describing the interesting sequence of renovations and explaining the devotional motivations underlying the changes. X-radiograph images revealing the underlying versions could be included to increase understanding of the repaintings.

When early hybrid works of the kind discussed in this study are treated and presented with an eye to balancing their aesthetic and historical dimensions, a renewal of interest in the special qualities of the images can be brought about. Objects formerly considered unfortunate because of their mixture of stylistic moments instead can be appreciated for the insight their physical structures provide into the function of images in early Italian society. Indeed, the way this group of early Tuscan paintings manifest, through their renovations, the specific circumstances of their religious and civic lives may prove to be of broader significance with our increasing modern understanding of images as cultural signs.

Notes

CHAPTER 1. INTRODUCTION: THE PRESTIGE OF THE ORIGINAL

1. Carli and Cecchini (1962), p. 80; to be discussed in greater detail in Chapter 3.
2. See Gomez-Moreno et al. (1969). This example is discussed in depth in Chapter 4.
3. Crowe and Cavalcaselle (1908–9), vol. 2, p. 60, n. 1; see discussion in Chapter 6.
4. Tintori (1980).
5. One exception is the Dugento Redeemer dossal attributed to Meliore that still carries small late-Quattrocento painted additions probably added by Cosimo Rosselli. These additions may have been retained because they hardly interfere with aesthetic contemplation of the original.
6. The ideology underlying European galleries like the Uffizi, galleries that developed out of princely collections in the late eighteenth century, has been connected with Enlightenment thought by Bazin (1967), pp. 141–67, and Holst (1967), pp. 204–14. These authors trace the conception of the art object as representative of a moment within the new classification of works according to national schools and periods, and the separation of the object from its original context, back to Enlightenment values. Duncan and Wallach (1980) relate the concurrent notion of the object as the manifestation of one artistic personality, to the middle-class concern with individual genius as the "essence of human history" (p. 456). Their article includes insightful comments about how art museums to this day control the viewing experience (esp. p. 463).
7. The local repainting has been attributed to the circle of Pacino di Buonaguida.
8. The provenance of the panel cannot be traced before 1881 when it was listed in the inventory of the Gallerie Fiorentine as from the Convent of SS. Annunziata in Florence; Marcucci (1958), p. 53. However, the panel was probably associated with one of the Franciscan establishments in Florence, perhaps from the outset as the two tiny donor figures at the feet of St. Luke represent a Franciscan friar and nun.
9. On the restoration carried out by G. Lo Vullo, see Procacci (1936).
10. "intervenendo nella struttura del polittico, portavano a una diversa dimensione le figure di Giotto, che si inserivano in uno spazio assai maggiorato e perdevano non poco della loro forza d'impianto," Baldini and Poggetto (1972), p. 24. See also the comments in Baldini (1958), pp. 11–12, and Baldini (1967). The altarpiece was restored in 1957–8 by Leonetto Tintori; see Vigorelli and Baccheschi (1966), p. 97.
11. Baldini and Poggetto (1972), p. 25.

12. See *Italian Primitives* (1972).
13. Seymour (1970), pp. 37–9.
14. Baldini and Poggetto (1972), p. 19.
15. "volgare ridipintura," Procacci (1953), p. 32.
16. "opera non disprezzabile," ibid.
17. "In questi casi è quasi, direi, un'opera di carità il distruggere le ignobili ridipinture per giungere al recupero del nascosto originale," ibid., p. 31.
18. On the complex fabric of the past and our responses to it, see Lowenthal (1985), esp. pp. 263–362.
19. Keith Christiansen (1982b), p. 174, argues, on the contrary, that the figure of St. Catherine was added solely "to balance the asymmetrical picture field which resulted from the sixteenth-century alignment with the window above."
20. The record of the fresco's devotional power appears in an early eighteenth-century manuscript describing the cathedral and its decoration; see Riccetti (1989), p. 542, n. 13.
21. Christiansen (1989), p. 541.
22. See Bull and Plesters (1990), pp. 21–43, esp. p. 43.
23. Brandi and Carli (1951).
24. "L'opera d'arte infatti si presenta alla nostra conscienza con due istanze, quella storica e quella estetica, nè l'una può essere sacrificata a scapito dell'altra," Brandi (1950), p. 164.
25. Written communication from Norman Muller, Art Museum, Princeton University.

CHAPTER 2. THE REPAINTING OF TWO *MAESTÀ* ALTARPIECES

1. It should be noted that a second *maestà* altarpiece attributed to Coppo, the *Virgin and Child Enthroned* in Orvieto, was also selectively repainted but in an oil medium. As the repainting seems to be considerably later, perhaps as late as the eighteenth century when similar consciously historical restorations were carried out in Florence, it was not appropriate to include in this discussion. See Polzer (1984).
2. Brandi (1950). The precise identity of the Ducciesque master responsible for these additions has been much debated and almost every possibility has been suggested. Pèleo Bacci attributed the repaintings to Segna; see Stubblebine (1979), vol. 1, p. 118; Weigelt (1911), pp. 211–12, n. 1, chose the Master of Città di Castello; Brandi (1948), pp. 18–19, says Niccolò di Segna; Coor-Achenbach (1952), p. 312, says the Master of Badia a Isola; and Stubblebine (1979), vol. 1, p. 118, suggests the Vertine Master, named from the *Madonna della Misericordia* at Vertine (Chianti), now on view in the Pinacoteca in Siena.
3. Brandi and Carli (1951). In this instance, the repaintings are again difficult to attribute to a specific Ducciesque master. Crowe and Cavalcaselle (1903–14), vol. 3, p. 24, suggested Ugolino da Siena, as did Berenson (1968), vol. 1, p. 206; whereas, most recently, Stubblebine (1979), vol. 1, p. 83, attributes the additions to the Master of Badia a Isola, and dates them c. 1320.
4. See Cole (1973).
5. See Muratori (1900), vol. 15, pt. 6, p. 313.
6. See Hans Belting's related theory that the two Dugento Madonnas were given the physiognomy of the new cathedral *Maestà* to identify them also as the patroness of the city, "Blessed Mary of Siena"; Belting (1990), p. 440.
7. See Ciatti in *Capolavori e Restauri* (1986), pp. 419–22, and Baldini (1982), pp. 62–5.
8. Santi (1969), p. 43. See also Conti (1973), p. 42.
9. Garrison (1949), p. 63, no. 114.
10. "Petrus Tedeschi restauravit 1805 – ora pro eo."
11. See Cellini (1950), Morey (1954), and Kitzinger (1955).
12. See, in particular, Kitzinger (1966), Stubblebine (1966), and Weitzmann (1966, 1984).
13. Belting (1982), and Hoenigswald (1982). The hybrid style and technique evident in the *Kahn Madonna* may, in fact, be the work of a second-generation Byzantine artist living in Tuscany rather than a first-generation immigrant.
14. See Margaritoff (1967).
15. Xyngopoulos (1964), pp. 244–5, no. 184.
16. Hamilton (1954), p. 69, attributed the practice of repainting icons to the Byzantine use of varnishes that temporarily brightened the colors but then discolored, making the figures illegible, and also to the presence of layers of candle soot. However, as Margaritoff (1967), p. 145, pointed out in the case of an Athenian icon of the sixteenth century repainted

in 1710, the hidden earlier icon, when exposed, was discovered to be clean, suggesting that the artist of c. 1710 removed all the soot and varnish before he began his own work. Therefore, in this case, repainting was not necessitated by the presence of dirt or discolored varnish.

17. Uspenskij (1976), p. 16.
18. See Skalova (1987).
19. Galavaris (1981), p. 2.
20. Ouspensky (1978), pp. 64, 73.
21. Galavaris (1981), p. 2.
22. Uspenskij (1976), p. 10.
23. Smirnova (1989), p. 278.
24. Illuminating though distant parallels can be drawn between the Byzantine tradition of repainting icons and certain aboriginal practices. For example, a group of tribes of aboriginal peoples in Northwestern Australia periodically retouch paintings in rock shelters in order to activate the supernatural powers represented. See Elkin (1930), and Crawford (1968), esp. pp. 25–37. A perhaps similar practice, performed by the Dogon in Western Sudan, is to cover ritual wooden sculptures with coatings of sacrificial materials to activate supernatural potential. See Ezra (1988), esp. pp. 48, 57, and 59. The theme of widespread, cross-cultural religious practices involving images is discussed by Freedberg (1989).
25. See Fabbri and Rutenburg (1981).
26. Extract from the Anonymous Chronicle transcribed in Muratori (1900), vol. 15, pt. 6, p. 90. See also Brandi (1951), p. 86.
27. Kitzinger (1955), pp. 147–50, citing L. Duchesne, *Le Liber Pontificalis*, vol. 1, p. 419 (Paris, 1886).
28. The document survives in two transcriptions found in O. Panvinio, *De gente Fregepania libri quatuor*, Cod. Barb. lat. 2481 (16th cent.), fols. 100v–101v, and in N. Cassiani's treatise on pictures of the Virgin by St. Luke, Cod. Vat. Reg. lat. 2100 (late 16th or early 17th cent.), fols. 13r–14r; see Kitzinger (1955), p. 147.
29. Kitzinger (1955), pp. 147–50.
30. Ibid., p. 148.
31. Another example of a St. Luke Madonna that was repainted early on in its cult history is the *Panagia Chalkoprateia* now housed in the cathedral of St. Mary and St. Korbinian in Freising. An x-radiographic examination of the icon suggests that it may have been painted as early as 1100 in Constantinople, where, before 1235, it was rewarded with a silver-gilt and enameled frame that still survives intact. A Latin inscription added to the frame in the early fourteenth century explains that the icon was an imperial gift to Duke Gian Galeazzo Visconti of Milan; and it seems it was during this period in Italy that the icon was totally repainted by a Byzantine artist. See Belting (1990), p. 373 and fig. 201; and Beckwith (1986), p. 295.
32. A. D. MCC.LXI. COPP.dFIORENTIA. MEPIXIT. The original inscription on the frame was recovered during the restoration work of 1948.
33. *Foglio volante* (Siena, 1895), cited by Coor-Achenbach (1946), p. 235.
34. Coor-Achenbach (1946), p. 234, referring to C. Paoli, *Il Libro di Montaperti* (Florence, 1889), p. 22.
35. Corrie (1990), p. 66.
36. Wieruszowski (1944), p. 18.
37. Lusini (1908), p. 2. Also Pino (1972, 1977).
38. Fra Jacopo was prior general of the Servite order from 1257 to 1265. See Pino (1972).
39. The commune paid for 50,000 bricks and provided additional funding as well. For documents, see Lusini (1908), p. 3, nn. 8–11. E. Casalini's claim that the altarpiece was made for another small Servite church on the via Romana remains unsubstantiated; Casalini (1983), pl. V. See also Corrie (1990), p. 61.
40. In a document of Feb. 22, 1260, for example, the church is referred to as "ecclesie beate Virginis"; Lusini (1908), p. 3, n. 8. For evidence that devotion to San Clemente continued, see the discussion of Bernardino Fungai's new high altarpiece of 1498–1501 for the Servi church, a *Coronation of the Virgin* with *Scenes from the Life of San Clemente* in the predella, in Christiansen, Kanter and Strehlke (1988), pp. 352–8.
41. *Foglio volante* (Siena, 1895), as cited by Coor-Achenbach (1946), p. 235.
42. This view was first expressed by Gaetano Milanesi, ed., Vasari (1878–85), vol. 1, p. 266, n. 1, in opposition to the earlier theory that the name came from the Bordoni family who supposedly owned the chapel in which the painting was located in the late sixteenth and early seventeenth century; see Gargani (1874). Milanesi found no archival record proving the existence of a family of that name

during the period specified. The earliest textual reference to the painting, in the manuscript of Fabio Chigi dated 1625, describes the altarpiece as on the altar of the "Rondoni" family; see Biblioteca Apostolica Vaticana, Ms. Chigiano. I.I.11, published by Pèleo Bacci, ed., Chigi (1939), p. 312, and the manuscript as transcribed by Faluschi (1821), fol. 41v. In a later manuscript, Pseudo-Buondelmonte (18th cent.), fol. 9v, the name of the altarpiece, the *Madonna del Bordone*, is traced back to the ownership of the chapel by the Bordoni family, but this is not fully reliable.

43. See, among others, Casalini (1983), pl. V.
44. On the Orvieto Madonna, see Coor-Achenbach (1946); and Polzer (1984), who argues in an unconvincing way for an earlier dating. M. Boskovits' contention that the Orvieto altarpiece is not by Coppo is equally unconvincing; see Boskovits (1977). Another copy is the reduced size Madonna in Pomarance attributed by Garrison to a Pisan master c. 1265–75; see Garrison (1949), p. 45, no. 26. See also Corrie (1990), p. 72, n. 28.
45. "maxima devotione motus erga sacram imaginem," as quoted in Coor-Achenbach (1946), pp. 234–5. See also Vasari (1878–85), vol. 1, p. 266, and Lusini (1908), p. 43.
46. Although it seems most likely that the altarpiece, because of its large size and importance, was originally designed for the high altar of San Domenico, it should be noted that the early history of the work is not clear due to the lack of sufficient documentary material and the mistakes in certain available sources. One of the earliest references to the painting – as an altarpiece "molto devota e bella" – in the *Bisdomini Chronicle* (15th cent.), fol. 41v, records that the work was brought on December 17, 1221, to San Domenico for the altar of the Malavolti family. In this case, the chronicler has been confused by the date of 1221 on the altarpiece. We know from archival sources that the land for San Domenico was only donated in 1225, and the church was still under construction but being completed in 1262. By 1286, when a structure was set up in honor of Beato Ambrogio Sansedoni in the middle of the church, the building must have been virtually complete. See Lusini (1906), esp. pp. 264, 271, and 274. Sigismondo Tizio in his *Historiarum Senensium* of 1528, vol. 10, fol. 67, describes the *Palazzo Pubbico Maestà* as then housed in the Capacci chapel in San Domenico, but as originally from the parochial church of San Gregorio supposedly previously occupied by the Dominicans, another error due to the inscribed date of 1221. For a transcription of the passage, see Milanesi (1873; rpt. 1973), p. 90, n. 1. See also Brandi (1951), pp. 101–3.
47. The fragmentary inscription, partially lost when the dossal was cut down at either end, reads: . . . X . . . AMENIS.QUE.XTS.LENIS.NULLIS.VELIT. ANGERE.PENIS:ANNO.DNI.MILLESIMO.DUCENTESIMO. SEPTUAGESIMO. . . . See Offner (1950), and Stubblebine (1964), p. 38.
48. Brandi and Carli (1951), p. 253.
49. Carli (1955), p. 177.
50. Hager (1962), pp. 137–8.
51. Stubblebine (1964), p. 40, and Gardner (1979). One aspect of Stubblebine's hypothesis, and an idea recently reiterated by Hans Belting, that the present inscription was added at the same time as the early Trecento repaintings, is disproved by the technical evidence. See Belting (1990), p. 441.
52. The *Virgin of Vladimir* was covered in this way until early this century when the icon was fully revealed. The Christ Icon from the Sancta Sanctorum in the Lateran in Rome was also enclosed in a cover of this kind; see Wilpert (1907), and Belting (1990), pp. 80–1.

CHAPTER 3. ENSHRINING THE REMAINS OF REVERED IMAGES

1. See Borsook (1970), p. 6. The technical information is summarized by R. Proto Pisani and Cecilia Filippini in *Maestri e Botteghe* (1992), pp. 212–13.
2. The Biagio d'Antonio collaborator active here may be the "Maestro di Marradi." See Zeri (1971), p. 66, and Conti (1973), p. 211. On this group of artists closely associated with Domenico Ghirlandaio, see also Fahy (1976), pp. 181–5, 204–11.
3. Garrison (1949), pp. 89–95.
4. Conti (1973), p. 211, first suggested that the central panel of the Lecceto triptych was Dugento in origin, in contrast to Borsook

(1970), p. 6, who cited the conclusions of the conservator Barbara Schleicher that the head disc was all that remained of the earlier image.

5. R. Proto Pisani in *Maestri e Botteghe* (1992), p. 212.
6. The panel was recently examined at the private restoration studio in Florence, Centro Internazionale di Firenze per il Restauro, where the altarpiece had been held for the past ten years pending minor structural restorations. The dense intermediary layer is probably either gesso or white lead paint.
7. This attribution was ventured by Dott.sa Rosanna Proto Pisani of the Soprintendenza in Florence. She told me, however, that Bruno Santi prefers an attribution to Giovanni da Milano. It is interesting to note that Carocci (1895), p. 16, in his early guidebook to the area, described the style of the central panel as "di maniera Giottesca."
8. Borsook (1970), p. 9.
9. "Servus meus es tu: quia elegi te, et in te gloriabor," in Razzi (1543), p. 561. The story is easily accessible in Razzi, but is recorded also earlier in the first *vita* of the saint by Piero Del Castagno (midfifteenth century), which is the primary source of all subsequent lives; see Petrus Andreas Del Castagno, *Vita Beati Andreae de Corsinis de Florentia Ordinis Carmelitarum et Episcopi Fesulani*, Biblioteca Vaticana, cod. Vat. Lat. 3813, fols. 28v-47v, or P. Domenico di Gesù, *Acta canonizationis S. Andreae Corsini* . . . (Paris, 1638), pp. 171–224; see also Saggi (1961), p. 90.
10. On the history of the church, see Bacchi (1926).
11. Ibid., pp. 9–14; Caioli (1929), p. 35.
12. Bacchi (1926), p. 14; Caioli (1929), p. 36.
13. Bacchi (1926), p. 15.
14. Ibid.
15. Neri di Bicci (1976), p. 19.
16. Marle (1923–38), vol. 10, p. 545.
17. Carocci (1895), p. 13; and Borsook (1970), p. 8.
18. Bacchi (1926), p. 14.
19. Most recently, Angelo Tartuferi (1990), p. 87, attributed the altarpiece to the St. Agatha Master, as had Garrison tentatively in 1949.
20. "portata dal Levante da quei molti Pittori, che a Firenze vennero; o da i Fiorentini, che per ragioni di commercio colà andavano," Richa (1762), vol. 10, p. 40; see also *Capolavori e Restauri* (1986), p. 424.
21. On the location of the panel from the fifteenth to the eighteenth century, see Mesnil (1912), and Procacci (1932).
22. The earliest description comes from Monsignor Bossio, who saw the Madonna on the altar of the Cioli family in 1575; see Bossi (1575), fol. 689v. See also Lusini (1907), p. 45, and Os (1987), p. 129.
23. Os (1984), p. 37.
24. See Boase (1939–40). See also Cannon (1987), p. 20.
25. Borsook (1970), p. 8.
26. Archivio di Stato di Firenze, Strozziane V, 22, c. 80v; transcribed in Borsook (1970), p. 19, document 63. At the same time, a wax image was also sent to the chapel of the Virgin at SS. Filippo e Giacomo in Lecceto.
27. See Borsook (1970), p. 5.
28. "considerando nui frati de santa maria delle Selve . . . el prudente e nobile homo philippo di matheo di Stroze essere devoto ela capella de la vergine m. posta nelachiesa nostra . . . avolerla adornare efarla bella solum deaccessori et arme . . . ," transcribed in Bacchi (1926), p. 16.
29. Borsook (1970), pp. 17–18, documents 39–43.
30. "per dipintura della cortina . . . per aconciare detta cortina dinanzi alla detta tavola di Nostra Donna," transcribed in Borsook (1970), p. 17, document 41.
31. VIRGINI GENITRICI PHILIPPUS STROZZA SUI IN SALUTEM CONDIDIT; see Borsook (1970), p. 5, and document 38 on p. 17.
32. VI[R]GO SI[N]GULARIS I[N]TER O[MN]ES MITIS NOS CULPIS SOLUTOS MITES FACET CASTOS; expanded in Borsook (1970), p. 6, n. 63.
33. On Montano d'Arezzo and the dating of the panel, see Bologna (1969), pp. 102–7, and Leone de Castris (1986), pp. 196–201. On the image, see also the brief account in Lorenzetti (1936–7), p. 423.
34. PP. Benedettini di Montevergine (1904), pp. 18–19, and PP. Benedettini di Montevergine (1905), pp. 54–5.
35. PP. Benedettini di Montevergine (1904), pp. 13–14.
36. Tropeano (1978), p. 179.
37. Mongelli (1967), and Tropeano (1978), p. 179. See also Mongelli (1965).
38. See Mongelli (1967), p. 443.

39. Tropeano (1973), pl. V.
40. Garrison (1949), p. 92, no. 227. Earlier datings, as early as the beginning of the thirteenth century, have been suggested by Mongelli (1967), pp. 440–1, and Quintavalle (1934), pp. 16–17, but these cannot be seriously considered.
41. Garrison (1949), pp. 89–95, nos. 210–39.
42. I would like to thank Pierluigi Leone de Castris for allowing me to examine the x-radiographs.
43. Bologna (1969), p. 104. His further suggestion that the overlying *Maestà* was executed in two separate stages, a first Cimabuesque stage in the early fourteenth century when the entire work was painted, and a second moment c. 1320–30 when elements of the composition such as the marble throne and metal plaque background were added by a follower of Cavallini, is not convincing; ibid., pp. 104–5.
44. Garrison (1949), p. 43, no. 18.
45. Tropeano (1978), pp. 173–4.
46. Léonard (1954), pp. 51–6, 157–70.
47. Tropeano (1978), pp. 174–5.
48. Ibid., p. 174.
49. Montevergine, Archivio, perg. no. 2619; cited by Tropeano (1978), p. 174.
50. Tropeano (1978), pp. 175–6.
51. Canc. Ang., reg. Rob. 1310E, fol. 27t; cited in Leone de Castris (1986), p. 205, n. 6.
52. The fresco was moved in 1588; see Tropeano (1978), p. 185.
53. The foundation document of the church, dated August 25, 1314, records Bartolomeo di Capua's financial bequest and the dedication. See Arch. MV., perg. no. 2866; partially cited in Tropeano (1978), p. 183.
54. On the Byzantine origins of this kind of gilding technique, see Frinta (1981).
55. I owe this information to Joseph Polzer, University of Calgary.
56. Garrison (1949), p. 43.
57. "nella testa e nel collo della Vergine riscontransi i caratteri della scuola senese di Duccio e dei suoi seguaci, metre è chiaro che tutto il rimanente del dipinto appartiene ad altra mano . . . ," as quoted in Carli and Cecchini (1962), p. 80.
58. For the attribution to Simone Martini, see Carli and Cecchini (1962), p. 83, and Carli (1963). For Memmo di Filippuccio, see Boskovits (1975), p. 293.
59. See Carli and Cecchini (1962), p. 83.
60. Pecori (1853; rpt. 1975), p. 552.
61. Carli and Cecchini (1962), p. 80. On this attribution, see the interesting early observations of Crowe and Cavalcaselle (1903–14), vol. 2, p. 250, who identify the frescoes in the church and oratory of San Lorenzo as by the same artist – "Cenni of Volterra" – responsible for the cycle at Volterra, but do not fully distinguish this Gaddiesque master from Cennino Cennini.
62. On Cenni di Francesco, see Boskovits (1975), pp. 76–8, 126–8, 285–94; Fremantle (1975), pp. 381–90; Poggetto (1963), pp. 36–7.
63. See Carli and Cecchini (1962), p. 80; Jannella (1989), p. 8; and Pecori (1853; rpt. 1975), p. 552.
64. Fiumi (1961), p. 274.
65. Ibid.
66. Carli and Cecchini (1962), p. 80.
67. Ibid.
68. For Simone Martini's will, see Archivio di Stato di Siena, Gabella de'Contratti 29, fol. 292v, published with minor errors in Milanesi (1854–5; rpt. 1969), vol. 1, pp. 243–4, and in Bacci (1944), pp. 185–7. See also Martindale (1988), p. 6, who provides a tentative family tree.
69. Martindale (1988), p. 6.
70. For an account of the later history of this kind of enshrined image, or "bildtabernakel," see Warnke (1968). Another early Tuscan example is the fourteenth-century *Madonna and Child* of Sienese origin at the Chiesa di Panzano, inserted as the central focus of a fifteenth-century Florentine *sacra conversazione*; see *Fiesole* (1986), pl. 159.
71. The literature on the cult of relics is extensive. For a concise account with a good bibliography, see Chiovaro (1967). Detailed recent discussions can be found in Kriss-Rettenbeck (1985), and Kroos (1985).
72. This legend recalls, of course, the story of Veronica's veil. See Stuart (1975), p. 31, for an account of the legend; and also Kitzinger (1976).
73. One example can be found in the Romanesque psalter, probably from Hildesheim and dating c. 1235, in Donaueschingen, Fürstlich-Fürstenbergische Hofbibliothek, Cod. 309; see *Ornamenta Ecclesiae* (1985), vol. 3, pp. 162, 164.

74. The tabernacle is in Christ Church Library, Oxford; see Garrison (1943–5).

CHAPTER 4. REVISING THE PORTRAITS OF TWO PATRON SAINTS

1. Brown (1981), p. 50.
2. On the partial shift from graveside to altar worship, see Vauchez (1981), pp. 519–29.
3. The most recent extended discussion of this subject is Krüger (1992).
4. Nine are catalogued by Garrison (1949), pp. 50–2, nos. 51–8 and 60. Another is the panel attributed to the workshop of Margarito d'Arezzo in the Kunsthaus in Zurich, recorded by Torriti (1977; rpt. 1980), p. 47. One final panel of St. Francis is attributed to the St. Gregory Master and housed in the Louvre in Paris; see Offner (1952).
5. See Offner (1952), pp. 129–33, and Scarpellini (1982), pp. 107–8.
6. Before the repainted nature of the image was recognized and before Margarito d'Arezzo's stylistic development was clarified by Anna Maria Maetzke, the panel was dated as early as c. 1230–40 by Longhi and as late as c. 1270–80 by Garrison and others. See Maetzke (1973); Longhi (1948), p. 38; and Garrison (1949), p. 50, no. 51. Margarito d'Arezzo's career is now generally believed to span the years c. 1240/50–c. 1270/80.
7. Garrison (1949), p. 50, no. 54.
8. (1) Castiglion Fiorentino, from S. Francesco, now Museo, 102 × 39 cm; (2) Montepulciano, from monastery of S. Francesco, now Museo Civico, 120 × 46.5 cm; (3) from Gangereto, S. Francesco, now Arezzo, Museo Diocesano, 127 × 45 cm; (4) Rome, S. Francesco a Ripa, Cella di S. Francesco, 129 × 52 cm; (5) Rome, Pinacoteca Vaticana no. 2, 122 × 40 cm; (6) Siena, Pinacoteca Nazionale, 95 × 37 cm; (7) Zurich, Kunsthaus. See Garrison (1949), pp. 50–2; and Torriti (1977; rpt. 1980), p. 47. It has been suggested that all these versions, including the repainted Arezzo *St. Francis*, follow a now lost original, but this seems unlikely. It would be difficult to explain why the Arezzo panel was repainted to reproduce an earlier original that acted as the inspirational source behind the other replicas.
9. Early images of Francis vary as to whether they show only three knots on the saint's belt or include a fourth knot at his waist. In the early dossal of *St. Francis and Four Miracles from his Life* given to the Maestro del Tesoro (Assisi, Tesoro della Basilica di San Francesco), seven knots are depicted, but this is unusual. On the iconography of St. Francis, see Schmucki and Gerlach (1968–76).
10. On Celano's learned use of previous written sources to shape his account of Francis's life and physical appearance, see Brooke (1967), esp. pp. 182–3.
11. Thomas of Celano, *Vita Prima*, 83; see Habig (1972), pp. 298–9.
12. Celano, *Vita Prima*, 112; in Habig (1972), p. 326. This idea was developed by Saint Bonaventure in his *Legenda major*, XV, 2; see Habig (1972), p. 742. See also Goffen (1988), p. 14 and n. 7.
13. See also Scarpellini (1982), p. 93, who believes that the Arezzo *St. Francis* and its replicas capture Francis's portrait likeness realistically for the first time.
14. On the recent restoration findings, see Maetzke (1973), p. 108; Maetzke et al. (1974), p. 29; Maetzke et al. (1987), p. 37, no. 3.
15. I disagree with Maetzke, who attributes the repainting to a Florentine artist close to the Magdalen Master; see Maetzke et al. (1974), p. 29, and Maetzke et al. (1987), p. 37. The repainting follows Margarito's original so closely as to indicate the work of a student. Further, the preservation of Margarito's signature makes sense if the renovation was carried out by a shop artist who worked under this banner. Also, the repainted version became the model for subsequent images of St. Francis produced by Margarito's shop.
16. Maetzke et al. (1974), p. 29.
17. Originally, Francis's face may have resembled more closely the male type used by Margarito for St. John in his *Crucifix* (Arezzo, Pieve di S. Maria), with very large, deeply set eyes, a thin, medium-length nose, and small thick lips.
18. If the repainted Arezzo *St. Francis* was the prototype for several of the smaller portraits of the saint produced by Margarito's shop, such as the Castiglion Fiorentino *St. Francis* and the panel in the Museo Civico di Montepulciano, these portraits all have to date

after the repainting of c. 1270–5. I am inclined to disagree with Laura Martini who, following the recent cleaning of the Montepulciano panel, would like to date it contemporary with the Arezzo *St. Francis*, c. 1260, and attribute the image to Margarito himself. See Martini et al. (1990), p. 31. Krüger (1992), p. 212, argues, to my mind unconvincingly, that all the versions were issued in a short span of years, c. 1260 (–1270), corresponding with the likely date of the underlying Arezzo image.

19. Hager (1962), pp. 88–100; Os (1983).
20. Hager (1962), pp. 88–100; Os (1983).
21. Bonaventure, in part two of the *Legenda major*, recounts the story of a Roman matron who kept a painted image of St. Francis in a private room of her house and prayed to it in secret. He relates how the stigmata miraculously appeared on the image where they were absent before, and how they later disappeared again to convince the doubting woman of the miracle; see *Legenda major*, part two, I, 4, in Habig (1972), pp. 749–50; and Vauchez (1981), p. 525, n. 19. On the proliferation and necessity of these images for the followers of St. Francis, see also Goffen (1988), p. 13.
22. See Offner (1930–84), sect. III, vol. V, p. 94, n. 1; Hager (1962), p. 91; and Os (1983), p. 334.
23. A number of early wooden sculptures of saints were included in the exhibition *Scultura Dipinta* held in Siena in 1987, notably a seated figure of a pope, perhaps San Clemente, attributed to an Umbrian follower of Arnolfo di Cambio and dated c. 1290–1300, and a standing figure of St. Thomas Aquinas by a Sienese master c. 1323. See *Scultura Dipinta* (1987), nos. 2 and 9. For the twelfth-century wooden Crucifixes in Arezzo, see Maetzke et al. (1974), pp. 124–8, and Maetzke (1979), pp. 11–14.
24. "ed a Sargiano, convento dei Frati de'Zoccoli, in una tavola, un San Francesco ritratto di naturale, ponendovi il nome suo," Vasari (1878–85), vol. 1, pp. 359–67, at 361. See also Scarpellini (1982), p. 108.
25. Maetzke et al. (1987), p. 37.
26. Salmi (1951), p. 172.
27. I have not been able to discover when the Convento di Sargiano was founded. It was suppressed in the nineteenth century. On the Montepulciano *St. Francis*, see Martini et al. (1990), pp. 31–5.
28. Os (1983), p. 336, suggests that portraits of this kind would have been used primarily by the "spirituals" who believed that they were the saint's true disciples and preserved his living memory.
29. Moleta (1983), p. 31.
30. It is interesting to note that in the records of the canonization procedures for Italian saints during the fourteenth century, there are numerous references to saints appearing in visions just as the witness had seen them depicted on panel or in fresco in the local church. See Vauchez (1981), p. 528 and n. 30.
31. See Os (1974), who discusses several later images of *Franciscus Alter Christus* and the textual and theological underpinnings. Also Goffen (1988), ch. 2.
32. Ten crosses of this kind with St. Francis at Christ's feet survive and the Perugia Crucifix seems to be the prototype. See Sandberg-Vavalà (1929; rpt. 1980), pp. 823–7. See also Goffen (1988), p. 22 and n. 52.
33. Saint Bonaventure, *Legenda major*, XIII, 3; in Habig (1972), pp. 730–1. See also Os (1974).
34. On the popularity of cult images of the face of Christ in Byzantium and in Italy, see Belting (1990), pp. 233–52.
35. The cuffs and lower border of Francis's robe were also outlined, drawing attention to the stigmata and once again emphasizing Francis's closeness to Christ. This outlining was repeated subsequently in several of the replicas.
36. Brooke (1967), pp. 177, 185.
37. Lehner (1964), p. 1.
38. For the *Libellus*, see ibid., pp. 5–89.
39. Bologna (1962; rpt. 1978), colorpl. 57.
40. Bologna (1969), p. 59.
41. Mark 16:15. See Kaftal (1965), col. 356.
42. Garrison (1949), p. 76, cat. no. 169. Toesca (1927), vol. 2, p. 1032, n. 33, says in a brief note that the provenance leads back to the Dominican church at Gaeta, whereas Bologna (1969), p. 59, suggests it may have been made for the original church of S. Pietro Martire a Castello in Naples, erected under Carlo II beginning in 1294.
43. Bologna (1969), pp. 58–9, and figs. 65, 66, reviews the literature on this painting. A dating of the panel to the late thirteenth

century was suggested first by Schultz (1860), vol. 3, p. 148. See also Garrison (1949), p. 127, cat. no. 337. Krüger (1992), p. 76, suggests it may originally have formed part of a larger work.
44. Lehner (1964), p. 11.
45. See R. D. Buck's examination report of May 8, 1942, in the conservation file at the Fogg. See also the fundamental study of the technical aspects of this panel-painting by Gomez-Moreno et al. (1969), pp. 364–5.
46. The reconstruction was published in Gomez-Moreno et al. (1969), fig. 2.
47. Ibid., p. 366, and Garrison (1949), p. 155, cat. no. 405.
48. For the cycle on the Naples altarpiece, see Kaftal (1965), cols. 356–60.
49. See Gomez-Moreno et al. (1969), pp. 365–6.
50. Ibid., p. 363.
51. Ibid., pp. 363–4 and fig. 1.
52. Examination report by E. Jones, dated July 15, 1960, in the conservation file at the Fogg Art Museum.
53. See Stout (1929).
54. Some of the earliest haloes employing full tooling can be found in Simone Martini's *Pisa Polyptych* of 1319.
55. Frinta (1971). For a survey of Ugolino di Nerio's activity, see Coor-Achenbach (1955).
56. Frinta (1971), p. 306. On the Sta. Croce altarpiece, see Loyrette (1978); Gardner Von Teuffel (1979), p. 48; Gordon and Reeve (1984); Bomford et al. (1989), pp. 98–123.
57. See Cannon (1982), pp. 87–91.
58. The painting passed through the hands of F. Mason Perkins, was sold to Bernard d'Hendecourt representing Durlacher Brothers, and was then bought by the Fogg. Notes on the provenance of the panel can be found in the archives of the Fogg.
59. This hypothesis was suggested tentatively by Stubblebine (1964), p. 87, and explored further by Gomez-Moreno et al. (1969), p. 364. I know of no other possible early Dominican locations in Siena or nearby.
60. Chigi (1939), pp. 322–4.
61. There was a serious fire in San Domenico in 1531 that destroyed areas of the interior. The altarpiece could have been partly ruined in such a fire and only the central portion salvaged.
62. See Lusini (1906), and Gardner (1979), p. 107.
63. Lusini (1906), p. 279 and n. 1.
64. Ibid., pp. 263–95.
65. Gomez-Moreno et al. (1969), p. 364. Krüger (1992), p. 77, contends that an initial date of c. 1250–60 is more plausible because the earliest textual evidence for official Dominican interest in images of their founder comes from the years 1247, 1254, and 1256.
66. Gomez-Moreno et al. (1969), p. 364.
67. See Crowe and Cavalcaselle (1903–14), vol. 3, p. 24; and Berenson (1968), vol. 1, p. 206.
68. Lehner (1964), pp. 160–3.
69. Ibid., pp. 183–4.
70. Gomez-Moreno et al. (1969), p. 364.
71. Ibid.
72. Seymour (1970), pp. 11–12.
73. For the dating, I am following White (1979), pp. 46ff. For an excellent discussion of the triptych, see Davies, rev. by Gordon (1988), pp. 14–16.
74. Cannon (1980), pp. 270 and 315, n. 240.
75. One further early Tuscan image of St. Dominic should be noted. A miracle from the saint's legend appears on the Gallerani Reliquary Shutters in the Pinacoteca in Siena, attributed by James Stubblebine to the St. Peter Master, a follower of Guido da Siena, and dated to the mid-1270s. St. Dominic is shown praying for the cure of Blessed Reginald, who is in turn rewarded by the Virgin with a Dominican habit. The panels most likely formed part of the structure of an altar dedicated to Blessed Andrea Gallerani, a tertiary Dominican and a Sienese cult figure. In this instance, St. Dominic's brown hair and beard have a slight reddish cast. On the shutters, see Stubblebine (1964), pp. 69–71.

CHAPTER 5. THE REFRAMING OF GOTHIC ALTARPIECES DURING THE RENAISSANCE

1. For the dating of the original altarpiece, see Ladis (1982), pp. 150–1.
2. See Newbery, Bisacca, and Kanter (1990), p. 23.
3. Christiansen (1982a), p. 7. The label next to the altarpiece in the gallery is written in the same tone: "The result is an unfortunate mixture of Gothic and Renaissance that

sadly compromises Taddeo Gaddi's original intentions."

4. Procacci (1962). Figure 4 on p. 15 shows the altarpiece "liberata dalle aggiunte quattrocentesche."
5. Poggi (1903), and Procacci (1962).
6. Offner (1930–84), sect. III, vol. 1, p. 68. Cohn (1957) introduced the attractive hypothesis that this *Maestà* was originally designed as a replacement for the first Madonna of Orsanmichele, destroyed in the fire of 1304. In this context, the image would have acquired a reputation for devotional efficacy that may in part explain the subsequent desire to renovate it.
7. Conti et al. (1983), p. 7. More recently, an attribution to Bartolomeo di Giovanni, a collaborator with Domenico Ghirlandaio, has been put forward by Everett Fahy. See Nicoletta Pons in *Maestri e Botteghe* (1992), p. 214.
8. Examples are: Follower of Bernardo Daddi, *Madonna and Child Enthroned with Saints* (Rome, Conte Alessandro Contini Collection), see Offner (1930–84), sect. III, vol. 4, p. 48; Remote Follower of Bernardo Daddi, *Madonna Enthroned with Saints* (S. Godenzo Mugello, Basilica di S. Godenzo), reframed in 1530 or a little later, see Offner (1930–84), sect. III, vol. 4, p. 148; attributed to Bernardo Daddi, *Madonna and Child with Four Saints* (San Martino a Lucarelli, Radda in Chianti), reframed in the late 15th century with spandrel panels in the manner of Botticelli representing, from left to right, St. Peter, the Annunciation, and St. Jerome, see *Fiesole* (1986), p. 331, colorpl. 150.
9. One example not discussed in this chapter is Giovanni del Ponte's *Annunciation Triptych* in Santa Maria di Poppiena, Pratovecchio, which seems to have been renovated in the 1480s by the Ghirlandaio workshop.
10. Procacci (1966). The central panel of the original triptych, a *Madonna and Child*, is now in Geneva, Musée d'Art et d'Histoire.
11. One of the first to document a number of these reframings and to comment on the underlying motivations was Offner (1930–84), sect. III, vol. 5, p. 88, n. 10. Offner drew a distinction between the earlier Trecento practice of selectively repainting religious images and the Renaissance fashion for architectural reframings. He remarked that these Renaissance remodelings reveal an attitude of appropriation: "[they] betray the last effort the Renaissance was to make at reclaiming Gothic by adapting it to its own forms." Most recently, a large number of examples have been discussed by Filippini (1992). She acknowledges the religious impulse underlying many of these renovations although she rarely examines the specific devotional contexts in any detail.
12. Burckhardt (1929; rpt. 1958), vol. 1, p. 250.
13. "la quale tavola fu g[i]à fatta antichamente chon civori e fogliami sechondo s'usavano a quello anticho tenpo, ed io la fe' rachonc[i]are e riducere a l'uso d'ogidì, c[i]oè cholonne da.llato e di sopra architrave, freg[i]o e chornic[i]one . . . ," Neri di Bicci (1976), pp. 382–3.
14. On the attribution and dating of the altarpiece, see Gardner (1971), pp. 107–8, and Skaug (1971–2).
15. The removal of the gable with God the Father need not be interpreted as an act of sacrilege. Devotional panels were often cut and reassembled in radical ways. There was a more utilitarian conception of the sacred object. The gable from the central panel is now in the Fine Arts Gallery in San Diego, California. See Zeri (1957), and Vigorelli and Baccheschi (1966), p. 118, fig. 149G.
16. On the dating of the *San Bartolo Altar*, see Lein (1988), pp. 117–18.
17. Gilbert (1977), pp. 13–14. For a renovation project of 1457 in which Giuliano da Maiano did the reframing for Neri di Bicci, see Neri di Bicci (1976), pp. 66–7.
18. Lein (1988), pp. 73–93.
19. Gardner (1971), p. 100.
20. Conti (1988), p. 15, attributes the repainted portions of the *Baroncelli Altarpiece* to Ghirlandaio with no explanation.
21. The chapel of Santa Fina in the Collegiata at San Gimignano represents one such collaboration. Designed by Giuliano da Maiano, the chapel includes an important tomb monument by Benedetto da Maiano dated 1475, but also painted prophet figures with scrolls that seem to have been executed by Sebastiano Mainardi working as part of the Ghirlandaio shop. See Lein (1988), p. 31, and Carl (1978). On projects involving both the Ghirlandaio and da Maiano workshops, see also Fahy (1976).

22. See Cassidy (1988), pp. 179–80.
23. On the family in Quattrocento Florence, see Kent (1977).
24. Cohn (1988), esp. pp. 58–71.
25. For an analogous argument concerning the mid-Trecento, see Cohn (1992).
26. "Arrechò l'arte nuova, lasciò la roccza dc' Greci," Lorenzo Ghiberti, "I Commentarii," in Schlosser (1912), p. 35.
27. See Krautheimer (1969), and Baxandall (1971), esp. pp. 51ff.
28. I would like to thank Megan Holmes for drawing to my attention a document of November 16, 1442, involving the restoration of a "large panel by Giotto" to be performed in the joint workshop of Fra Filippo Lippi and his temporary partner Giovanni di Francesco. See Holmes (1993), pp. 302–4 and 542–3, and Ruda (1993), pp. 520–2.
29. Several punch motifs that Lippo used in his early works – the *Glorification of St. Thomas* (Pisa, Sta. Caterina) and the *Madonna of Mercy* (Orvieto, Duomo) – appear for the first time in Simone's works in the *Orvieto Polyptych* of c. 1324, signaling that around this time a collaboration between the two artists began; see Polzer (1983), esp. p. 241.
30. Archivio di Stato di Siena, Consiglio Generale, no. 92, fols. 121v–122v. See also Bennett (1979), p. 113.
31. On the cult history of Lippo Memmi's panel in Sta. Maria dei Servi and the role of the Luti family, see Lusini (1908), in this case at p. 34.
32. Ibid., p. 18.
33. Archivio di Stato di Siena, Patrim. dei Resti, 10 gennaio 1470, no. 1335; A.S.S., Conventi 2612, c. 22r; and Lusini (1908), p. 18.
34. For the stemma of the Servites, see Macci, fol. 123v.
35. Sa.Ma.MATER. DEI. ORA. PRO. POPULO. INTERVENI. PRO.CLERO.
36. For the history of the church, see Baroni (1866), in this case at pp. 13–15. See also Raspini (1977).
37. Baroni (1866), p. 18.
38. Archivio di Stato di Firenze, Diplomatico, Badia di Firenze, 26 marzo, 1451.
39. Baroni (1866), p. 18.
40. A stylistic comparison can be made between the prophet added in the third spandrel to the right on the triptych and the St. Anthony Abbot in Rosselli's *Madonna and Child with Sts. Nicholas and Anthony Abbot* (Florence, Uffizi, Inv. 1890, no. 3941).
41. Raspini (1977), p. 41.
42. Attributed to him are the *Madonna and Child with Sts. Andrew and Sebastian* on the altar patronized by the Cecchini family, the fresco abovc of thc *Crucifixion*, and somc frcscocs in the private chapel of the bishop. See *Fiesole* (1986), pp. 347–8.
43. On Rosselli and the Zati family at San Ambrogio, see Borsook (1981), p. 176.
44. On the artist, see Boskovits (1975), p. 379, and Klesse (1957–9). Bellosi (1985) suggests that the artist may be identifiable with the documented Florentine master, Francesco di Michele.
45. On the attribution and dating of the altarpiece, see Ladis (1982), p. 222.
46. The prophet figures in the S. Martino a Mensola triptych closely resemble the saints in Mainardi's *Madonna and Child in Glory with Saints* (San Gimignano, Museo dell'Opera del Duomo). However, Conti (1973), pp. 39–40, attributes the painted additions to Cosimo Rosselli, whereas Filippini (1992), p. 202, suggests instead an artist in Rosselli's circle.
47. Archivio di Stato di Firenze, Conventi Soppressi no. 78, filza 250, c. 99; largely transcribed in Baroni (1866), pp. 29–30.
48. According to Sinibaldi and Brunetti (1943), p. 463, a nineteenth-century manuscript preserved in the parochial archives at San Martino a Mensola records a Quattrocento document stating that the altarpiece was renovated (*fatto fare*) in 1482 as part of the testamentory bequest of Giusto d'Antonio di Michele Betti di Corbignano. I have not been able to locate the nineteenth-century manuscript or the original Quattrocento document.
49. Ladis (1982), p. 222.
50. As suggested by Raspini (1977), p. 45.
51. "Circa anno Domini 1501 . . . tabula altaris majoris renovata est et reducta in quadrum et additae picturae, aer super picturas superius et ornamenta tabulae per singularem pictorem Laurentium de Credis," quoted in Gigliolì (1933), pp. 24–5. See also Pope-Hennessy (1974), p. 189, and Marchese (1854), vol. 1, p. 229, n. 1.
52. Baldini (1977).
53. Ibid., pp. 236–7. The original predella, sold before 1827, was replaced by a nineteenth-

century copy. On the predella, see Davies (1961), pp. 16–31.

54. Original pilaster figures by Fra Angelico are believed to have been replaced at some point by the present ones attributed to Lorenzo Monaco. See Pope-Hennessy (1974), p. 189.
55. "Dipinse, similmente, a San Domenico di Fiesole la tavola dell'altar maggiore: la qual, perchè forse pareva che si guastasse, è stata ritocca da altri maestri e peggiorata," Vasari (1878–85), vol. 2, pp. 509–10. Quoted also by Pope-Hennessy (1974), p. 189.
56. "Circa anno Domini 1501, tempore prioratus Fra Dominici de Mugello . . . renovata est tribune capellae majoris in duobus arcubus, et remotum est altare majus, et positum iuxta murum . . . et tabula altaris majoris renovata est . . ."; quoted in Pope-Hennessy (1974), p. 189.
57. Ferretti (1901), pp. 13–14.
58. Ibid., pp. 39–40.
59. Ibid., p. 46.
60. Ibid., p. 47.
61. See also the comments of Filippini (1992), esp. pp. 199, 206, and 209.

CHAPTER 6. RESTORING WALL-PAINTINGS

1. Wackernagel (1938, 1981), pp. 45–8. Vasari tells a version of the story; Vasari (1878–85), vol. 3, pp. 260–2. For a detailed study of the patronage, see Simons (1987).
2. One example recorded in documents is the restoration of a Trecento fresco cycle of *Uomini Famosi* in the Sala dei Gigli of the Palazzo Vecchio, Florence, for which Fra Filippo Lippi was paid on April 19, 1451. See Nelson (1992), n. 35. I would like to thank Megan Holmes for this reference.
3. The document reads: "Libro de le memorie dei Quatro di Biccherna Simone dipentore die' dare di venti d'ottobre [tre e quindici] prestamo contanti viij fiorini d'oro. Anco die' dare di dodici di dicembre contanti prestamo in sua mano v libre. . . ." Archivio di Stato di Siena, Biccherna, no. 377 (1315), c. 27, as published by Bacci (1944), p. 134.
4. Mazzoni (1936), pp. 146, 153–4.
5. Martindale (1988), pp. 14–17.
6. Tintori (1986), p. 13, first drew attention to this evidence. The technical findings have been discussed more recently by Bagnoli (1988), p. 113 and fig. 1.
7. Southard (1979), p. 49.
8. Os (1984), p. 45.
9. See Rubinstein (1958), p. 179, and Southard (1979), p. 50.
10. Borsook (1980), p. 20.
11. This summary is based on Bowsky (1981), and Waley (1991).
12. Bowsky (1981), p. 85.
13. Ibid., pp. 97–9, and Waley (1991), pp. 50–1.
14. See Bowsky (1981), p. 100, and the rebuttal by Waley (1991), p. 49.
15. On the technique of Simone's *Maestà*, see Bagnoli (1988), pp. 109–12.
16. "Mezzedima addì xxx del mese di dicembre. Anco al maestro Simone Martini dipentore e quali doveva avere per sè e per li suoi gignori et per oro e colori per raconciatura la *Maestà* la quale è dipenta ne la Sala del Palazzo de Nove. xxvij libre" [1321, 30 dicembre – Archivio di Stato di Siena, Biccherna, no. 142 (1321), c. 79]. "Die mercurij, xxx mensis dicembris (1321). Item, xxvij libras magistro Simony Martini pictori quos [denarios] habere debebat pro se et pro suis discipulis et pro auro et coloribus pro reactatione figure *Majestatis* que picta est in Sala Palatii doninorum Novem" [A.S.S., Biccherna, no. 143 (1321), c. 79]. In Bacci (1944), p. 136.
17. Leonetto Tintori's diagram of the replaced areas can be found in Borsook (1980), p. 19, fig. 3. As Bagnoli (1988), p. 116, n. 8, points out, to the areas detected by Tintori, the small portion of the Christ Child's tunic should also be added. Hueck (1968) argues that the new areas were painted by Simone himself. For a thoughtful rebuttal to Martindale's recent contention that the 1321 payment is too large to relate to the replaced heads alone, see Gordon (1989), p. 371.
18. See Gordon (1989), p. 371.
19. Tintori (1986), p. 13.
20. Borsook (1980), p. 21.
21. See, for example, ibid., pp. 20–3, esp. n. 24.
22. This may be partially implied in ibid., p. 21.
23. Cf. Gordon (1989), p. 371.
24. Translated in Larner (1971), pp. 113–14.
25. See, for example, the wording of the documents advocating the enlargement of the cathedral in the early to mid-Trecento "for

the honour of God and of the blessed Virgin Mary, his most holy mother, who ever was, is, and will be in future, head of this city of Siena . . ."; translated in Larner (1971), p. 69.

26. For the document, see Davidsohn (1896–1908), vol. 2, p. 312.
27. For remarks on the attribution, see Bennett (1979), p. 62.
28. Ibid., pp. 29–30.
29. Carli and Cecchini (1962), p. 70.
30. Vasari (1878–85), vol. 3, pp. 50–1.
31. Crowe and Cavalcaselle (1908–9), vol. 2, p. 60, n. 1. The inscription reads: BENOTIUS FLORENTINUS PICTOR RESTAURAVIT ANNO DOMINI MCCCCLXVII. For the document of 1466, see Pecori (1853; rpt. 1975), p. 650.
32. Soprintendenza per i Beni Artistici e Storici di Siena e Grosseto (1981), pp. 30–1.
33. Ibid., p. 31.
34. My source is Leonetto Tintori's unpublished technical study of Lippo's *Maestà*: Tintori (1980).
35. Ibid., p. 4.
36. Both Bartolo di Fredi and Benozzo Gozzoli were most likely selected to perform the renovations because they were San Gimignano's communal artists at the time. As early as the 1270s, San Gimignano had engaged communal artists for a period of one year or more. See Davidsohn (1896–1908), vol. 2, p. 310, for document of Sept. 13, 1271, and Wieruszowski (1944), pp. 29–30 and p. 30, n. 1.
37. Pecori (1853; rpt. 1975), p. 567.
38. A comparable, though later, example is Taddeo Gaddi's *Tabernacolo dei Teri*, a frescoed image of the Madonna and Child Enthroned to which Sebastiano Mainardi added figures of St. Nicholas and St. Michael Archangel in the late 1480s. See L. Venturini in *Maestri e Botteghe* (1992), pp. 214–15.
39. On the civic cult of saints, see Vauchez (1986), pp. 59–80. On the cult worship of Bartolo of San Gimignano, see Castaldi (1928), p. 72.
40. Archivio di Stato di Siena, Deliberazioni del Consiglio Generale, l. 107, fol. 33v, as translated in Bowsky (1981), p. 263.
41. A.S.S., Deliberazioni del Consiglio Generale, l. 107, fol. 33v, as cited by Vauchez (1986), p. 74.
42. Fiumi (1961), p. 171.
43. Pecori (1853; rpt. 1975), pp. 165–6.
44. Ibid., p. 188.
45. Soprintendenza di Siena (1981), p. 31.
46. See Caraffa (1962), and Bennett (1979), p. 68.
47. On her life and cult, see Imberciadori (1979).
48. Pecori (1853; rpt. 1975), pp. 367–8.
49. On his life, see Castaldi (1928).
50. Pecori (1853; rpt. 1975), pp. 448–9.
51. Ibid., p. 543.
52. Attwater (1965; rpt. 1973), pp. 219–20.
53. See Bowsky (1981), pp. 35, 160.
54. "Item. Mettere di bianco tutto il resto della faccia de la sala, dove sono dette pitture, cioè dal fregio di esse, al canto dove seghono e' capitani, e cosi di sotto dal fregio di esse al canto dell'uscio de la sala," cited in Pecori (1853; rpt. 1975), p. 651. However, the whitewash has been subsequently removed, for the late-thirteenth-century decoration on this wall is now visible.
55. Amerighi (1982), pp. 207–8; cited also by Trexler (1972), p. 28.
56. For a detailed discussion of the activities of Florentine artists in San Gimignano during the period of Onofrio di Pietro's position as *operaio*, 1464 to 1489, see Krohn (1992).

CHAPTER 7. CONCLUSION: LIVING IMAGES

1. Brandi (1950), p. 164, as cited also in Chapter 1.
2. Procacci (1953), p. 32.
3. Bergeon (1990), p. 170. I would like to thank Kate Helwig for pointing out this reference to me.
4. Bergeon and Mognetti (1977), p. 268.
5. Ibid., p. 267.
6. Bergeon (1990), pp. 186–7.

References

Amerighi, Chiara, ed. 1982. *Facezie, Motti e Burle del Piovano Arlotto*. Florence: Libreria Editrice Fiorentina.

Attwater, Donald. 1965; rpt. 1973. *The Penguin Dictionary of Saints*. Harmondsworth, Middlesex: Penguin Books.

Bacchi, G. 1926. *Sta. Maria delle Selve (Lastra a Signa)*. Florence.

Bacci, Pèleo. 1944. *Fonti e commenti per la storia dell'arte senese*. Siena: Accademia degli intronati.

Bagnoli, Alessandro. 1988. "I Tempi della 'Maestà.' Il Restauro e Le Nuove Evidenze." In *Simone Martini: atti del convegno*. Siena, March 27–9, 1985. Ed. L. Bellosi. Florence: Centro Di, pp. 109–18.

Baldini, Umberto. 1967. "Restauri Giotteschi." In *Giotto e il Mugello 1967*. Florence: Giorgi e Gambi, pp. 55–60.

Baldini, Umberto. 1977. "Contributi All'Angelico: Il Trittico di San Domenico di Fiesole e Qualche Altra Aggiunta." In *Scritti di Storia dell'Arte in Onore di Ugo Procacci*. 2 vols. Milan: Electa, vol. 1, pp. 236–46.

Baldini, Umberto, ed. 1958. *Mostra di Opere d'Arte Restaurate*. Exhibition catalog. Flor ence: Giuntina.

Baldini, Umberto, ed. 1982. *Metodo e Scienza: Operatività e Ricerca nel Restauro*. Florence: Sansoni.

Baldini, Umberto, and P. dal Poggetto, eds. 1972. *Firenze Restaura: Il Laboratorio nel suo Quarantennio*. Florence: Sansoni.

Baroni, Giovanni Francesco. 1866. *La Parrocchia di S. Martino a Mensola: Cenni Storici*. Florence.

Baxandall, Michael. 1971. *Giotto and the Orators*. Oxford: Clarendon Press.

Bazin, Germain. 1967. *The Museum Age*. Trans. J. van Nuis Cahill. New York: Universe Books.

Beckwith, John. 1986. *Early Christian and Byzantine Art*. Harmondsworth, Middlesex: Penguin Books.

Bellosi, Luciano. 1985. "Francesco di Michele, il Maestro di San Martino a Mensola." *Paragone*, 419–23: 57–63.

Belting, Hans. 1982. "The 'Byzantine' Madonnas: New Facts About Their Italian Origin and Some Observations on Duccio." *Studies in the History of Art*, 12: 7–22.

Belting, Hans. 1990. *Bilt und Kult: Ein Geschichte des Bildes vor dem Zeitalter der Kunst*. Munich: C. H. Beck.

PP. Benedettini di Montevergine. 1904. *La Prodigiosa Immagine di Maria SS. di Montevergine, Tradizioni e Memorie*. Rome.

PP. Benedettini di Montevergine. 1905. *Montevergine. Guida – Cenni Storici*. Rome.

Bennett, Bonnie Apgar. 1979. "Lippo Memmi, Simone Martini's 'Fratello in Arte': The Image Revealed by his Documented Works."

Ph.D. diss., University of Pittsburgh, 1977. Ann Arbor.

Berenson, Bernard. 1968. *Italian Pictures of the Renaissance: Central Italian and North Italian Schools.* 3 vols. London: Phaidon.

Bergeon, Ségolène. 1990. *"Science et patience" ou la restauration des peintures.* Paris: Editions de la Reunion des musees nationaux.

Bergeon, Ségolène, and Elisabeth Mognetti. 1977. "La restauration des Primitifs italiens du musée du Petit Palais d'Avignon: Quelques problèmes rencontrés." *Revue du Louvre*, 4: 264–70.

Bisdomini Chronicle. 15th cent. Siena, Bibl. Com., Ms. A.III.23.

Boase, T. S. R. 1939–40. "A Seventeenth Century Carmelite Legend Based on Tacitus." *Journal of the Warburg and Courtauld Institutes*, 3: 116.

Bologna, F. 1962; rpt. 1978. *La Pittura Italiana delle Origini.* Rome: Editori Riuniti.

Bologna, F. 1969. *I pittori alla corte angioina di Napoli, 1266–1414 e un riesame dell'arte nell'età fridericiana.* Rome: U. Bozzi.

Bomford, David, Jill Dunkerton, Dillian Gordon, and Ashok Roy, with contributions from Jo Kirby. 1989. *Art in the Making: Italian Painting Before 1400.* London: National Gallery.

Borsook, Eve. 1970. "Documenti Relativi alle Cappelle di Lecceto e delle Selve di Filippo Strozzi." *Antichità viva*, 9: 3–20.

Borsook, Eve. 1980. *The Mural Painters of Tuscany: From Cimabue to Andrea del Sarto.* 2d ed. Oxford: Clarendon Press.

Borsook, Eve. 1981. "Cults and Imagery at Sant'Ambrogio in Florence." *Mitteilungen des Kunsthistorischen Institutes in Florenz*, 25: 147–202.

Boskovits, Miklòs. 1975. *Pittura Fiorentina alla vigilia del Rinascimento 1370–1400.* Florence: Edam.

Boskovits, Miklòs. 1977. "Intorno a Coppo di Marcovaldo." In *Scritti di storia dell'arte in onore di Ugo Procacci.* 2 vols. Milan: Electa, vol. 1, pp. 94–105.

Bossi, F. 1575. *Visita apostolica di monsignor Bossio 1575.* Siena, Archivio arcivescovile, Ms. 21.

Bowsky, William M. 1981. *A Medieval Italian Commune: Siena Under the Nine, 1287–1355.* Berkeley, Los Angeles, London: University of California Press.

Brandi, Cesare. 1950. "Il Restauro della Madonna di Coppo di Marcovaldo nella Chiesa dei Servi di Siena." *Bollettino d'Arte*, 35: 160–70.

Brandi, Cesare. 1951. *Duccio.* Florence: Vallecchi.

Brandi, Cesare, ed. 1948. *V Mostra di Restauri.* Istituto Centrale del Restauro. Exhibition catalog. Rome.

Brandi, Cesare, and Enzo Carli. 1951. "Relazione sul Restauro della Madonna di Guido da Siena del 1221." *Bollettino d'Arte*, 36: 248–60.

Brooke, Rosalind. 1967. "The Lives of St. Francis of Assisi." In *Latin Biography.* Ed. T. A. Dorey. London: Routledge and Kegan Paul, pp. 177–98.

Brown, Peter. 1981. *The Cult of the Saints: Its Rise and Function in Latin Christianity.* Chicago: University of Chicago Press.

Bull, David, and Joyce Plesters. 1990. *The Feast of the Gods: Conservation, Examination, and Interpretation.* Studies in the History of Art, 40. Washington, D.C.: National Gallery of Art.

Burckhardt, Jacob. 1929; rpt. 1958. *The Civilization of the Renaissance in Italy.* 2 vols. New York: Harper.

Caioli, Paolo. 1929. *S. Andrea Corsini Carmelitano Vescovo di Fiesole, 1301–1374.* Florence.

Cannon, Joanna. 1980. "Dominican Patronage of the Arts in Central Italy: the Provincia Romana, c. 1220–1320." Ph.D. diss., Courtauld Institute, University of London.

Cannon, Joanna. 1982. "Simone Martini, the Dominicans and the Early Sienese Polyptych." *Journal of the Warburg and Courtauld Institutes*, 45: 69–93.

Cannon, Joanna. 1987. "Pietro Lorenzetti and the History of the Carmelite Order." *Journal of the Warburg and Courtauld Institutes*, 50: 18–28.

Capolavori e Restauri. 1986. Florence, Palazzo Vecchio. Florence.

Caraffa, Filippo. 1962. "Antonio Abate." In *Bibliotheca Sanctorum.* Rome, vol. 2, cols. 106–14.

Carl, Doris. 1978. "Der Fina-Altar von Benedetto da Maiano in der Collegiata zu San Gimignano. Zu seiner Datierung und Rekonstruktion." *Mitteilungen des Kunsthistorischen Institutes in Florenz*, 22: 265–86.

Carli, Enzo. 1955. *Dipinti Senesi del contado e della Maremma.* Milan: Electa.

Carli, Enzo. 1963. "Ancora dei Memmi a San Gimignano." *Paragone*, 14/159 (March): 27–44.

Carli, Enzo, and Giovanni Cecchini. 1962. *San Gimignano.* Milan: Electa.

Carocci, Guido. 1895. *Monumenti e Oggetti d'Arte nei Comuni Toscani: Comune di Lastra a Signa.* Florence: Tipografia Minori Corrigendi.

Casalini, E. 1983. *L'ordine dei Servi di Maria e la sua nascita in Firenze (1233).* Florence.

Cassidy, Brendan. 1988. "The *Assumption of the Virgin* on the Tabernacle of Orsanmichele." *Journal of the Warburg and Courtauld Institutes*, 51: 174–80.

Castaldi, E. 1928. *Santo Bartolo, il Giob della Toscana.* Florence: Casa Editrice Giannini.

Cellini, Pico. 1950. "Una Madonna Molto Antica." In *Proporzioni. Studi di Storia dell'Arte a cura di Roberto Longhi*, III. Florence: Sansoni, pp. 1–6.

Chigi, Mons. Fabio. 1939. "L'Elenco delle Pitture, Sculture e Architetture di Siena compilato nel 1625–26." Ed. Pèleo Bacci. In *Bullettino Senese di Storia Patria*, n.s. 10: 297–337.

Chiovaro, F. 1967. "Relics." In *New Catholic Encyclopedia.* New York: McGraw-Hill, vol. 12, pp. 234–40.

Christiansen, Keith. 1982a. "Fourteenth-Century Italian Altarpieces." *The Metropolitan Museum of Art Bulletin*, 40/1 (Summer): 3–56.

Christiansen, Keith. 1982b. *Gentile da Fabriano.* Ithaca, N.Y.: Cornell University Press.

Christiansen, Keith. 1989. "Revising the Renaissance: 'Il Gentile Disvelato.'" *Burlington Magazine*, 131 (August): 539–41.

Christiansen, Keith, Laurence B. Kanter, and Carl Brandon Strehlke. 1988. *Painting in Renaissance Siena 1420–1500.* Exhibition catalog. Metropolitan Museum of Art. New York.

Cohn, Samuel K., Jr. 1988. *Death and Property in Siena, 1205–1800: Strategies for the Afterlife.* Baltimore and London: Johns Hopkins University Press.

Cohn, Samuel K., Jr. 1992. *The Cult of Remembrance and the Black Death: Six Renaissance Cities in Central Italy.* Baltimore and London: Johns Hopkins University Press.

Cohn, W. 1957. "La seconda immagine della Loggia di Orsanmichele." *Bollettino d'Arte*, 42: 335–8.

Cole, Bruce. 1973. "Old in New in the Early Trecento." *Mitteilungen des Kunsthistorischen Institutes in Florenz*, 17: 229–48.

Conti, Alessandro. 1973; 2d ed., 1988. *Storia del restauro e della conservazione delle opere d'arte.* Milan: Electa.

Conti, Alessandro, et al. 1983. *Domenico Ghirlandaio: Restauro e storia di un dipinto.* Exhibition catalog. Fiesole: Opus Libri.

Coor-Achenbach, Gertrude. 1946. "A Visual Basis for the Documents relating to Coppo di Marcovaldo and his son Salerno." *Art Bulletin*, 28: 233–47.

Coor-Achenbach, Gertrude. 1952. "A Dispersed Triptych by the Badia a Isola Master." *Art Bulletin*, 34: 311–16.

Coor-Achenbach, Gertrude. 1955. "Contributions to the Study of Ugolino di Nerio's Art." *Art Bulletin*, 37: 153–65.

Corrie, Rebecca W. 1990. "The Political Meaning of Coppo di Marcovaldo's Madonna and Child in Siena." *Gesta*, 29/1: 61–75.

Crawford, I. M. 1968. *The Art of the Wandjina: Aboriginal Cave Paintings in Kimberley, Western Australia.* Melbourne: Oxford University Press.

Crowe, J. A., and G. B. Cavalcaselle. 1903–14. *A History of Painting in Italy.* 2d ed. 6 vols. London: J. Murray.

Crowe, J. A., and G. B. Cavalcaselle. 1908–9. *A New History of Painting.* 3 vols. London: J. M. Dent.

Davidsohn, Robert. 1896–1908. *Forschungen zur Geschichte von Florenz.* Berlin: E. S. Mittler und Sohn.

Davies, Martin. 1951; 2d ed., 1961. *National Gallery Catalogues: The Earlier Italian Schools.* London: National Gallery.

Davies, Martin, rev. by Dillian Gordon. 1988. *National Gallery Catalogues: The Early Italian Schools before 1400.* London: National Gallery Publications.

Duncan, Carol, and Alan Wallach. 1980. "The Universal Survey Museum." *Art History*, 3: 448–69.

Elkin, A. P. 1930. "Rock-Paintings of North-West Australia." *Oceania*, 1/3: 257–79.

Ezra, Kate. 1988. *Art of the Dogon: Selections from the Lester Wunderman Collection.* Exhibition catalog. Metropolitan Museum of Art. New York: Abrams.

Fabbri, Nancy Rash, and Nina Rutenburg. 1981. "The Tabernacle of Orsanmichele in Context." *Art Bulletin*, 63: 385–405.

Fahy, Everett. 1976. *Some Followers of Domenico Ghirlandajo*. Ph.D. diss., Harvard University, 1968. New York and London: Garland.

Faluschi, Giovacchino. 1821. *Memorie, Descrizioni, ecc.* Siena, Bibl. Com., Ms. E.VI.20.

Ferretti, P. Lodovico. 1901. *La chiesa e il convento di San Domenico di Fiesole*. Florence: Tip. S. Giuseppe gia Q. Ciardi.

Fiesole: Una Diocesi nella Storia. saggi, contributi, immagini. 1986. Florence: Corradino Mori.

Filippini, Cecilia. 1992. "Riquadrature e 'Restauri' di Polittici Trecenteschi o Pale d'Altare nella Seconda Metà del Quattrocento." In *Maestri e Botteghe: Pittura a Firenze alla Fine del Quattrocento*. Exhibition catalog. Florence, Palazzo Strozzi. Milan: Silvana, pp. 199–211.

Fiumi, Enrico. 1961. *Storia Economica e Sociale di San Gimignano*. Florence: L. S. Olschki.

Foglio volante. 1895. Siena.

Freedberg, David. 1989. *The Power of Images: Studies in the History and Theory of Response*. Chicago and London: University of Chicago Press.

Fremantle, Richard. 1975. *Florentine Gothic Painters from Giotto to Masaccio*. London: Secker and Warburg.

Frinta, Mojmìr S. 1971. "Note on the Punched Decoration of Two Early Painted Panels at the Fogg Art Museum: *St. Dominic* and the *Crucifixion*." *Art Bulletin*, 53: 306–9.

Frinta, Mojmìr. 1981. "Raised Gilded Adornment of the Cypriot Icons, and the Occurrence of the Technique in the West." *Gesta*, 20: 333–47.

Galavaris, George. 1981. *The Icon in the Life of the Church*. Leiden: Brill.

Gardner, Julian. 1971. "The Decoration of the Baroncelli Chapel in Santa Croce." *Zeitschrift für Kunstgeschichte*, 34: 89–113.

Gardner, Julian. 1979. "Guido da Siena, 1221, and Tommaso da Modena." *Burlington Magazine*, 121: 107–8.

Gardner Von Teuffel, C. 1979. "The Buttressed Altarpiece: A Forgotten Aspect of Tuscan Fourteenth Century Altarpiece Design." *Jahrbuch der Berliner Museen*, 21: 21–65.

Gargani, G. 1874. "Un pittore fiorentino anteriore a Giovanni Cimabue." *Il Buonarroti*, ser. 2, 9: 157–66.

Garrison, Edward B. 1943–5. "A New Devotional Panel Type in Fourteenth-Century Italy." *Marsyas*, 3: 15–69.

Garrison, Edward B. 1949. *Italian Romanesque Panel Painting: An Illustrated Index*. Florence: L. S. Olschki.

Giglioli, Odoardo H. 1933. *Catalogo delle cose d'arte e di antichità d'Italia: Fiesole*. Rome: Libreria dello stato.

Gilbert, C. 1977. "Peintre et menusier au début de la Renaissance en Italie." *Revue de l'Art*, 37: 9–28.

Goffen, Rona. 1988. *Spirituality in Conflict: Saint Francis and Giotto's Bardi Chapel*. University Park and London: Pennsylvania State University Press.

Gomez-Moreno, Carmen, Elizabeth H. Jones, Arthur K. Wheelock, Jr., and Millard Meiss. 1969. "A Sienese *St. Dominic* Modernized Twice in the Thirteenth Century." *Art Bulletin*, 51: 363–6.

Gordon, Dillian. 1989. "Martini Shaken and Stirred." *Art History*, 12/3: 370–3.

Gordon, Dillian, and Anthony Reeve. 1984. "Three Newly-Acquired Panels from the Altarpiece for Santa Croce by Ugolino di Nerio." *National Gallery Technical Bulletin*, 8: 36–52.

Habig, Marion A., ed. 1972. *St. Francis of Assisi, Writings and Early Biographies: English Omnibus of Sources for the Life of St. Francis*. Chicago: Franciscan Herald Press.

Hager, Hellmut. 1962. *Die Anfänge des Italienischen Altarbildes*. Munich: A. Schroll.

Hamilton, George Heard. 1954. *The Art and Architecture of Russia*. Baltimore: Penguin.

Hoenigswald, Ann. 1982. "The 'Byzantine' Madonnas: Technical Investigation." *Studies in the History of Art*, 12: 25–31.

Holmes, Megan. 1993. "'Frate Filippo di Tommaso Dipintore' – Fra Filippo Lippi and Florentine Renaissance Religious Practices." Ph.D. diss., Harvard University, 1993.

Holst, Niels von. 1967. *Creators, Collectors and Connoisseurs*. Trans. B. Battershaw. London: Thames and Hudson.

Hueck, Irene. 1968. "Frühe Arbeiten des Simone Martini." *Münchner Jahrbuch der bildenden Kunst*, 19: 29–60.

Imberciadori, Jole Vichi. 1979. *Fina dei Ciardi: Un simbolo nella realtà storica e sociale di*

San Gimignano. San Gimignano: Comitato Celebrazioni S. Fina.

Italian Primitives: The Case History of a Collection and its Conservation, An Exhibition Celebrating the Centenary of Yale University's Acquisition of the Jarves Collection. 1972. Yale University Art Gallery. New Haven.

Jannella, Cecilia. 1989. *Simone Martini.* Florence: Scala.

Kaftal, George. 1965. *Iconography of the Saints in Central and South Italian Schools of Painting.* Florence: Sansoni.

Kent, Francis William. 1977. *Household and Lineage in Renaissance Florence: The Family Life of the Capponi, Ginori, and Rucellai.* Princeton: Princeton University Press.

Kitzinger, Ernst. 1955. "On Some Icons of the Seventh Century." In *Late Classical and Mediaeval Studies in Honor of Albert Mathias Friend, Jr.* Ed. K. Weitzmann. Princeton: Princeton University Press, pp. 132–50.

Kitzinger, Ernst. 1966. "Byzantium and Western Art in XIIth and XIIIth Centuries." *Dumbarton Oaks Papers,* 20: 27–47.

Kitzinger, Ernst. 1976. "The Cult of Images in the Age before Iconoclasm." In *The Art of Byzantium and the Medieval West: Selected Studies.* Ed. W. Eugene Kleinbauer. Bloomington: Indiana University Press, pp. 91–156.

Klesse, Brigitte. 1957–9. "Der Meister des Hochaltars von S. Martino a Mensola." *Mitteilungen des Kunsthistorischen Institutes in Florenz,* 8: 247–52.

Krautheimer, Richard. 1969. "The Beginnings of Art Historical Writing in Italy." In *Studies in Early Christian, Medieval, and Renaissance Art.* New York and London: New York University Press, pp. 257–73.

Kriss-Rettenbeck, Ruth and Lenz. 1985. "Reliquie und ornamenta ecclesiae im Symbolkosmos der Kirche." In *Ornamenta Ecclesiae: Kunst und Künstler der Romanik.* Exhibition catalog. 3 vols. Cologne: Stadt Köln, vol. 3, pp. 18–24

Krohn, Deborah L. "Civic Patronage of Art in Renaissance San Gimignano." Ph.D. diss., Harvard University, 1992.

Kroos, Renate. 1985. "Vom Umgang mit Reliquien." In *Ornamenta Ecclesiae: Kunst und Künstler der Romanik.* Exhibition catalog. 3 vols. Cologne: Stadt Köln, vol. 3, pp. 25–49.

Krüger, Klaus. 1992. *Der frühe Bildkult des Franziskus in Italien: Gestalt- und Funktionswandel des Tafelbildes im 13. und 14. Jahrhundert.* Berlin: Gebr. Mann Verlag.

Ladis, Andrew. 1982. *Taddeo Gaddi: Critical Review and Catalogue Raisonné.* Columbia, Mo., and London: University of Missouri Press.

Larner, John. 1971. *Culture and Society in Italy 1290–1420.* London: Batsford.

Lehner, Francis C., ed. 1964. *Saint Dominic: Biographical Documents.* Washington, D.C.: Thomist Press.

Lein, Edgar. 1988. *Benedetto da Maiano.* Diss., Bochum University, 1987. Frankfurt: Lang.

Léonard, Émile. 1954. *Les Angevins de Naples.* Paris: Presses Universitaires de France.

Leone de Castris, Pierluigi. 1986. *Arte di Corte nella Napoli Angioina.* Florence: Cantini.

Longhi, Roberto. 1948. "Giudizio sul Duecento." *Proporzioni. Studi di Storia dell'Arte a cura di Roberto Longhi,* II. Florence: Sansoni, pp. 5–54.

Lorenzetti, Costanza. 1936–7. "La corrente pittorica romana e senese e la tradizione locale in alcuni dipinti inediti della campania." *Bollettino d'Arte,* 30: 417–36.

Lowenthal, David. 1985. *The Past Is a Foreign Country.* Cambridge: Cambridge University Press.

Loyrette, H. 1978. "Une source pour la Reconstruction du Polyptyque d'Ugolino da Siena à Santa Croce." *Paragone,* 29/343 (September): 15–23.

Lusini, V. 1906. "San Domenico in Camporegio." *Bullettino Senese di Storia Patria,* 13: 263–95.

Lusini, V. 1907. *La Chiesa di S. Niccolò del Carmine in Siena.* Siena.

Lusini, V. 1908. *La Basilica di S. Maria dei Servi in Siena.* Siena.

Macci, Girolamo. *Memorie.* Archivio di Stato di Siena, Biblioteca, Ms. D.107.

Maestri e Botteghe: Pittura a Firenze alla fine del Quattrocento. 1992. Eds. M. Gregori, A. Paolucci, and C. Acidini Luchinat. Exhibition catalog. Florence, Palazzo Strozzi. Milan: Silvana.

Maetzke, A. M. 1973. "Nuove Ricerche su Margarito d'Arezzo." *Bollettino d'Arte,* 58: 95–112.

Maetzke, A. M., ed. 1979. *Arte nell'Aretino: Seconda Mostra di Restauri dal 1975 al 1979.* Exhibition catalog. Arezzo, San Francesco, 1979–80. Florence: Edam.

Maetzke, A. M., et al. 1987. *Il Museo Statale d'Arte Medievale e Moderno in Arezzo.* Florence.

Maetzke, A. M., et al., eds. 1974. *Arte nell'Aretino: Recuperi e Restauri dal 1968 al 1974.* Exhibition catalog. Arezzo, San Francesco, 1974–5. Florence: Edam.

Marchese, P. Vincenzo. 1854. *Memorie dei più insigni pittori, scultori e architetti domenicani.* 2 vols. Florence: Presso A. Parenti.

Marcucci, Luisa. 1958. *Gallerie Nazionali di Firenze: I Dipinti Toscani del Secolo XIII.* Rome: Istituto Poligrafico dello Stato.

Margaritoff, Tasso. 1967. "A New Method for Removing Successive Layers of Painting." *Studies in Conservation*, 12: 140–6.

Marle, Raimond van. 1923–38. *The Development of the Italian Schools of Painting.* 19 vols. The Hague: M. Nijhoff.

Martindale, Andrew. 1988. *Simone Martini.* Oxford: Phaidon.

Martini, Laura, et al. 1990. *Museo Civico di Montepulciano: Storia e Restauri.* Chiusi: Edizioni Luì.

Mazzoni, Guido. 1936. "Influssi danteschi nella Maestà di Simone Martini (1315–16)." *Archivio Storico Italiano*, 94: 144–62.

Mesnil, J. 1912. "Per la storia della Cappella Brancacci." *Rivista d'Arte*, 8: 34–40.

Milanesi, G. 1854–5; rpt. 1969. *Documenti per la Storia dell'Arte Senese.* 3 vols. Siena; rpt. Holland: Davaco Publishers.

Milanesi, G. 1873; rpt. 1973. *Sulla Storia dell'Arte Toscana: Scritti Vari.* Siena: Tip. sordo-muti di L. Lazzeri.

Moleta, Vincent. 1983. *From St. Francis to Giotto: The Influence of St. Francis on Early Italian Art and Literature.* Chicago: Franciscan Herald Press.

Mongelli, G. 1965. *Storia di Montevergine e della Congregazione Verginiana: Dalle Origini alla Fine della Dominazione Angioina.* 2 vols. Avellino.

Mongelli, G. 1967. "L'autore dell'immagine della 'Madonna di Montevergine' alla luce della critica storica." In *Il contributo dell'archidiocesi di Capua alla vita religiosa e culturale del Meridione, Atti del Convegno Nazionale di Studi Storici promosso dalla Società di Storia Patria di Terra di Lavoro, 1966.* Rome, pp. 439–90.

Morey, C. R. 1954. "The Madonna of Sta. Francesca Romana." In *Studies in Art and Literature for Belle da Costa Greene.* Ed. Dorothy Miner. Princeton: Princeton University Press, pp. 118–21.

Muratori, L. A., ed. 1900. *Rerum Italicarum Scriptores.* n.s. 28 vols. Città di Castello: S. Lapi.

Nelson, Jonathan. 1992. "Dante Portraits in Sixteenth Century Florence." *Gazette des Beaux-Arts*, ser. 6, 120 (September): 59–77.

Neri di Bicci. 1976. *Le Ricordanze (10 marzo 1453–24 aprile 1475).* Ed. B. Santi. Pisa: Marlin.

Newbery, Timothy H., George Bisacca, and Laurence B. Kanter. 1990. *Italian Renaissance Frames.* Exhibition catalog. Metropolitan Museum of Art. New York.

Offner, Richard. 1930–84. *A Critical and Historical Corpus of Florentine Painting.* 14 vols. New York and Berlin: New York University.

Offner, Richard. 1950. "Guido da Siena and A. D. 1221." *Gazette des Beaux-Arts*, ser. 6, 37: 61–90.

Offner, Richard. 1952. "Note on an Unknown *St. Francis* in the Louvre." *Gazette des Beaux-Arts*, 94: 129–33.

Ornamenta Ecclesiae: Kunst und Künstler der Romanik. 1985. Exhibition catalog. 3 vols. Cologne: Stadt Köln.

Os, H. W. van. 1974. "St. Francis of Assisi as a Second Christ in Early Italian Painting." *Simiolus: Netherlands Quarterly for the History of Art*, 7: 115–32.

Os, H. W. van. 1983. "The Earliest Altarpieces of St. Francis." In *Francesco d'Assisi nella Storia, Secoli XIII-XV.* Ed. S. Gieben. Atti del Primo Convegno di Studi per L'VIII Centenario della Nascita di S. Francesco (1182–1982). Rome, vol. 1, pp. 333–8.

Os, H. W. van. 1984. *Sienese Altarpieces 1215–1460.* Vol. 1. Groningen: Bouma's Boekhuis.

Os, H. W. van. 1987. "The case of the twin Madonnas." In *Historische Avonden.* Groningen, pp. 125–33.

Ouspensky, Leonid. 1978. *Theology of the Icon.* Crestwood, N.Y.: St. Vladimir's Seminary Press.

Pecori, Luigi. 1853; rpt. 1975. *Storia della Terra di San Gimignano*. Florence; rpt. Rome: Multigrafica.

Pino, Franco-Andrea dal. 1972. *I Frati Servi di S. Maria dalle origine all'approvazione (1233 ca.–1304)*. 3 vols. Louvain: Bureau de Recueil, Bibliothèque de l'Université. Vol. 1: *Storiografica – Fonti – Storia*.

Pino, Franco-Andrea dal. 1977. "I Servi di S. Maria a Siena." In *Mélanges de l'École Française de Rome. Moyen Age – Temps Modernes*. Rome, vol. 89/2, pp. 749–55.

Poggetto, P. dal. 1963. *Arte in Valdelsa*. Certaldo.

Poggi, Giovanni. 1903. "Dall'Archivio della Badia fiorentina." *Miscellanea d'Arte*, 145–6.

Polzer, Joseph. 1983. "A Contribution to the Early Chronology of Lippo Memmi." In *La Pittura nel XIV e XV Secolo. Il Contributo dell'Analisi Tecnica alla Storia dell'Arte*. Eds. H. van Os and J. R. J. van Asperen de Boer. Atti del XXIV Congresso Internazionale di Storia dell'Arte, III, 1979. Bologna, pp. 237–52.

Polzer, Joseph. 1984. "The Virgin and Child Enthroned from the Church of the Servites in Orvieto Generally Given to Coppo di Marcovaldo: Recent Laboratory Evidence and a Review of Coppo's Oeuvre." *Antichità viva*, 23/3: 5–18.

Pope-Hennessy, J. 1952; 1974. *Fra Angelico*. London; Ithaca, N.Y.: Cornell University Press.

Procacci, Ugo. 1932. "L'incendio della Chiesa del Carmine del 1771." *Rivista d'Arte*, 14: 141–232.

Procacci, Ugo. 1936. "Restauri ai dipinti della Toscana." *Bollettino d'Arte*, 29: 364–9.

Procacci, Ugo. 1953. "Distacco di Tempere Ducentesche Sovrapposte." *Bollettino d'Arte*, 38: 31–7.

Procacci, Ugo. 1961–3. "La Tavola di Giotto dell'Altar Maggiore della Chiesa della Badia Fiorentina." In *Scritti di Storia dell'Arte in Onore di Mario Salmi*. 3 vols. Rome: De Luca, vol. 2, pp. 9–45.

Procacci, Ugo. 1966. "Cinque Opere Inediti di Arte Toscana." In *Arte in Europa: Scritti di Storia dell'Arte in Onore di Edoardo Arslan*. 2 vols. Milan: Artipo, vol. 1, pp. 303–5.

Pseudo-Buondelmonte. 18th cent. *Memorie di S. Maria dei Servi*. Siena, Bibl. Com., Ms. B. VII. 14.

Quintavalle, Armando O. 1934. "Contributi allo studio della pittura romanica in Campania." *Crisopoli*, 2: 3–19.

Raspini, Giuseppe. 1977. *San Martino a Mensola: La Chiesa, Il Museo, Il Monastero*. Florence: Libreria Editrice Fiorentina.

Razzi, Silvano. 1543. *Vite de'Santi e Beati Toscani*. Florence.

Riccetti, Lucio. 1989. "'Dolci per Gentile': New documents for Gentile da Fabriano's 'Maestà' at Orvieto." *Burlington Magazine*, 131 (August): 541–2.

Richa, Guiseppe. 1762. *Notizie istoriche delle chiese fiorentine divise ne'suoi quartieri*. Vol. 10. Florence: P. G. Viviani.

Rubinstein, N. 1958. "Political Ideas in Sienese Art: The Frescoes by Ambrogio Lorenzetti and Taddeo di Bartolo in the Palazzo Pubblico." *Journal of the Warburg and Courtauld Institutes*, 21/3–4: 179–207.

Ruda, Jeffrey. 1993. *Fra Filippo Lippi: Life and Work with a Complete Catalogue*. London: Phaidon.

Saggi, L. 1961. "Andrea Corsini, santo." In *Dizionario biografico degli italiani*. Rome, vol. 3, pp. 88–92.

Salmi, M. 1951. "Postille alla Mostra di Arezzo." *Commentari*, 2: 93–7, 169–95.

Sandberg-Vavalà, Evelyn. 1929; rpt. 1980. *La Croce Dipinta Italiana e L'Iconografia della Passione*. Verona; rpt. Rome: Multigrafica.

Santi, Francesco. 1969. *Perugia, Galleria Nazionale dell'Umbria: Dipinti, Sculture e Oggetti d'Arte di Età Romanica e Gotica*. Rome: Istituto Poligrafico dello Stato.

Scarpellini, Pietro. 1982. "Iconografia francescana nei secoli XIII e XIV." In *Francesco d'Assisi: Storia e Arte*. Ed. F. Porzio. Milan: Electa, pp. 91–126.

Schlosser, Julius von, ed. 1912. *Lorenzo Ghibertis Denkwürdigkeiten*. Berlin: J. Bard.

Schmucki, O., and S. Gerlach. 1968–76. "Franz von Assisi." In *Lexikon der Christlichen Ikonographie*. 8 vols. Rome: Herder, vol. 6, cols. 260–315.

Schultz, H. W. 1860. *Denkmäler der Kunst des Mittelalters in Unteritalien*. 4 vols. Dresden: W. H. K. Schultz.

Scultura Dipinta: Maestri di Legname e Pittori a Siena 1250–1450. 1987. Exhibition catalog. Siena, Pinacoteca Nazionale. Florence: Centro Di.

Seymour, Charles, Jr. 1970. *Early Italian Paintings*

in the Yale University Art Gallery. New Haven and London: Yale University Press.
Simons, Patricia. 1987. "Patronage in the Tornaquinci Chapel, Santa Maria Novella, Florence." In *Patronage, Art, and Society in Renaissance Italy.* Eds. F. W. Kent and Patricia Simons. Canberra and Oxford: Oxford University Press, pp. 221–50.
Sinibaldi, G., and G. Brunetti. 1943. *Pittura Italiana del Duecento e Trecento. Catalogo della Mostra Giottesca di Firenze del 1937.* Florence: Sansoni.
Skalova, Suzana. 1987. "The 17th Century Icon 'Mother of God of Smolensk' Rediscovered." *ICOM Committee for Conservation, Preprints.* 8th Triennial Meeting, Sydney, Australia, Sept. 1987. Los Angeles: Getty Conservation Institute, pp. 1127–31.
Skaug, Erling. 1971–2. "Contributions to Giotto's Workshop." *Mitteilungen des Kunsthistorischen Institutes in Florenz,* 15: 141–60.
Smirnova, E. S. 1989. *Moscow Icons: 14th–17th Centuries.* Trans. A. Shkarovsky-Raffe. Oxford: Phaidon.
Soprintendenza per i Beni Artistici e Storici di Siena e Grosseto. 1981. *Mostra di opere d'arte restaurate nelle province di Siena e Grosseto,* II. Exhibition catalog. Genoa: Sagep.
Southard, Edna Carter. 1979. *The Frescoes in Siena's Palazzo Pubblico, 1289–1539: Studies in Imagery and Relations to other Communal Palaces in Tuscany.* Ph.D. diss., Indiana University, 1978. New York and London: Garland.
Stout, George L. 1929. "A Puzzling Piece of Gold Leaf Tooling." *Fogg Art Museum Notes,* 2/4 (June): 140–52.
Stuart, John. 1975. *Ikons.* London: Faber.
Stubblebine, James H. 1964. *Guido da Siena.* Princeton: Princeton University Press.
Stubblebine, James H. 1966. "Byzantine Influence in Thirteenth-Century Italian Panel Painting." *Dumbarton Oaks Papers,* 20: 87–101.
Stubblebine, James H. 1979. *Duccio di Buoninsegna and His School.* 2 vols. Princeton: Princeton University Press.
Tartuferi, Angelo. 1990. *La Pittura a Firenze nel Duecento.* Florence: Bruschi.
Tintori, Leonetto. 1980. "Relazione tecnica sulla Maestà di Lippo Memmi nel Palazzo Civico di S. Gimignano." Florence. Manuscript.
Tintori, Leonetto. 1986. "Segnalazioni sul costante progresso tecnico nelle pitture murali di Simone Martini (1315–30?)." In *Tecnica e Stile: esempi di pittura murale del Rinascimento italiano.* Atti del Seminario, Villa I Tatti 23–24 maggio, 1983. Eds. E. Borsook and Fiorella Superbi Gioffredi. 2 vols. Milan: Silvana, vol. 1, pp. 11–16.
Tizio, Sigismondo. 1528. *Historiarum Senensium.* Siena, Bibl. Com., Ms. B.III.15.
Toesca, Pietro. 1927. *Storia dell'Arte italiana, I, Il Medioevo.* 2 vols. Turin: Unione tipografico-editrice torinese.
Torriti, Piero. 1977; rpt. 1980. *La Pinacoteca Nazionale di Siena: I Dipinti dal XII al XV Secolo.* Genoa: Sagep.
Trexler, Richard. 1972. "Florentine Religious Experience: The Sacred Image." *Studies in the Renaissance,* 19: 7–41.
Tropeano, Placido Maria. 1973. *Montevergine nella Storia e nell'arte 1266–1381.* Naples: A. Berisio.
Tropeano, Placido Maria. 1978. "Un affresco trecentesco di Montano d'Arezzo replica della 'Maestà' di Montevergine?" *Rivista Storica del Mezzogiorno,* 13: 171–89.
Uspenskij, Boris. 1976. *The Semiotics of the Russian Icon.* Lisse.
Vasari, Giorgio. 1878–85. *Le vite de' più eccellenti pittori scultori ed architettori.* Ed. G. Milanesi. 9 vols. Florence: G. C. Sansoni.
Vauchez, André. 1981. *La Sainteté en Occident aux Derniers Siècles du Moyen Age.* Rome: Ecole française de Rome.
Vauchez, André. 1986. "Patronage des saints et religion civique dans l'Italie communale à la fin du Moyen Age." In *Patronage and Public in the Trecento: Proceedings of the St. Lambrecht Symposium.* Ed. Vincent Moleta. Florence: L. S. Olschki, pp. 59–80.
Vigorelli, Giancarlo, and Edi Baccheschi. 1966. *L'opera completa di Giotto.* Milan: Rizzoli.
Wackernagel, M. 1938; 1981. *The World of the Florentine Renaissance Artist: Projects and Patrons, Workshop and Art Market.* First German ed. Leipzig; English trans. Princeton: Princeton University Press.
Waley, Daniel. 1991. *Siena and the Sienese in the Thirteenth Century.* Cambridge: Cambridge University Press.
Warnke, Martin. 1968. "Italienische Bildtabernakel bis zum Frühbarock." *Münchner Jahrbuch der Bildenden Kunst,* 19: 61–102.

Weigelt, Curt. 1911. *Duccio di Buoninsegna: Studien zur Geschichte der frühsienesischen Tafelmalerei.* Leipzig: K. W. Hiersemann.

Weitzmann, Kurt. 1966. "Icon Painting in the Crusader Kingdom." *Dumbarton Oaks Papers*, 20: 49–83.

Weitzmann, Kurt. 1984. "Crusader Icons and the Maniera Greca." In *Byzanz und der Westen. Studien zur Kunst des Europäischen Mittelalters.* Ed. I. Hutter. Vienna, pp. 143–70.

White, John. 1979. *Duccio: Tuscan Art and the Medieval Workshop.* London: Thames and Hudson.

Wieruszowski, Helene. 1944. "Art and the Commune in the Time of Dante." *Speculum*, 19: 14–33.

Wilpert, Josef. 1907. "L'Acheropita ossia l'immagine del Salvatore nella cappella del Sancta Sanctorum." *L'Arte*, 10: 161–77, 247–62.

Xyngopoulos, Andreas. 1964. "Icons." In *Byzantine Art: A European Art.* Athens: Zappeion Exhibition Hall, pp. 227–90.

Zeri, Federico. 1957. "Due Appunti su Giotto." *Paragone*, 8/85 (January): 75–87.

Zeri, Federico. 1971. *Diari di Lavoro I.* Bergamo: Emblema.

Index

Note: Page numbers in italics refer to illustrations. Colorplates precede Chapter 1.